PENHALL
WORLD SPEEDWAY CHAMPION

STEVE JOHNSON

TEMPUS

First published 2005

Tempus Publishing Limited
The Mill, Brimscombe Port,
Stroud, Gloucestershire, GL5 2QG
www.tempus-publishing.com

© Steve Johnson, 2005

The right of Steve Johnson to be identified as the Author
of this work has been asserted in accordance with the
Copyrights, Designs and Patents Act 1988.

All rights reserved. No part of this book may be reprinted
or reproduced or utilised in any form or by any electronic,
mechanical or other means, now known or hereafter invented,
including photocopying and recording, or in any information
storage or retrieval system, without the permission in writing
from the Publishers.

British Library Cataloguing in Publication Data.
A catalogue record for this book is available from the British Library.

ISBN 0 7524 3400 4

Typesetting and origination by Tempus Publishing Limited
Printed in Great Britain

CONTENTS

ACKNOWLEDGEMENTS

First and foremost, a sincere thanks to Bruce for sparing me his time, and offering tremendous support throughout writing the book. And on behalf of all those people who stood on the terraces between 1973 and 1982, thanks for the entertainment and the memories! For assisting me in the course of much research, my appreciation also goes to the following people in particular: Dan McCormick, Chris Van Straaten, Eddie Bull, Ryan Evans, Carrie Hancock and Brian Burford. Thanks go to Pete Foster for his valuable help and support, and also to all those people who have responded to my calls and e-mails in request for information, of whom there are far too many to mention here. I would like to acknowledge the photographers of all the images printed in the book, although special thanks go to John Hall for the time and trouble he devoted to helping me out. If any breach of copyright has occured it is entirely unintentional and please contact the publisher to rectify the situtaion. And last, but of course not least, many thanks to my mum and dad, Pam and Phil Johnson, and to my wife Caroline, for all their advice and encouragement.

PROLOGUE

WEMBLEY, 1981

'We're going to have an American World Champion. It's going to be Bruce Penhall; going over the line on his back wheel; there he goes; and Penhall it is. The people's choice for champion, Bruce Penhall from the USA is the pin-up World Speedway Champion of 1981.'
Dave Lanning, commentator

It is every speedway rider's ultimate wish. The fulfilment of an eight-year dream for Bruce Penhall. Crossing the line for the final time on the mild, clear evening of 5 September 1981, Penhall had made it and 92,000 fans inside Wembley Stadium roared with approval. It capped a phenomenal performance on a truly unforgettable night and the blonde, blue-eyed golden boy of America was carried triumphantly from the track, being hailed as arguably the most popular champion there has ever been. Twice he had fought from behind to overhaul his closest rivals in two of the most memorable speedway races in World Championship history. Twice he had looked beaten, only to produce equally remarkable rides to snatch victory with quite literally inches of the 344-metre track to spare. With his unique style of 'making the straights longer', Penhall had clearly demonstrated his abundant skills as the complete natural motorcyclist and a man born to race, and, more significantly, to succeed. A crescendo of air horns filled the night sky to create an atmosphere fitting of the occasion, and a buzz of adrenalin that anyone there on that evening can probably still feel in the goose pimples and hairs on the back of their neck, whenever the moment is relived.

In less than five years, this twenty-four-year-old sunny Californian had turned from British League novice to World Speedway Champion. On his way, he had been the catalyst for the small, unfashionable and unsuccessful Cradley 'Heathens' club in an unknown industrial corner of the West Midlands to become the most exciting and successful team in the country. He had scooped virtually every team and individual prize available to collect; he did it all on the back of huge personal tragedy after the death of both his parents in a private plane crash when he was just eighteen years old; and he did it with the style of the Hollywood movie star he would eventually become, not to mention with the charm, charisma and personality that is not only so rare in someone so tremendously successful, but totally unrivalled in the eyes of many who witnessed and couldn't help but adore the magnetic appeal of Bruce Lee Penhall.

ONE

THE BEGINNING OF THE DREAM

It was on Bruce Penhall's sixteenth birthday, 10 May 1973, at Irwindale, California, that he lined up at the tapes for his first competitive senior speedway meeting. American motorcycle speedway thrived on individual racing, so it was young Penhall against the rest of the Thursday night third division field, with his first real opportunity to make people sit up and notice. Understandably nervous, but full of confidence and after around eight months' practice on the junior scene, it was a chance he wasn't keen to let slip, and he carved his way through the opposition to qualify for the evening's main final. Not satisfied with that already impressive debut achievement, he completed the action with a tremendous victory in the final itself. It was a remarkable opening, setting a perfect tone for the hugely successful ten-year career which would follow.

Speedway US-style was concentrated around a handful of tracks mainly located in Bruce's home of California. Although circuits existed elsewhere, the sport has never been massively popular in the States compared to the likes of baseball, basketball and American Football, and the support that was attracted was generally on the west coast and in the southern part of California. The same core group of riders would compete four or five times a week around the same main venues, always on an individual basis and often using a system of handicap racing. Consequently, after Bruce's swashbuckling start at Irwindale on that Thursday night, it was off to Costa Mesa for the young hopeful to try and do it all over again on the Friday night. Unfortunately, the follow-up performance did not turn out to be quite so impressive. With the nerves a little less intense and the confidence bubbling over, Bruce attacked the first bend of his first race and went in too fast and too hard. He slid to the deck and saw his hopes for the evening crash out with him. It was disappointing, but brought the youngster back down to earth – quite literally – and there would be another chance to pick things up again the following week.

Bruce had undeniably been bitten by the speedway bug much earlier than that night of his senior debut at sixteen. He enjoyed a close childhood friendship with Dennis Sigalos, someone who would later follow him into both the British League and International World Championship racing. The boys' parents also shared a close social relationship and their fathers would take them down to nearby Costa Mesa together every Friday night of the summer to watch the action. The two boys lapped it up and soon became big fans of the sport. They had always enjoyed the same hobbies and had already started racing motocross together. Bruce was a couple of years older, but looked upon Dennis as the more able motorcyclist and even envied the natural ability that his friend, 'Siggy', demonstrated on the bike. They would spend weeks on end in each others company through the school holidays and although they never competed officially against each other on the motocross bikes, due to the slight age difference, they would always practise together. Gradually, the relatively small sport of speedway began to take a hold of the two kids' interests, and before long they began to fantasise about becoming speedway stars. They would watch their heroes race at Costa Mesa and then dream up ways to imitate them on their bicycles. Bruce recalls cutting off the handlebars of his push-bike for a closer resemblance to speedway handlebars. They also had a great regular hang-out for 'playing speedway'. The Sigalos family home had a huge garage, so Bruce and Dennis would pull out all of the cars onto the driveway and soak the polished concrete floor. It made for an ideal surface to slide their bicycles round in circles, just like the real speedway riders, and they did it for hours on end! The boys both agreed that Siggy had the best house for them to indulge in their favourite hobbies and to have the most fun; As well as the garage-cum-speedway track, there were four acres of land for them to ride their dirt bikes. In return, Bruce lived at the beach, so when they eventually got tired, they would take off to the Penhall residence to soak up the sun, sand and surf instead.

Bruce had been born in 1957 in Anaheim, home of Disneyland and just a few miles from the celebrated coastline of the Pacific

Ocean. The city of Anaheim is one of around thirty that make up the Orange County in California, south-east of Los Angeles. The County enjoys a truly Mediterranean climate virtually all year round with little rain and an abundance of glorious sunshine. When he was twelve, the family moved a little further south, and right onto the coast itself in Newport Beach. Still in Orange County, it is the place that Bruce would call 'home' throughout the rest of his childhood and, in fact, right through his speedway career until his eventual retirement from the sport.

In 1969, the boys' fathers were introduced to a man called Ed Schafer, who at the time was working as mechanic to one of the American first division riders, Rick Woods. The Woods brothers, Rick and Gene, were two of the top stars in the late 1960s and early 1970s. As a result of meeting with Schafer, a sponsorship deal was struck for the men to provide backing for Rick Woods for two seasons. The acquaintance grew and during the 1970 season, Schafer built four junior speedway bikes on which Bruce and Dennis would get to ride. The frames were scaled-down Jawas mounted with chainsaw motors. They were a handful to control to say the least, but the boys had the time of their young lives trying to tame the wild machines.

Bruce was extremely fortunate to be in a position where his love for the sport, and increasingly serious ambitions, could be supported by those around him both financially and otherwise. To have use of the junior bikes would alone have been fantastic, but the deal would get even better. Both Bruce and Dennis now had the machines to ride upon, they had already acquired a boyhood love for the sport that many speedway fans the world over will be able to relate to, and they even had some natural talent on two wheels just beginning to shine through. The icing on the cake was a place to practise just about any time they had to spare – after finishing their daily chores and jobs of course. Their fathers, who couldn't fail to notice the enormous pleasure their kids were getting from sliding sideways on a speedway bike, constructed a miniature oval track on some land behind the Sigalos' business premises. The place was there for the kids to throw their bikes around as often as they could afford the time. They gradually added a makeshift starting gate, an old catering truck with a watering tank to water the track and an electric generator for power. Progressing from the pedal bicycles and the motocross bikes, Bruce remembers spending hours and hours riding speedway at this age, but still just never getting enough of it.

In 1972, Bruce turned fifteen years old, and looking back on the time with hindsight, sees it as the season where his dedication to speedway really emerged. There were no shortage of temptations for a talented and good-looking kid in California. Growing up in the city of Anaheim and later Newport Beach, and living right next to the beach itself, he spent a considerable amount of his youth engaged in some sporting pursuit. His early interests and hobbies included baseball, tennis, swimming and surfing. With the golden beaches barely a stone's throw, or pebble's skim, away, the surf would always provide a means to burn off some energy, and swimming came just as naturally, given the location. Baseball was a less obvious route, but Bruce played in the high school team and there is even the suggestion that he could have taken up the sport professionally, had it not been for speedway. He was eventually forced to make a choice between the two sports, as the amateur baseball regulations would not allow players involved professionally in another sport. When the choice had to be made, it was speedway racing that won prominence.

The baseball bat and the surfboard began to receive less use and the time spent practising on the speedway bikes became more and more. When Bruce was fifteen, his buddy Dennis was just turning thirteen, so it was the elder of the two friends who first began to think more seriously about his future. Sigalos still enjoyed playing around on the motocross bike, mixing it up now and again with taking a spin around the speedway track. But Bruce left the motocross behind with the pedal bikes and began to really focus on racing speedway. The junior bikes on which they had started out were very fragile machines. With two enthusiastic youngsters hammering them for all they were worth, it was hardly surprising that these machines were in frequent need of repair, both physically and mechanically. The boys' fathers hence made the decision to buy them a pair of 500cc two-valve Jawas. It was time to step up a notch and the local racing scene was not far away. Bruce knew that he could not turn professional until his sixteenth birthday, but by September 1972, he had set his sights on one of his first speedway goals. He had eight months of practice on the junior scene and the training track, but was already riding the same specification 500cc machine on which his older and more experienced rivals would be mounted. It was his practice season and he had those eight months in which to learn his trade before aiming for the four or five nights a week schedule that the top American riders competed. He was ambitious, even at a young age, and knew that speedway was where he wanted to seek success.

He still didn't really know just how big speedway was internationally. The British and European leagues were the place where the most money could be made and where the best riders in the world could be found, often working an even more punishing schedule riding in meetings in a long list of different cities and countries, and travelling thousands of miles per week to race. But there was very little connection between that and the high-excitement, high-entertainment thrills and spills of small-track US speedway. Even when the occasional American riders made the transition to British speedway, it was easier to think they had simply disappeared than moved on to bigger and better competition. None of that was even in Bruce's mind in those early stages, but it wouldn't be long at all before he would make that professional debut and be dreaming of becoming World Champion.

When delving only a little deeper into the Penhall family tree, it is not surprising at all that the racing instinct flowed freely through his blood. His father, Leroy, raced Second World War fighter aircraft as well as cars and boats in various capacities and his brother, Jerry, took up off-road motorcar racing. With Bruce's speedway, it made for quite a variety of family pursuits, even if they did follow a similar high-adrenalin theme. Crucially, behind it all was Bruce's mother Bonnie. Although she hated watching any of them race and disapproved of the dangerous high-risk activities, she remained the heart and soul behind the family. It was Bonnie who would drive Bruce to the training track at least three or four times a week during his practice season, despite being frightened to death of the speed at which her young son ·was hurtling around the track. It is probably every mother's nightmare and yet at the same time, she could not have been more proud.

Those eight months of preparation for racing against the professionals quickly passed by. Bruce would be practising regularly on the training track, never losing interest or enthusiasm for what he was doing, while at the same time watching each week the riders whom he dreamt of lining-up alongside. Soon enough, his sixteenth birthday approached and it happened to be Irwindale that staged their weekly event on a Thursday night. After that, and the Costa Mesa blip, Bruce began winning races and meetings elsewhere. As well as Irwindale on Thursdays and America's number-one track at Costa Mesa on Fridays, there was Bakersfield on Saturdays, Ventura on Tuesdays and San Bernadino on Wednesdays.

The riders at the time were all categorised as either first, second or third division. There were no strict rules or regulations stipulating in which division a rider would compete, but all the top guys would be in the first division and the rookies would start out in the third division. They would then move up or down, largely depending on recent form, and would only usually compete against other riders in the same bracket as themselves, ensuring close competitive racing. Following the whirlwind week of Bruce's third division debut, he settled down to some great performances, winning at all the different tracks. Within a few weeks, he had made enough of a name for himself and the promoters moved him up to become a second division rider. The standard was a little higher, but by then Penhall's already outstanding talent was propelling him along. He spent a further three months competing in the second division, before making another move up the ladder into the first division. Having reached the highest level in such a short space of time, he was competing against some of the top riders in the States while still aged just sixteen. By his next birthday, he was a fully-fledged first division rider, winning more than his share of main events around the tracks, at both the handicap and scratch formats. By any standard, he was emerging as a hugely talented rider. He was well on the way along his extraordinary speedway journey, but there was much more in store just around the corner.

TWO

TRIUMPH OVER ADVERSITY

1974 was an exciting year as it was Penhall's first full season as a first division rider. Having spent the previous campaign working his way up from the bottom, he started this one with the full expectation on his shoulders that he would be mixing it with the best talent US speedway had to offer. Furthermore, while developing his own following of fans on the terraces, he was rapidly establishing himself among that top echelon of riders on the track.

At the same time, he had also been working hard away from the track. During summer holidays from school, both Bruce and his brother Jerry were made to work for the thriving family demolition company, which performed tasks such as tearing down bridges, breaking up concrete structures and putting rain grooves in roads and highways. In Bruce's case, he continued to work for the business in his early speedway days, even when racing five nights a week. It was never an easy job as he would be working with huge power tools, such as backhoes or power saws. One of the hardest to handle was the jackhammer, a hand-held machine weighing around ninety pounds, which would be used for breaking up concrete pavements. While being wholly supportive, his parents were also very strict, and the boys would be up at 3 or 4 a.m. some mornings to start work for an eight or ten-hour day. Part of the reason was that Bruce's father knew what the racing life could be like, and really didn't want either of his boys to become professional racers in any sport. He knew the risks all too well, knew the slim chances of actually making a successful career out of something like speedway racing and maybe above all, he had his own dreams of Bruce and Jerry taking over the running of the company one day. Despite all that, it was also still clear to him that racing was in the boys' blood and there was never going

15

to be much that anyone could do about that. Eventually, he realised how serious Bruce was about racing motorbikes, and if he was going to have any chance of making anything out of speedway, it would require a full-time devotion to the sport.

As 1974 progressed, Bruce's reputation grew and grew. He notched an increasing number of victories and battled hard on track no matter who he was up against. He developed a particular love for handicap racing, where riders would start from staggered points along the home straight of the track. The challenge of trying to weave through from the back of the field to the front and the need to find a way past riders, rather than make the quickest start, would really get the Penhall adrenalin flowing. And he always looks back with the view that handicap racing was the best possible experience for his early career; a fast-gating rider in Britain learns to do just that – get out of the gate, or away from the starting tape, fast. If a quick enough start can be made, a British rider can concentrate on going fast and keeping the opposition behind him. American riders have to learn to make their way 'through the traffic', creating a whole different approach to racing. And it was always that racing gene that made Bruce tick, so a lightning getaway from the starting tapes – although undoubtedly useful – was not his first priority. Consequently when he later moved to England, if he happened to make a poor start to a race, he was confident and capable of fighting his way from the back where some of his European counterparts struggled. Back in the USA, he proved his ability to win the scratch main events (those without handicap), but the fans who soon referred to him as 'Super Bruce', did so due to his exploits in battling his way from the back.

Everything was going well and when Bruce turned eighteen years old in May 1975, with two years of professional speedway behind him and a world of possibilities opening up ahead of him, life couldn't have been much better. So it was the worst possible time for the most traumatic event imaginable to devastate the Penhall family. In a routine flight home from a ski trip with Bruce's mother and father on board, their private aeroplane crashed, tragically killing both parents. His brother Jerry was due to be on the same plane, but had stayed behind for an extra day. The mother of his best friend Dennis Sigalos was also involved in the accident and she too lost her life.

For a teenager, so close to his parents, and coming from such a tight-knit family, the trauma is incredibly difficult for anyone else to comprehend. Bruce was the youngest of three children; his brother Jerry was a year older and their elder sister Connie was herself only twenty-two at the time. For several months, the news remained almost impossible to come to terms with. The three siblings were drawn even closer together by the tragedy than they were previously, with Connie becoming a mother figure to her two younger brothers. Their extended family were hugely supportive and Bruce's aunt and uncle moved into the family home in Balboa to take over running the house. In the face of such tragic adversity, it was Bruce's remaining family who became the backbone of all his future success. Speedway racing could quite understandably have been cast aside as the last thing he wanted to think about. With quite the opposite effect however, it became an outlet where he could focus his energy and his thoughts. Connie and Jerry fully encouraged his speedway dreams; his uncle Kenny raised him like a son and Bruce pledged all his future racing success to the memory of his mother and father. He had made them a promise that he would become World Champion and from then on, always raced with the presence of them both watching over him. After a period of time, Bruce felt that the accident eventually made him a stronger person both mentally and physically. 'At first you just don't understand, then you become mad. You just keep asking yourself 'why?' The deep pain never really goes away. There isn't a day that goes by that I don't think of them' he admits. 'But then you start remembering the good times and the love. I'm glad my parents raised me as they did. They were just the greatest people. They would have wanted me to go on, so that's what I did.'

It was from that point that he wanted nothing more than to win every race for his parents, who had spent so much time and money taking him to and from the tracks and giving him the upbringing in which he still places tremendous credit and importance. To this day, elder sister Connie has remained a mother figure and the whole family have continued to get along extremely well, sticking rigidly together through thick and thin.

As young Bruce gradually came to terms with the terrible family heartbreak, he continued to throw himself unequivocally into his racing. After the understandable initial setback, he maintained his rapid level of progress. There was a period around 1975 where Bruce may have snapped up an easy route into taking a break from racing, as controversy struck the setup at Costa Mesa's Orange County Fairgrounds, promoted by Harry Oxley. Harry would later become known as 'The Godfather' in American speedway and was the man that brought many major developments and an international focus to the sport Stateside. Back in the earlier days of the 1970s though, he was faced with a rider revolt as the competitors, largely from the top end of the first division, banded together to demand an increase in the prize money that was on offer. The sport was enjoying something of a 'rebirth' with attendance figures on the increase and an upsurge of interest running through promoters, riders and fans alike. Wanting their share of the success, a significant number of riders called a strike against the Costa Mesa promotion, refusing to ride in any of their meetings, unless the purse on offer for prize money was increased from thirty per cent to thirty-five per cent of the gate money. The top riders, including Steve and Mike Bast and Bill Cody, sat out the start of the season in protest. Bruce, however, chose not to participate in the strike and rode on regardless, along with a bunch of the other younger riders such as Bobby Schwartz, Mike Faria and the Moran brothers, Kelly and Shawn. He steadfastly adhered to his principles and did not agree with the action that his more experienced colleagues had taken; besides, he was young and enthusiastic and frankly just wanted to be out there enjoying the action first-hand. Unfortunately for the elder brigade, the youngsters actually filled their shoes impeccably and the stands were packed every week. It wasn't long before most of the protesting riders returned, although the break was enough for some never to bother riding again.

Sending ripples of interest and debate on a much wider scale in 1975 were radical plans to revolutionise the whole setup of speedway in the USA. A consortium of mainly businessmen with little real experience of speedway announced their plans to capitalise on the growing popularity of the sport by introducing league racing. It wasn't the first time the notion had been considered in the country, but trials a few years earlier had fallen flat. The new proposals, and in particular the method of

18

franchising promotions for huge sums of money, caused immediate rifts between the newcomers and established promoters such as the Oxleys at Costa Mesa. Harry Oxley, who was very successfully promoting the existing individual format of meetings and regularly attracting sell-out crowds to the Orange County venue – with or without the biggest names on the track – had his own ideas and did not co-operate with the new plans. A scheduled season start of June never materialised and by the end of the year the new consortium had given up and dropped the idea.

It shouldn't have come as much of a surprise then, when in November of the same year, Oxley announced his own plans for a new American Speedway League, with five tracks already signed up for an inaugural 1976 season. He was ambitious and had dreams of staging the World Championship on his side of the Atlantic, away from its traditional European home. A domestic league was seen as the next stepping stone and this time, the setup was right and the local promoters were on board. Tracks would be involved at Irwindale, where Bruce had made his sensational first-night debut, Bakersfield, Ventura, San Bernadino and Oxley's own Costa Mesa – all the existing and thriving Californian speedway circuits agreed and the wheels were in motion for a full-scale switch away from the popular individual scratch and handicap racing to team events and league racing. The rest of the world was forced to take notice of the American developments and British promoters in particular, who were used to having a monopoly on the best riders from all around the globe, were given a shake when Oxley attempted to recruit a crux of foreign riders to compete in the new setup. First to sign up was loveable Scotsman Bert Harkins, who pledged his 1976 season to racing in the States.

Also taking notice, though, were the country's main sanctioning body, the American Motorcycle Association (AMA), who were affiliated to the FIM, the international governing body for all forms of motor sport. The organisation had a lot of clout and were the only administration who could officially license speedway tracks in the country for any international events. Although Oxley had promoted the US National Championship and other meetings with the AMA's approval, he was unhappy that the authority had never showed any real interest in the sport until it began showing the promise of a revival. Returning fire, the AMA refused to license the tracks unless all meetings and competing riders were affiliated to the association, therefore having to pay a significant financial subscription. Oxley publicly declared his contempt and the battle headed to the American federal courts to be decided. He insisted that the league was definitely going ahead regardless, and the riders, including Penhall, were forced to sit and wait for developments to determine how and where their speedway would be ridden in 1976.

Caught up in the ongoing dispute however, was an international series of meetings jointly organised by Oxley along with former World Champions Ivan Mauger and Barry Briggs, in which Bruce could have been lined up to compete. The Champions Series was launched in 1974 by Mauger and Briggs and involved a touring troupe of top European-based riders visiting Australia, New Zealand and the USA. The series was envisaged to be an annual event during the British winter time and was expected by the organisers to eventually go worldwide. The plan for the beginning of 1976 was for the participating riders to race a number of individual events in Australasia, and then band together into a Rest of the World Select side against a hosting American team on the Californian circuits. The Mauger and Briggs partnership had already promoted a similar USA *v.* The Rest of the World match at the Houston Astrodome in Texas a year earlier, and also an individual event at the same venue a year before that. Penhall had not been called up by the American team organisers in 1975 but his significant strides over the intervening twelve months hadn't gone unnoticed, so he was in contention for a place in the line-up for 1976. The problem was that while Ivan, Barry and the rest of the troupe, including other former world champions Anders Michanek of Sweden and Denmark's Ole Olsen, were racing their way around the tracks of Australia and New Zealand, the wrangling over events in the USA forced the cancellation of the American leg of the tour. Wielding their axe of power, the AMA refused Oxley's request to sanction the Californian tracks that were scheduled to host the Test matches, meaning any riders competing in the matches could have been handed a worldwide racing ban from all FIM events. Naturally, the best riders in the world were not willing to risk being thrown out of the World Championship events for the season ahead, let alone potentially jeopardise their places in the bread and butter of their income, the British League. The meetings were cancelled, the riders made other plans and Oxley began preparations for a court battle with the authorities. For Bruce, the cloud that initially seemed to represent a missed opportunity to try his hand against the very best opposition did turn out to have more than a trace of silver lining.

In response to the disappointment of the cancelled events, Barry Briggs hastily turned his promoting intentions elsewhere. Keen to take the sport to new locations, plans evolved to take a troupe of riders to the Middle East instead of California, but to stage the same USA versus The Rest of the World meetings which had been wiped out in the Yanks' home country. What's more, Bruce was called up for the American team to get his very first taste of competitive racing outside the States, and it was a lucky break that would lead to much greater things. The main man behind the new venture was actually Allan Becker, who had been one of the joint organisers with Mauger and Briggs of the Houston Astrodome events. Becker had previously lost money experimenting with the promotion of basketball in the Middle East, but undeterred, he had opened negotiations regarding the idea of motorcycle racing in the country of Israel. A motocross show was quickly ruled out due to the requirement of too many riders and no suitable venues, so speedway was the next idea. He contacted Barry Briggs to see if Briggo could provide The Rest of the World side while Becker organised the Americans, and the plans were put into place. The greatest obstacle facing the promoters, not to mention the riders who were soon signed up to compete, was that competitive motorcycle racing was completely new to the Middle East. In fact, at the time, there was no racing there whatsoever – no cars, bikes, dogs or even horses. Not only would the riders have to adapt to new purpose-built temporary tracks, but they would be trying to entertain and win the hearts of a totally new public who had never seen anything like it before. Quite a challenge for them all, but most of all for eighteen-year-old Bruce in his first foreign racing trip!

Six meetings in total were contested on the Middle East tour, a five-match Test series between the USA and The Rest of the

World, rounded off by an individual meeting under the banner of 'The 1976 Israel Open Championship'. All but one of the meetings were held in Tel Aviv. Although it had been hoped to stage further matches in Jerusalem, Haifa and Iran, the unforeseen problems mounted up from the off. An Israeli bank had sponsored the tour with the purchase of fourteen brand new Jawa bikes and a wide range of spares, and in addition all travel and accommodation costs were met for the riders. Unfortunately, the authorities were not used to shipments of that many speedway bikes arriving, or any amount of speedway bikes for that matter, let alone the unusual quantities of fuel and other racing equipment. In all, there were lots of logistical problems and trouble satisfying the bewildered Israeli police and other authorities, both for the riders and organisers.

During a gap in the schedule of the trip, Bruce and some of his teammates decided on a trip to the coast, hoping to explore a little of the strange country while they were there. Driving with Sonny Nutter, Mike Curuso and Rick Woods and having just crossed the Jordanian border, the four unlikely Americans had aroused suspicion. They were promptly pulled over by armed guards with machine-guns pointed at their heads. Only after a terrifying hour of questioning and interrogation were their stories believed and the four men released to go about their business!

On the track, despite the language barriers, the unfamiliar machinery, the undesirable track surfaces and, thrown in for good measure, three days of constant rain to start the tour, things went well! The intention by Briggs was always to avoid disrupting British League racing, even though the trip took place over the end of March and beginning of April – just when the British season had got underway. Subsequently, the 'World' team had an unfamiliar look about it, but still a fair smattering of some recognisable speedway greats. Certainly it was no less than a wonderful opportunity and experience for young Bruce to measure just how much progress he was making. Briggs himself starred and pulled off something of a coup in tempting five-times World Champion Ove Fundin out of retirement especially for the venture. Then there was the American League's first foreign capture Bert Harkins, a couple of other riders with some British League experience who were not tied to contracts in 1976 and the numbers were made up with New Zealander Frank Shuter, formerly of the Exeter Falcons in Britain, who was working as an engineer in Israel at the time and also heading for the US League later that year. Shuter's local knowledge from living in the country and his own transport was a huge help and surely helped to guarantee his place in the septet! The Americans featured Woods, Curuso and Nutter along with Dubb Ferrell, Steve Bast, Scott Sivadge and Penhall himself. Tracks were made from granite, which Bruce recalls as looking like a dark cinder that wouldn't hold together properly as shale does on a conventional track, laid on top of an athletics surface. There was no ideal equipment to construct the tracks so they came apart very early in the meetings with huge ruts being formed all around them. Bruce loved it! He was used to deep tracks and had no problems in having to pass from the back due to the handicap racing in America. While some riders treated the competition as demonstration races, Bruce wanted to win regardless and the highly enthusiastic crowds very quickly warmed to his all-action style.

The two teams exchanged victories over the first two tests with Bruce top scoring for the USA in both matches. After being so eager to do well in the first one though, he was approached by Briggs and Fundin with some useful words of caution and advice. Impressed by his talent, the two former World Champions said they were sure that there would be several big races ahead of him in his career – but he might want to slow down a little in order to live long enough to experience them! Buoyed by simply sharing the pits with such successful international stars, he teamed up with Rick Woods in the third match – the same guy who had been at the centre of Bruce's first forays into racing – to lead the Yanks to a second victory and a 2-1 series lead, scoring nine behind Woods' tally of eleven. The last two matches went evenly one apiece to each team, giving the USA a 3-2 aggregate score. Bruce chipped in with more modest returns of four and six respectively, but earned himself plenty of admirers both on the terraces and in the opposition camp of the 'World' side.

He was determined to make the most of every aspect of the trip and by the time the sixth and final meeting came around, he was hooked on the European-style racing on the bigger tracks with his next goals firmly set on more international ventures. Bowing out in style, he pitched in a battling performance in the Israel Open, to bid his new fans a fitting farewell. The same riders from the team events all competed for the individual prize and Bruce scored 7 points in the qualifying round of heats to earn himself sixth spot and a place in the semi-final races. He then won his semi after Briggs had suffered an engine failure while leading, beating Sweden's Bengt Larsson and compatriot Sonny Nutter. Overall glory was a just a step too far, but he went on to finish third in the final behind winner Oyvind Berg and the maestro Ove Fundin, who had clocked two maximum scores in the Test matches, leaving Larsson in last. It still rates for Bruce as one of the greatest trips he ever had in speedway. He enjoyed some great performances, even though still just a 'rookie', and the chance to race against the like of Briggs and Fundin were more than an aspiring young rider could have dreamed of. While he was revelling in pitting his wits and developing track skills against the all-time greats, they were in return experiencing first-hand the relatively raw talent and untapped potential, from a British club point of view, that Penhall was displaying. 'A fabulous rider and the most impressive of the Americans' enthused the defeated Open semi-finalist and proud organiser, Barry Briggs, after the end of the tour, 'one of the hottest properties in America right now'. And so Penhall would be. Returning home to prepare for the rapidly approaching start of the experimental US League season, he would also have to prepare himself for the steady flow of offers that would be coming his way from eager British League promoters who were already beginning to be alerted to his outstanding ability.

THREE

THE LA SPROCKETS

Bruce returned from Israel in April 1976 and the tapes went up on the new American League season a little over a month later. Each of the five participating clubs were building their teams from scratch, so it was decided to pool all available riders together and allow the promoters to pick their riders in turn, one by one. Ironically, Bruce was chosen to ride for the Los Angeles Sprockets at Irwindale, so his home track turned out to be around the same circuit as his first professional meeting three years earlier. It was a good omen, and better news was that he would be teaming up with multi-US National Champion Mike Bast, pretty much the best rider on the domestic circuits at the time. Bast would become the next great influence on young Bruce's career. 'I can honestly say that Mike was so very important to my success in speedway',s he admits now. 'I really benefited riding under him for the season and he taught me more than anyone could ever imagine, including Mike Bast himself.'

So, the teams were decided, and the Irwindale outfit boasted Bast and Penhall, along with Gene Woods (Rick's brother, who later followed a successful speedway career with NASCAR and Monster Trucks). Joining them was Frank Shuter, the former British Leaguer who had been up against Bruce's US side on the Israel tour, and a few lesser lights who never fulfilled any great rise to fame. The top riders of the time were shared around and gave the league a well-balanced look. Bakersfield Bandits were installed as early favourites though, featuring not only the highly promising talent of Jeff Sexton and Dubb Ferrell, but the travelling Scot, Bert Harkins. Ventura Sharks were led by the popular Sonny Nutter along with the up-and-coming Bobby Schwartz, while San Bernadino signed up Bruce's buddy, Dennis Sigalos, who had now followed him into professional speedway and was making noticeable strides of his own. Costa Mesa's Orange County Eagles had a fascinating look, combining the proven ability of Rick Woods, Bill Cody and Alan Christian with former TV-star turned speedway rider, Billy Gray. Gray was better known for playing the part of Bud in the American sitcom *Father Knows Best*, but was beginning to carve out an impressive niche on the speedway tracks too.

It was rather symbolic of the way the league racing experiment would turn out that many of the opening meetings of the season were marred by heavy rain. Irwindale's opening meeting barely survived the weather after two days of downpours completely decimated the track surface. It had to be scraped and covered with 100 tonnes of decomposed granite, dumped over the rain puddles. Despite windy conditions hampering proceedings further, the match was staged as planned, albeit with a rather problematic spongy new surface. From the start, Bruce was keen to prove himself both as a quality rider and a useful team member. He found the league setup exciting, but not as exciting as the adoring public soon found him. Racing was, and still is, very close because the circuits are so small and tricky. There simply isn't enough room on a 180-yard track to pull too far away from the chasing pack. Added to the fact that teams and riders were very evenly matched and it made for typically action-packed heats, close contact, and plenty of falls and crashes – but relatively very few serious injuries, partly due to less chance of building up any dangerous speed. Mike Bast took Bruce under his wing and the young pretender flourished with the guidance of the seasoned professional. The pair quickly established themselves as a winning combination and within a few weeks were recognised as the top two riders in the league. Penhall had edged his way up the individual rankings, surpassing the likes of Sexton, Ferrell, Woods and Christian – all of whom had flirted with British League promoters to varying extents. The top two Sprockets riders were among the first on the domestic American scene to switch to the new four-valve bikes that were just earning prominence in the British Leagues at that time. It was another factor that helped to set them apart from the rest of the pack.

All five competing league tracks reported initial success and the crowds were encouraging. Despite being used to the individual racing diet, the supporters could take both the teams and their favourite riders to heart. American fans are a much bigger part of the show than their British counterparts; there are lots of banners and plenty of leaping up and down cheering on their heroes. Just as in Israel, Bruce's full-on determined style endeared him to the locals. Extrovert American announcer Larry Huffman, who dreamed up all the riders' nicknames, christened Bruce 'The Fox', largely because of his extraordinary good looks. The American promoters had also dreamed up some extra features to add to the all-important entertainment show. The smart yet simple idea of teams wearing matching racing suits and helmets in team colours for meetings, was a concept which British League promoters finally came round to adopting some twenty-five years later! Bruce's first team colours for Irwindale were blue and yellow. In an interesting race format, league meetings were staged over thirteen heats with six-man teams. Each of the six riders would have four programmed rides with a seventh 'reserve' rider on standby. Heat thirteen was a nominated race, but a fourteenth heat was also programmed in as a decider, should it be required. The Yanks decided there would be no drawn matches and a match-race between one rider from each team would decide the outcomes. Penhall and Bast regularly featured for Irwindale in heat thirteen, and the chances to shoot-out for the match points in heat fourteen were usually shared. The top couple of riders in every team were the stars of the league and would frequently find relatively easy pickings among the bottom end of their opposition teams, while the best contest in a match was naturally between the top two from each side. Bruce, The Fox, was second best to Bast, but as a pair they were feared by many other sides, especially with the perfect combination of Bast's renowned lightning starts and Penhall's attacking manoeuvres from the back.

No team managers were employed, so it was down to the team captains to choose riders for heat thirteen. The initial intentions were to allow no guest riders or rider replacement as in the more complicated rules of the British League and there were no riders' averages to worry about, as American speedway fans were far less statistically orientated than Europeans. They wanted the show and they wanted to be entertained. People rarely bothered to even fill in a programme, in stark contrast to the meticulous details completed in Britain. Halfway through the season however, the league was forced into adopting a rider replacement rule to cover for the build-up of injuries in certain teams. The treatment tables were so full that San Bernadino even lost every single team member to injury at one point or another during the six-month season. Hardly surprising for Sigalos's team though: the track was built on a former county rubbish dump and whenever Bruce seemed to visit, he remembers that the junk would regularly work its way to the surface creating lumps, bumps and holes where you'd least expect. It was just another step along the learning curve though, and Bruce was gradually earning more and more respect, both in the US and from his long-distance admirers.

At the end of the season, he was approached by Barry Briggs to join the next annual Champions Troupe, this time touring Australia and New Zealand and eventually taking in a similar US leg to that which had been cancelled twelve months earlier. The same promoters would be involved and Bruce was beginning to build up a good relationship with both Harry Oxley in the States and Briggs, who was still based in Britain. He had done enough on the Israel tour, combined with those impressive performances throughout the rest of 1976, to warrant the full call-up to the troupe, and would be lining-up in some more highly esteemed company, including 1976 British World Champion Peter Collins, multi-World Champion Ole Olsen and the biggest names of all, Briggs and Mauger. Before he left however, there was the highly prestigious matter of the US National Championship to race.

The 1975 final had been held at the LA Coliseum, and although deemed to be a success, the atmosphere was lacking in comparison to the ever-popular Costa Mesa circuit. So, in 1976 the National Championship moved back to the Orange County Fairgrounds in front of a 10,000 capacity crowd. Bruce's new status on the American circuits was confirmed when he was installed as pre-meeting favourite for the title. If there was anyone at all who could knock reigning champion Mike 'The Bike' Bast off his perch, then it was his Irwindale teammate and colleague, Bruce. Among the great banners in the crowd that night, one stood out: 'Beat 'em all, Penhall' it read, and for the first time in any major competition, Bruce was riding under the pressure and the expectation of a potential favourite rather than an outsider. It was something that he would certainly get used to over the years and would learn to live with much more than virtually any other rider. On the night of the National, however, the unfamiliar pressure was a factor from the beginning. He made a poor start in his opening race and got thoroughly filled in with mud from the back wheels of Bobby Schwartz and Larry Shaw on a well-watered track. But there was encouragement for 'Super Bruce' as Bast opened with a second place behind Alan Christian. The title of National Champion was one of the first goals that Bruce had set himself to achieve in honour of his late parents and the possibility came a little closer when Shaw finished third in his next ride, giving further hope to both Penhall and Bast. It all came down to heat nineteen, with Bruce knowing a victory over 'Mike the Bike' would force a three-man run-off for the championship, along with Shaw. The top two Irwindale teammates produced one of the most electrifying races in Nationals history, passing and repassing each other time and time again for four laps, side by side and never more than a bike length apart. In the end, it was the more experienced Bast who edged over the line ahead and took the overall victory with 14 points, securing his fourth title. A thoroughly dejected Bruce was relegated to third on 12, a point behind surprise-package Shaw.

Although it hadn't quite turned out as planned, it was another great performance and a good enough return to boost Bruce's confidence before the forthcoming World Champions Series. He was still young, enthusiastic and relatively inexperienced, but he was extremely focused on his goals and lacked no determination in his will to eventually succeed. Drafted into the squad for Australia and New Zealand at a relatively late stage and still with only the Middle East tour in his competitive foreign racing CV, the trip down under would be a huge experience that was almost enough in itself to prepare him for the challenges of European racing. Bruce knew by that point that to make real progress on the world stage, he would sooner or later have to make the move across the Atlantic to Britain, and he was determined to maximise the opportunity of spending time with internationally established stars and former world champions. Starting out in New Zealand, Bruce eased his way into the series, finding some difficulty at first adapting to the speed and size of the racing tracks down under, which were in many cases at least twice the size of Costa Mesa. Riders competed on an individual basis through a series of qualifying heats, leading up to semi-finals and a final at the end of each meeting, with series points awarded based on overall finishing positions. By the time the troupe reached the end of round three of the ten-round series, in Wellington, Bruce had made it to his first final and took third place behind Mauger and Czech rider Jiri Stancl, beating World Champion Collins into fourth. It was the first of his tour results that people really noticed, but his performances had stood out once again from the very start. On paper, he shouldn't have been given a hope against the quality and experience of the opposition he faced, but rookie Penhall fitted in perfectly and rarely looked out of place among a group of riders who were at the very top of the sport. 'One highlight of the tour so far', commented Briggs again, a year after Israel, 'has been the riding of Bruce Penhall, the blonde wonder from California. He settled in straight away and has been a big hit with the crowds wherever we have gone.'

He qualified for the final four in the next round as well, followed by consecutive semi-final appearances in the next two, placing him fifth in the series standings at the halfway stage, out of a total of ten regular riders and a number of wild-card entries. Moving over to Australia, the troupe were faced with torrid weather conditions from one extreme to another with a 100-degree heatwave in Adelaide followed by torrential rain and flooding that forced the cancellation of round nine in Newcastle. In between though, Mauger had done enough to clinch the overall Champions Trophy with an eighth-round victory in Bundaberg. Rounding off the tour in Melbourne, Bruce missed out on a last semi-final spot after losing a run-off with the victorious Mauger. It meant that in the final series standings, the relatively unknown outsider finished joint seventh. It was below all the rest of the riders who had managed to compete in every round, but the experience was truly invaluable. The emerging American took many scalps during the tour, defeating riders who should in theory have been streets ahead of him. He beat Ivan Mauger in the first meeting in New Zealand and even defeated Peter Collins from the back in a dashing ride at Wellington. He consistently gave a thoroughly good account of himself, both on the track, and most significantly off the track too. During the series, he struck up a great friendship with Collins and invited Peter and his wife Angie to stay at his Newport Beach family home when the riders moved on to California for the USA *v.* The Rest of the World Test series. Peter would offer much advice on Bruce's best options in considering a move to the UK and, to this day, still remains a close friend, staying with Bruce and his family whenever visiting the States.

While in Australia and New Zealand, the riders involved with the Champions Series were invited to take part in a number of other meetings, which all provided more practice for Bruce. There was a benefit match for Ronnie Moore, involving Canterbury State (NZ) versus an Overseas Select, in Christchurch, where Bruce scored a creditable 5 and the visitors won 32-22 over nine heats, and then a contrasting performance in an open meeting in Perth a week later where he failed to score from four rides. In the same week there was another open event at Liverpool, New South Wales. Although he notched just 5 points once again, he looked impressive and his tally included a noteworthy opening-race victory over Aussie John Boulger and Swede Bernt Persson, two internationals both at the time riding for Cradley Heath in the British League. Some of the best behind-the-scenes experience was also earned at the Australasian final, held in Sydney in between rounds seven and eight of the Champions Series. While some of the troupe's riders took a rest or watched the action from the other side of the fence, Bruce was thrilled to be asked by Ivan Mauger to help out in his camp in the pits during the meeting. Watching the preparation in the pre- and post-race tasks carried out would all rub off on the youngster. In actual fact, he was soaking it up like a sponge.

From Australia, it was back to the United States to round off the tour for all the riders. At last there was a USA *v.* The Rest of the World Test series on the Yanks' home turf. Bruce was keen to show a little more of what he could do on the tracks that he was infinitely more familiar with, and top-scored for the hosts in the opening clash, scoring a fantastic 14 points. The rest of the mainly young, inexperienced Americans were no match for the international visitors, even with the home track advantage at Costa Mesa, and the World side ran out 55-35 winners. Only the more-established Scott Autrey provided any consistent stern defence for the USA in the Second Test at Irwindale, although Bruce clocked a worthy 8 points, followed by 6 in a surprise home victory in the third and final meeting in Ventura.

When first starting out, it had taken Penhall, from being a complete rookie, around a year or two to earn the respect of his fellow riders on the American racing scene. It had now taken him the period of two foreign racing tours to merit the admiration of the international speedway community. And the world of speedway racing had certainly noticed him now.

FOUR

OFFERS FROM THE BRITISH LEAGUE

American riders had no modern tradition of success in the tough demands of the British League. The upsurge of the sport in the States had alerted British promoters to the prospect of spicing up their teams with some Californian flavouring, and the American League created little short of a frenzy of riders being mooted to try their hand in the UK. Few of those who actually made the trip across the waters lasted very long though. Two riders stood apart: Scott Autrey and Steve Gresham. Autrey in particular had made a name for himself with the Exeter Falcons since arriving on British shores in the winter of 1972/73. Two of his countrymen, Sumner McKnight and that man again, Rick Woods, had made the journey at the same time but none lasted more than a few matches. Woods in particular went home disillusioned after his spell with Newport, complaining of the weather, the conditions and the earnings, despite being one of the top-ranked riders in his home country at the time and winning the American Championship in 1968, 1970 and 1972. Gresham had carved out a few solid seasons in Britain, but most of the others who aspired for greater things in Europe in the 1970s had soon fallen by the wayside and ended up back home in the sun. For Bruce then, there were no shortage of hard-luck tales to listen to and more than enough riders who were willing to share their stories about why not to go to Britain. But he knew that if he was to have any chance of achieving such great feats as conquering the World Championship, then there was no doubt whatsoever in his mind that Europe, and in particular the British League, was *the* place to be. 'The early riders like Rick, Sumner and Dewayne [Keeter] did not last long. I think they thought things were going to be a lot different than they were. They were making great money back home and they had great-looking women chasing them all time! Plus, the furthest track for them to travel to was only two hours away with perfect eighty-five-degree weather. I was into one thing and that was going over to become World Champion, I never listen to the ugly stories. However, that is why it took a while to sign my contract. I wanted to think of only one thing: that was riding the motorcycle!' The first of the offers actually came at the beginning of 1976, almost twelve months before the tour of Australasia. It was from forward-thinking Hull promoter Ian Thomas, who has since become one of the most respected men administrating the sport in the UK, through a long and successful career. Hull even went as far as declaring 'new signing' Bruce Penhall in their 1976 line-up, and not just that. They also had Wolverhampton's reigning World Champion Ole Olsen in there too. Neither rider would ever eventually appear for the Vikings, but the British Speedway Promoters Association, the BSPA, confirmed them both in the 1-7 at their rider control meeting. At the time, Bruce claims that there had not even been any contact between Thomas and himself, although the promoter did later fly to Los Angeles when he was still trying to convince Olsen to move to Humberside. While Bruce insisted he was staying in the USA for at least the time being, and at eighteen years old wasn't quite ready for the transatlantic move, Olsen was insisting that he would only ride for Coventry Bees – who also desperately wanted him in their line-up – or he wouldn't be appearing in the British League at all. Bruce never genuinely considered the offer at such a relatively early stage of his career, and was at the time all geared up for racing in the new American League. After weeks of wrangling, Olsen was allowed to line up at Brandon for the Bees, and Hull instead signed Barry Briggs, alongside Mike Curuso in the place of Penhall.

It was around the time of Bruce's trip down under, early in 1977, where the chase for his signature really began to heat up. There had been that sparkling performance to earn third place in the US National, which alerted some observant British promoters to his potential. More significantly, news from the Aussie and New Zealand matches regularly filtered back to Britain through a variety of sources – riders, promoters, fans, journalists – and soon enough everyone in the UK was hearing about the new blonde, pin-up glamour boy of the USA, who could by the way ride a mean speedway race. He was first linked in the media with Halifax and Coventry, and then Wolverhampton and Exeter openly joined the hunt. In truth, offers and negotiations began to take place before any of the boys set off for the Champions troupe series, but from the outset, Bruce was always determined to take his time and seek not just the best deal but the best setup to suit his style in Britain. He sought advice from some of the biggest names around, and his likeable personality had earned him friendships in various quarters. The promoters in Britain all thought that they could use those allies to their own advantage. Exeter claimed to have an influence over Bruce through Ivan Mauger, who was riding for the Falcons at the time. Speculation then was that Mauger, who helped Bruce in many ways while with the troupe, would be trying to convince him to throw his lot in at the County Ground and join, not just Mauger, but fellow American Scott Autrey. The reality was that Ivan gave his advice and kept a watchful eye out for Bruce, but never gave him the 'hard sell' or got involved with any serious discussions on the subject. Wolverhampton also considered themselves to have some powers of persuasion, with Wolves rider Jimmy McMillan forming part of the touring troupe. Scotsman McMillan did indeed help in a big way with negotiations between the parties, but a deal with Wolves was never close, despite Jimmy Mac's involvement. Halifax seemed to have pulled out the trump card with their own insider, Chris Pusey. The Liverpool-born former Belle Vue rider was not with the troupe, but had made Penhall's acquaintance much earlier. Pusey made regular winter excursions to the States in search of brighter weather and some more laid-back relaxation in between British seasons. He also rode in the odd meeting at Costa Mesa and even ran his own training school in the US early in 1975. Around that time, Bruce's mechanic was John Mack, who previously tuned engines for Steve Bast. John would regularly house a few of the European riders during their visits to the States and Bruce was often introduced to them. When Pusey stayed, he took a liking to the bold young Penhall and invited him to visit the UK and stay with him. The ace in the pack for Halifax was that Bruce had taken up the offer and made that trip. The Dukes promoter Eric Boothroyd publicly announced that Penhall had already secretly practised at The Shay in 1975, while holidaying in the UK and staying with one of their riders, so naturally he would be joining them. Furthermore, he had clocked a time of roughly 69 seconds, compared to a track record at the time of about 64, which was not bad for a novice on his only visit. The news came as a setback to the rest of the clubs hoping to add Penhall to their 1977 line-up, but nothing had been decided for certain.

'I can remember the day [of the Halifax practice]. It was very cold and raining I could hardly hold on to the handlebars,' says Bruce, looking back. 'I thought Halifax was a cool track, fast and narrow with a great bank to it.' But he knew there was much more to the deal and he wanted everything to be right before making any firm commitment. It was a sensible, mature approach to what would be a well-planned and well-thought out move in his career, in stark contrast to other Americans who jumped at the chance to join the first British club who sought their services, and it would stand Bruce in good stead when he eventually made the transition. Even at that stage of his career, he would openly talk of his plans to spend only around five years in Britain, much less than would be expected of the top-class riders earning a living from the sport. 'That approach came from my father' he reflects. 'It's real simple; My father only wanted me to ride speedway for a short time and then take over the family business. This is such a short career, riding motorcycles, you can only do it while you're young. "Have fun, and if you screw it up or you get in trouble, you're not going to ride" – because he wouldn't allow it – "and take over the family business. That is a lifelong ambition, and you will do well, and you can run this business." I always kind of looked into that and made sure that was always in the back of my mind, and I knew it wasn't going to last forever. I wanted to be here [in California]. This is where all my family was, and I was very, very close to all my family. It was something that was always instilled in both my brother and sister and I. He really would have liked us to take over the family business. "Have fun while you're young but don't screw up because there's a lot of kids that look up to you. If you do, you're done with this." This is what my Dad wanted, and I actually somewhat wanted it too.'

As the weeks rolled by into the spring of 1977 and the start of the British season drew ever closer, Bruce was being mentioned every other week in the UK speedway press. He admitted to being 'a confused man', inundated with offers and with the whole move tempered by the fact that he owned a luxurious home in California with his brother and sister, whom he would have to leave behind. The lifestyle he had been lucky enough to enjoy while growing up was wonderful and his late parents provided a terrific living environment for their family.

'We lived on the beach in Balboa,' Bruce recalls with a smile. 'Beautiful water, beautiful girls and the greatest weather anywhere.' It needed to be a near-perfect offer to tempt him away, even with the consideration of his international and World Championship ambitions. Everyone had an opinion about where he would end up and the speculation grew to intense levels. Bruce talked to Harry Oxley and Barry Briggs in the US, two of the people who had shown great faith in him before anyone else. He also spoke to both Peter Collins and Doug Wyer, who had become good friends after their visits to the States. The pair of Englishmen offered advice about teams, locations and promoters. They discussed which tracks would suit Bruce's style. In the case of Collins in particular, it was the next development in what would become a lifetime friendship. Bruce explains: 'He was one of the most sincere guys. He would give the supporters more time than you could imagine and a he was a true fighter on the track. The only thing that held Pete back from winning more World Championships was that he didn't make good starts. But he was hell from the back! I learned a great deal from PC both on and off the track. To this day I consider him one of my true friends, more so than all but one of the American boys, and I always look forward to seeing him.' Towards the end of March, Halifax gave up on their efforts to lure Bruce to West Yorkshire for the time being at least. Even though Penhall remained undecided, the Dukes used their only foreign permit to entice twenty-three-year old Norweigan Tom Godal instead. Wolves also turned their attentions elsewhere and tried unsuccessfully to tempt Bobby Schwartz to Monmore Green. While the offers had appeared one by one, Bruce was never persuaded to take up any that didn't feel exactly right. In any case, his number-one intention all along was to stay in the States for 1977, but he was wise enough to court the British clubs and see what sort of deal they were prepared to come up with. He still didn't feel sure that he was ready for Britain and didn't want to join the list of riders – from the USA and elsewhere – who had tried and failed to cope with the demands of UK racing. Above all else though, he had already committed himself to a national sponsor in the States for the 1977 season and it would have taken an enormous deal to prise him away from that contract. The Wild West Stores were one of the first national chains to get involved with speedway in America at that time, but were only known on that side of the ocean. For Bruce to take their name and logo to Britain would have been no use to them whatsoever; they had agreed to back him on the basis that their brand would be advertised around the Californian speedway circles. In addition to the sponsorship, Bruce felt that one more season in the States would be enough to build up his level of equipment to the better standards required of the rigorous British League, and wanted one more crack at the US National Championship. Back in those days, the National was only open to American riders competing on the domestic US scene, so if Bruce moved to Europe, he would become ineligible and miss out on a dream target. The mêlée in Britain died down. All the clubs who had missed out on Penhall managed to recruit their teams and went on their way. Drawing a line under 'what might have been', as far as the British public were concerned, *Speedway Star* magazine took the almost unprecedented step of printing an action photograph of Bruce on their front cover near the end of April; something very unusual, to say the least, for a rider who had never competed officially in Britain and had little to no international experience.

So, it was back to normality in the 1977 American season – in more ways than one. Bruce settled down to racing on the domestic circuits again, without the pressures from abroad, and it was back to individual scratch and handicap racing for the Yanks after the early interest in league racing had gradually dwindled. There really weren't enough competitive riders to field five quality teams and the speedway show suffered because of it. The format was not popular with the fans because they were used to seeing all of the top stars every week at their local track riding individually. With the team setup, they only saw the top men every few weeks. Only four or five of the stars would be appearing on a single night, because any riders in the bottom half of each league team would not be the names to feature very prominently on the bill, had it been an individual meeting. Plus, handicap racing provided more passing and more crashes and tumbles. The fans wanted to see more of it, not find it pushed to a short second-half support event. 'It's a shame that team racing never took off in the States,' Bruce mused. 'I loved it!'

From a riders point of view, there were benefits in the return to an individual setup too. They would be seeing each other more often and a great social scene was present between them. Because the top riders met each other so often, there had to be a trust between them, and it didn't do any harm if they were friends off-track as well. One example of the camaraderie around the Californian scene was the craze of CB radios during the mid to late seventies. The top riders travelled to meetings in relative style, in comparison to some of their British counterparts at the time, with some rather plush vans to carry their bikes and equipment. Lots of riders had CB radios fitted and would be chatting away or winding each other up, en route to the track, all recognisable only according to their nicknames or 'handles'. Although he didn't really get into the craze too much, Bruce was known as 'Mr Wizard', due to being nicknamed 'The Pinball Wizard' by some of his riding pals. Getting in on the act as well as the other riders were 'The Hot Shoe Man' (the late Ken Maely, who was very well known for, among other things, his own very popular practice track, and for making all the riders' steel shoes) and of course there was 'The Godfather' (who else, but the man at the most successful promoting helm in the state, Mr Harry Oxley).

The true highlight of the season for Penhall was the World Championship qualifying meetings, beginning with the American final in July. This was a separate event to the US Nationals, which were usually raced at the end of the season, and was staged purely to decide on the riders who would represent the USA in subsequent rounds along the World final qualification route. The decision on whether to stage the meeting at all, or to seed the best riders directly to the Inter-Continental final, was always a contentious one. Many of the domestically based riders were not interested in pursuing the ensuing qualification dream because of the high cost of travelling to Europe for a single meeting and the even higher standard of competition when they got there. The

European-based Yanks, such as Scott Autrey, who by this time was edging ever closer to the quality required of a World finalist, disliked the idea of having to travel the same distance in the opposite direction, just to compete in the American qualifier. The same debate seemed to rage every single year in the late 1970s, but in 1977 the AMA ruled that the American qualifier would be staged and if Autrey or any other US rider for that matter, wanted a chance to progress towards the World final, then they would have to compete in the event. Autrey begrudgingly returned for the duty of riding in the meeting to ensure his safe passage via whatever means necessary. But things didn't quite turn out as planned for the experienced campaigner; he hadn't counted on the ambitions of Bruce Penhall. Mike Bast won the meeting, but it was Penhall who beat Autrey in a five-lap run-off for the second and final qualifying spot. To finish runner-up in the meeting was a fine accomplishment for twenty-year old Bruce in front of another capacity crowd. If he had been temporarily forgotten by the British public during the intervening months since the start of the UK season, then he was well and truly back in the headlines now. Moreover, preparations immediately ensued for his first serious racing trip to England.

Bruce and Mike Bast travelled to England together in August for the Inter-Continental final at London's White City venue. There was no Overseas final then, which was introduced as a stepping stone and extra qualifying round a few years later, so the Americans suddenly found themselves just five rides away from the World final. Competition in the event was fierce though, and only the top eight from sixteen could march on. Most riders were British-based and had the advantage of a mere car journey to get to the track, rather than having to acclimatise to a different country. A two-week stay was arranged, giving time for the pair of ex-Irwindale stars to settle down after their flights and prepare as best they could for one of the biggest meetings of either of their careers. There had also been the promise of some open meetings or guest appearances by promoter Reg Fearman to give them some more experience of British tracks, but this was frustratingly blocked by the Speedway Control Board. Harry Louis, then manager of the SCB, insisted that riders not contracted to British League tracks could only ride in FIM-inscribed meetings, of which there were none scheduled before the Inter-Continental final itself. Furthermore, to sign a contract they would first have to acquire a work permit. The gloss was immediately taken off the trip, but the guys still wanted to get in some racing practice before their much-hyped appearance at White City. They managed to have a spin on three or four different tracks, after watching the preceding league meetings at Wimbledon, Hackney and Leicester. Someone at Coventry didn't take too kindly to their efforts though, and the track lights were turned out on them while riding post-match at Brandon! They were also introduced to Alf Hagon, who gave them some workshop space in order to prepare their machines.

'For the most part, the British people were very good to me,' Bruce remembers. 'But I can honestly say that the way we were treated at a few of the tracks is another reason that I wanted to come back to England and prove that I could race with the best the world had to offer!'

When it came to the main job in hand, the occasion proved bigger than the pair of enthusiastic Americans imagined. The White City track was a huge difference to the tiny Costa Mesa circuit of their previous qualifying round and the attendance of 37,000 was bigger than that which would witness the World final itself in Sweden less than a month later. In the end, Bruce scored 3 points, finishing ahead of only two other riders. In last place, however, was his compatriot Bast, so after all the occasions of finishing second in the pecking order, this time it was Penhall who faired the marginally better of the two rivals, but it mattered little. Qualifiers from the meeting were dominated by an impressive array of the world's top stars including Peter Collins, who was the defending World Champion at the time and meeting winner, plus ex-champions Olsen and Mauger. Bruce had fallen in his first ride as Olsen equalled the White City track record, and his confidence was shattered; he suffered a last place in his next with Collins a distant winner, then mustered a third place and his first point in heat twelve by beating Phil Crump, who suffered machine problems. He beat Bast in his next for third again and grabbed another consolation point in his final heat ahead of Keith White. Even taking into account the top-class opposition, Bruce had struggled to turn any heads. The experience in hindsight however was absolutely vital, and would stand him in very good stead when that big permanent move across the pond was to arise. While Bruce was disappointed with his performance, there were still some British promoters whose interest in the rider had been rekindled. He was once again approached by Halifax, who offered him the chance to stay on and have an immediate crack at the rest of the UK domestic circuit. The deal once more didn't feel right though, and as a kid with a smart head on his suntanned shoulders, he wisely declined, still preferring to bide his time over the right move. More than that, and with the trip also costing him a lot of money from his own pocket, he felt at the time that he'd made something of a fool of himself in front of the British public. He left saying that he'd never come back. It had been a natural reflex reaction to the frustrations of the trip and it didn't take long for Bruce to refocus on his lifelong dreams and aspirations of speedway success once he was back home. He knuckled down for the remainder of the US season and built up a head of steam with some fine form leading into the National final in October. Unfortunately it was the same old story at Costa Mesa, with Mike Bast back on top and taking a record-breaking fifth title. Bruce went one better than the previous year and finished in second place after a run-off with the other Bast brother, Steve. Both finished on 13 points, just one behind the victorious Mike. At the end of the year, the Irwindale track, which had been such a prominent stage in Bruce's early career, was forced to close down. Irwindale itself is only a small, industrial town with a population of less than 1,500, so speedway crowds were never as high as some of the other Californian circuits. But, by the beginning of 1978, the land had been leased to the Miller Brewing Company for just $1, as the town knew it would reap subsequent benefits of tax money from the American beer giants.

During the British close season of 1977/78, the offers of a team place began to roll in once again for Bruce. Although negotiations this time were a little less frenzied, it was most of the same clubs as the previous season hoping that their similar packages might seem more appealing than twelve months earlier. Bruce was ready for a move to England now and was itching to get on the plane as soon as what he considered to be a reasonable deal was placed before him. Although he stayed in the USA, there was International action again in March 1978 when a condensed Champions Troupe was brought to the US by Mauger and Briggs. They had not toured Australasia as the British Test squad were racing against the Aussies, but six meetings were arranged around the Californian tracks for just before the start of the new British season. Unfortunately, the riders arrived in Los Angeles to some of the worst weather conditions in the state for decades. Torrential rain and flooding forced the postponement of the first four dates, before the Americans took three comfortable victories. Penhall scored 16 in the first match behind Mike Bast's top score of 18, while the World side struggled, with minor resistance coming from Ivan Mauger and Peter Collins. The Second Test was abandoned after eleven heats, but not before Bruce and his mate PC had fought out a titanic tussle in the rain while most of the San Bernadino crowd were rushing to find shelter. Although the first four meetings were rearranged, The Rest of the World squad was decimated by riders returning to Britain for the start of their UK commitments. Ove Fundin was called upon as a late addition and again came out of retirement and to the rescue for organisers Briggs and Mauger. As Bruce was clocking up another couple of double-figure returns against the weakened World squad, there was just enough time for one more club to fail in a bid to land his signature before the right deal actually came along. King's Lynn were the penultimate suitors to pitch their best offer, with a view to bringing him into the Stars team for the 1978 season, and once again they thought they had an inside contact to broker the deal. Bruce had become friends with Martin Hignett, the mechanic of Michael Lee, who was then riding for the Stars. Thus the link was forged between rider and club. Hignett had previously worked with Peter Collins and was later the team mechanic for the British Lions in their tour of Australia in 1978. In the years of Bruce's eventual British career, he would become another good friend. However, although opening discussions were held with Stars promoter Martin Rogers, Bruce claims that the club weren't in a position to offer what some of the other clubs had done already, so no deal was struck. Shortly afterwards, however, he finally signed a contract, not for any of the previously interested clubs, but instead opted to join Cradley Heath.

FIVE

THE HEATHENS

While the other interested British League clubs had been clambering over each other for a year or more, trying to capture the signature of Bruce Penhall, a revolution was underway in the sleepy Black Country town of Cradley Heath. The club was traditionally unfashionable, unsuccessful and its Dudley Wood base was certainly one of the less glamorous homes of speedway racing. Changes began at the start of 1977 though with the arrival of new promoter, Dan McCormick. Outspoken Glaswegian McCormick had taken the reins at Cradley, his first stab at promoting a speedway club, making wild promises of success and silverware. Many experts discarded his comments and gave his patchwork side precious little hope of even holding its own in the toughest League competition in the world. But Dan was a great, great character with a huge personality. He was already making waves in the waters of British speedway and quickly earned a tremendous amount of respect from a most significant proportion of the Cradley Heath supporters. He wasn't a newcomer to the sport, but had never worked in the role of promoter of a speedway club. His involvement began as general manager of the Newcastle Diamonds from 1963-70, where he gained a good working knowledge of the sport, and he then had a stint with Wolverhampton before making the big step up with Cradley at the beginning of 1977. Among his achievements before speedway however, he had promoted a massive range of events from showjumping, horse racing, world film premieres, cavalcades of speed, celebrity football matches and charity balls. He was a man with a true entertainment background and he had come to give the Heathens faithful a real show.

The Cradley team for 1978 was to be based around four existing Dudley Wood riders: captain Bruce Cribb, fast-improving talented young Englishman Steve Bastable, promising local youngster Dave Perks and Arthur Price. Although the club had boasted former World Champion Anders Michanek in their septet for around a dozen matches in 1977, he had been discarded as sensationally as he had been signed, along with crowd favourite and fellow countryman Bernie Persson, when the pair of Swedes began missing too many domestic matches. Much-sought-after Birmingham rider Alan Grahame was added to the line-up, but McCormick had been chasing a host of other top names, failing in separate bids to land Australasians Phil Herne, John Titman and Larry Ross in the close season. The outspoken promoter was also good friends with the great Ivan Mauger and the Heathens had been rather audaciously linked with the multi-World Champion before he instead moved from Exeter to Hull. It was Mauger though, who McCormick turned to, late in the winter of 1977/78 to seek his recommendation of any young riders around the world, who might be worth bringing to Cradley. One name in particular was discussed: Bruce Penhall.

Although Dan had a lot of confidence in Ivan's opinion, he wasn't quite one hundred per cent sure that it would be the way forward. He had been seeking an established number-one rider to lead the troops and while Penhall had earned a very good reputation, he was still untried in Britain. Another key factor in the move for Bruce was the surprising figure of Dudley Wood track photographer John Hipkiss, who had holidayed in the USA over the winter. He came back from his trip, raving about the talents of the young American, and more importantly had acquired contact details for Bruce. Dan decided to take the plunge and made the call to California. Club administrator Chris Van Straaten was sitting opposite McCormick on the afternoon of that momentous telephone call, and he remembers the conversation to be short but positive. It took a matter of minutes to sort out the deal to bring Penhall to Cradley Heath. Except for the formalities of signing the contract, fulfilling the terms and applying for a work permit, McCormick had just captured the signature of one rider who would flourish into one of the greatest champions and ambassadors for speedway that the sport had ever experienced. But did it break the bank to do it? 'It was a big gamble' says

McCormick in reflection now. 'But I had confidence. I used to be good at my job, you know!'

What Bruce wanted in order to finally make the move to British speedway was a virtually unique package at the time, but one that has become commonplace now among riders coming to compete in the UK. He didn't want to worry about breaking down en route to a meeting, or to be distracted by having to find a decent place to live in a new country where he had no experience. He was a fine speedway rider, albeit a little raw around the edges at that time, and he basically wanted to be able to put his backside on the saddle and ride. McCormick listened to what it would require to set Bruce up for his first season in Britain, and then he delivered it. In return, Dan told Bruce that Cradley Heath was not a glamorous club and the stadium was, in truth, rather shabby, but it was a club that was going places, with big ambitions and fantastic supporters. Van Straaten jokes that, considering the dilapidated office in which they were sitting and imagining the luxurious surroundings on Bruce's side of the conversation, that an advancement in the technology of video phones may well have scuppered the whole arrangement before it even got off the ground! Fortunately, both parties were equally as impressed with what each other had to say, and Penhall had become a Heathen.

By the time the new signature was announced to the Cradley supporters, the season had already got underway. The team had beaten both Wolves at home and Birmingham away, but lacked top-end strength in their line-up if they were going to challenge at the top of the league. Although the Penhall signing saw the American comfortably into the middle order of the squad, there would be a hint of pressure for him to provide some considerable scoring support for Bastable, Cribb and Grahame in the heat-leader roles. Bruce flew into Heathrow airport in the final week of March, accompanied by his brother-in-law, Mark Cherry, who would be acting as his mechanic and mentor for the first month. Cherry was an established rider himself in the USA, having ridden for San Bernadino in the American League and even appeared in a couple of matches for Birmingham in the British League two years earlier. Things had not worked out and he had returned home, getting married to Penhall's sister Connie in the intervening time. In fact the wedding had been barely a month before the two guys flew out to the UK. Hence, Connie's support of Bruce's racing ambitions was tested somewhat, but she agreed to her new husband accompanying her little brother to England, and Bruce of course, remains eternally grateful!

Waiting at Heathrow airport on that cold Thursday morning to pick them both up was McCormick himself, along with his son Barry. A house had been rented in Penn, Wolverhampton for Bruce to live, which was just a few yards from then-Cradley team manager Bob Wasley's garage business – not that there was any suggestion that the promotion wanted to keep a close eye on their new prize asset! Before they made it to the house however, Dan the Man whisked the two bewildered arrivals off to the nearby Goldthorne Hotel in Penn, where journalist and friend of Cradley speedway Tom Johnson was waiting for the first interview and photo call with the new star. A few other selected press associates had been assembled in order that Dan could further build up the hype surrounding the new acquisition. Bruce was photographed sipping a typically English cup of tea, complete with little finger sticking out!

Pat Foley, stadium announcer and radio presenter at the time for Beacon FM (then Beacon 303), was another one of the people to interview both Bruce and Mark that Thursday afternoon. The interview was recorded for the following day's *Friday Sport* show, and Bruce came up with the most delightful comparison of the different track sizes in Britain and the USA; he said that English tracks were 'so big you could eat a cheese sandwich down the back straightaway', while the size of those back home were 'like riding in a doughnut hole!' When Foley asked Mark how important he was to Bruce's success, the reply was that 'the bike looks after itself. I just try to get his head right!' Finally they were allowed to settle into their new accommodation, where they promptly asked how to turn up the heating, as they struggled to adapt to the slight change in temperature between California and Cradley! After a quick change, the boys were taken by McCormick to the Heathens' new sister-track Oxford, to spectate at the Cheetahs' opening meeting of the season and begin the job of acclimatising, not just to Britain, but to British speedway.

Bruce brought with him his two regular Jawa speedway machines from the States and almost immediately made plans to trial a Weslake bike once in the UK. On the team front, cosmopolitan-looking Cradley were forced into a minor reshuffle. They had already signed ultra-professional Dane Kristian Praestbro and promising young Finn Pekka Hautamaki to the squad, and were awaiting the arrival of Czech newcomer Zdenek Kudra. The authorities were quick to inform them that one of the foreigners must be released to accommodate Penhall and it was Kudra who never made it into a Heathens race jacket. Bruce's debut was to be Cradley's fourth home match of the season, a challenge match against Sheffield on Saturday 1 April. McCormick arranged for him to have some practice spins around Dudley Wood on the Saturday morning to get his first taste of the track, before the meeting that same night. Tongues had started to wag about the new arrival and a couple of local kids could be found peering over the stadium fence to be the first to sneak a look at the new guy. The session went well, but then the heavens opened and Penhall was treated to an early dose of the great British weather. Rain during the rest of the day, most notably a huge deluge which came down when half the fans had already arrived at the stadium, forced the postponement of the eagerly anticipated debut – but only for a couple of days. The fixture was hastily rearranged for two nights later on the Monday evening, 3 April, which did officially become Bruce's first match for Cradley Heath.

The evening came and the crowd packed into Dudley Wood to see just what the new import could do. Bruce was introduced to the fans before the meeting and received a tremendous reception, although his first words were to tell his new public that he was 'freezing his ass off' in the cold English weather! His first race didn't quite go as planned though, with clutch problems forcing him to a premature halt, but in his next outing he picked up his first point behind Doug Wyer and teammate Alan Grahame. Unfortunately, it turned out to be his only point of the evening, although he was unlucky enough to face a pair of Tigers heat-leaders in both of his remaining races. He was visibly trying and putting himself about the track, and he did enough to impress most people with his style and determination, but was disappointed with himself and expected more.

Not every supporter had been satisfied with the signing and some were still to be won over. After all, the Heathens had been linked – genuinely or otherwise – with a long list of established top riders. Penhall arrived largely unknown to many people in the Midlands, other than those who had followed his overseas progress or seen him in the Inter-Continental final. To that minority, the solitary score was vindication that McCormick had not attracted a rider of the top quality they were seeking. It was, without doubt, early days. In fact, for the fans who had stuck around for the second-half event, which followed the Sheffield match, there was a rapidly improving Penhall on display. In the scarcely reported post-match 'Star of the Night' support races, Bruce used his preceding four-rides experience to good effect by first winning his qualifying heat and then finishing second in the final, after passing club captain Bruce Cribb from behind and leaving Steve Bastable at the back! He was learning fast and his debut return of a single point would be by far his lowest club score of the season, and indeed the rest of his career. Never again would he score anything less than four in Heathens colours.

On Thursday of that week, Bruce began the first of what would eventually add up to many hundreds of public appearances, by attending the Midland Sportsman of the Year luncheon in Birmingham. He was joined by McCormick and Cribb to see West Bromwich Albion footballer Cyrille Regis receive the award, and took the opportunity to catch up with another invited guest, his mate Peter Collins. Two days later, back at Dudley Wood for his second Heathens match, he clocked up a fine score of 9 points from four rides to silence any premature critics. It was a remarkable performance in only his second competitive match for the club and now everyone knew he had well and truly arrived.

Fans were soon dazzled with the American style that Penhall bought with him to brighten up the industrial Black Country; the flash leathers emblazoned with Bel Ray, the sponsor that would eventually become synonymous with his success; there was the cowboy hat or the baseball cap, and even his brightly attired mechanic gained prominence. Everything seemed to set him aside from the majority, right down to the full-face helmet design that he sported and virtually pioneered, compared to the open-face versions with accompanying monkey masks worn by British riders of the time. Already, Bruce was so much more than just another speedway rider. He was an entertainer, a personality; he stood out both on and off the track and it is doubtful that any other rider has ever set so many tongues wagging. He had been brought into the middle part of the Cradley team and ended up providing the Heathens with another much-needed heat-leader. It was the sort of masterstroke signing to transform any club, a prize acquisition for whom speedway promoters have searched the world, both before and since.

Bruce settled into the setup at Dudley Wood very quickly. He was very pleased with his decision to hold out for the right deal and knew early on that he could feel at home with the Heathens for some years to come. 'Those Cradley fans took me to their heart, and most of 'em just never let me go,' he fondly recalls. 'All of the riders that had helped me with my decision had also agreed that the Cradley fans were the most loyal, and they were right. Plus the deal that Dan had offered was awesome and I must say everything that he and Derek Pugh offered, they came through with.'

With his blonde hair, blue eyes and wide American smile, he was a massive hit with the ladies. Then there was his grit and determination on the track, which endeared him just as perfectly to the men. In a handful of remaining matches through April, he chipped in with some useful middle-order scores. His gating was letting him down, but all that handicap practice in the US enabled him to confidently come from the back. He quickly became known for some stunning sweeps around the boards in those early days, always a rider who would be slow from the start but deadly from the back. Maybe a little wild at times, and the cause of a few worrying gasps as he scraped paint off the perimeter fence at sixty miles per hour, but he was always a rider who people wanted to watch.

There had to be a few unforeseen changes at the Wood however, as Bruce's popularity with the female population grew immediately into unprecedented proportions. After one of his home matches in that first month, he was literally pinned to the door of the dressing rooms as he appeared after the meeting, with a horde of around forty screaming girls lunging forward for his autograph, photo or just to get close enough to be within touching distance. Chris Van Straaten confirms that after the incident, the club had to take the previously unimaginable step of putting guards on the dressing room door to keep the masses under control! It was the beginning of a fixation with the blonde bombshell. In hardly any time at all, speedway found itself blessed with so many more female spectators than ever before. The oft-perceived image of flying shale and dusty faced spectators suddenly no longer mattered; this boy was worth getting dirty for! Away from the track, not only did Bruce get his good-looking features on the front cover of *Speedway Star* magazine, complete with cowboy hat, but he also did a photo shoot with the *Observer* newspaper, unusual to say the least for a speedway rider. The first whirlwind month was capped with an invitation to ride in the prestigious Superama meeting at Hackney. On his first visit to the London venue, he started with a last place but then got better and better with every ride, dazzling the crowd with two second places and then two victories, securing a completely unexpected fifth place overall in a high-quality field. The event was sponsored by the Superama chain of central London stores, with a string of unusual prizes being donated to heat winners by all the traders, including jewellery, champagne and travel accessories. One of the rewards that Bruce walked away with for his efforts was a pair of braces and a belt with the word 'BOSS' printed on. He gave them as a charming gesture to his Cradley promoter, Dan McCormick, who still treasures the gift to this day.

In comparison to all the overseas riders who have been signed by British League promoters both before and since Bruce Penhall's arrival, few, if any, have performed so consistently well so quickly against such quality opposition. In circumstances where the most informed of experts were allowing him some grace as a newcomer or a novice, he would time after time dumbfound the critics and produce the sort of sparkling displays that any seasoned professional could be proud of. He went to tracks that he'd never seen or heard of before, and came away notching victories against the top home riders who raced there week in, week out. It was a rollercoaster ride from the very beginning of Penhall's British League career, but most of the time he was going onwards and upwards.

One of the immediately apparent differences between the British League and the way team racing had been adopted in the USA, was that the UK rules were being increasingly governed by riders' calculated match averages. This had two direct effects for Bruce. Firstly, he dropped to one of the reserve positions at the beginning of May and secondly, it was declared that he had to aim for one of the top two averages by any American in the league by the start of June, if he was going to compete in the World Championship. His BL average, as was standard for a rider with no prior experience, was assessed at 6.00 and stayed at that figure until he had completed six competitive fixtures in order to obtain a true, and more accurate figure. The norm was that 6.00 was a reasonable figure for any newcomer to achieve, but the majority actually fell considerably short by the end of their debut season. In fact, the SRA (Speedway Riders Association) were forced to back down later in the season over their proposed ruling whereby any foreigners falling short of that figure at the end of June would have to return home. The British League would have found considerable difficulty coping with the loss of around twenty riders, should the ruling have been imposed, most of which had at least one season's experience in the competition. When new averages were calculated in May, Bruce's Cradley teammates, who had a head start on their matches before the American's arrival, had obtained new figures and all but one had made lightning starts to the year, which catapulted them above Bruce's 6.00 assessment. Consequently the team had to be reshuffled for the lowest two averaged riders to be at the bottom, giving him less programmed rides but the chance for more extra substitute rides should he maintain his good early form. Needless to say that by the time, the next month's figures were released in June, he had rocketed not just out of the reserve berth but straight up into a heat-leader role, with a figure comfortably in excess of 8.00.

The situation regarding the American contingent in the World Championship race was rather more complicated and contentious. After the disharmony of the previous season where Bruce had knocked out a disgruntled Scott Autrey after the Exeter man had been forced to travel back to the USA for the qualifying meeting, the system was changed for 1978. The AMA decided that the top two Yanks in the British League, as of the first week in June, would be seeded directly to the Inter-Continental final in Denmark without any further qualification necessary. With the experienced Autrey clearly at the top of the tree, and the struggling Mike Curuso and Kelly Moran firmly out of the running, it left just two remaining Americans, Penhall and Steve Gresham, battling it out with each other. Furthermore, their two respective teams, Cradley and Bristol, were racing against each other at Dudley Wood on the final day before the averages were calculated. When the sums were done, the official figures showed that Penhall had by that time ridden enough matches to establish his own average and had reached a highly creditable 8.37. Gresham had not yet competed in enough matches, and his official figure was listed as 7.06, taken from his final tally of the previous season. Great news for Bruce, until the AMA were provided with a different set of figures based on the actual 1978 matches, where Gresham, who had missed four away matches and clocked up most of his points on his home track, stood pretty with 8.76. Bad news for Bruce; he was out of the World Championship race, without even getting a chance of qualifying through the normal route. He was gutted, pointing out that World Championship qualification was a big factor in him coming to Britain and all he wanted was a fair crack of the whip to improve upon his performance of the previous year. Despite all the arguments that ensued, it was Gresham who went to Denmark where he failed to make the cut for the World final itself. Bruce's dreams were shattered for another year, without having turned a wheel in competition.

There was, however, still plenty to focus on. He was already becoming a big draw at away tracks and open meetings, and for the first time, the USA had entered the World Team Championship, providing at least some consolation for the disappointment dished out in the individual competition. America barely had the opportunity to field a whole team of riders in any European-based competition, without the considerable expense of flying several of their less-experienced California riders over specially. For the preliminary qualifying round, Bruce teamed up with Autrey, easily their leading light at the time, plus Gresham and Mike Curuso, now plying his trade with Poole. Only Kelly Moran of the British-based Yanks was not included, as he was deemed ineligible due to being younger than the minimum qualifying age of eighteen years. Bruce scored 3 points against esteemed opposition, as the USA came within one point of causing a major upset. The highly experienced England and Australia squads were expected to walk away with the two qualification positions for the final, and although the Brits were virtually untouchable, the USA took Australia right to the wire in an indication of what they would begin to offer over the coming years.

He may have agonisingly missed out on the chance to prove himself on the individual world stage rather earlier in the season than he anticipated, but as the determined young Californian beach boy gradually found his feet in the industrial heart of the West Midlands, he had already begun to make his mark. His Cradley Heathens team were upsetting a few of the odds and providing a surprise result or two, not to mention some superb racing and entertainment, as they strived to end the club's barren years without success. The United States, as a speedway nation, had made their first tentative steps back into the international arena with their World Team Cup endeavours, and were showing the early glimpses of a return to the sort of prominence that they had not enjoyed since the late 1930s. Above all, wherever Bruce appeared, whether representing his club, his country or as an individual, he was commanding respect from the discerning speedway patrons and attracting fresh adoration from a whole new public, who were being compelled to watch.

SIX

WONDERFUL, WONDERFUL CRADLEY HEATH

By mid-season, Bruce was scoring points around Dudley Wood as if he had ridden the track for years. He had made the move from Jawa bikes, which he had bought over from the States, to the British Weslake within about a month of his arrival. The machinery change had proved to be a significant turning point, and coupled with him linking up with a new mechanic, Eddie Bull, it gave Bruce the consistency that he lacked earlier on. His first experience of the Weslake around Dudley Wood was after a meeting, on a bike belonging to his first Cradley captain, Bruce Cribb. 'Now, take it easy because this thing's gonna be a little fast for ya,' Cribby had warned. Rather amusing when you consider that Penhall was already scoring as many points as his elder teammate on the apparently slower Jawa. It was an admirable gesture from the big New Zealander though, and it didn't take many practise laps for the difference to become clear to Penhall that he preferred the Weslake. He made the switch, describing it now as 'the best move he ever made' and he stayed loyal to them for the rest of his career, eventually being signed up as a factory rider.

It was roughly the same time when Eddie Bull came on board as the first of the Penhall back-room team. Both Bruce and Mark Cherry realised early on that they would need to find a mechanic to help with the bikes, especially as Mark would not be staying around for too long. Eddie had previously helped Anders Michanek when the Swede was at Cradley, and was still dabbling with some racing of his own in the second-half support races at Dudley Wood. While working full time in a motorcycle shop, he was introduced to Bruce, and took over the day-to-day maintenance of the bikes. He was to stay with Penhall for the rest of the American's speedway career and although other mechanics were brought in to help at different times or in different places, Eddie missed only a handful of Bruce's matches for the next five seasons. The two men became very good friends over and above their professional association, and Bruce spent a huge amount of time in the company of Eddie and his family. 'I think the world of them,' he says, referring to Eddie and his wife Betty. 'Eddie was definitely the main reason for my success both in England and the Continent. He not only maintained my motorcycles, he also had a strong influence on me mentally. Betty, Eddie's wife, also had a very strong parental influence on me. To this day we remain great friends.' Things were already working out well by the time that Mark left his brother-in-law in England and returned to the States. He had made the journey primarily to help Bruce settle in, as well as working on the bikes and helping out in other areas. 'His business savvy was impeccable, and mine wasn't,' admits Bruce. 'I didn't want to have to worry about contracts and things like that, and Mark was a good mechanic. He had a good mechanical knowledge.'

It was hugely beneficial for Bruce's racing that he had been fortunate enough to find assistance as good as Eddie Bull's before he was left to fend completely for himself. The pair quickly established a well-oiled working routine, where they each knew their roles and helped each other out equally to make sure that Bruce was in the best possible position to give the best account of himself, once out on the track. As Eddie worked in the shop during the day, Bruce would often clean the bikes from a previous evening's racing, enabling his mechanic to concentrate on the technical aspects of preparing the clutch and the engines. Eddie would do the driving, while on the way to a meeting Bruce would always sleep. Anything other than trying his best to get some rest and relaxation would result in some extremely unwanted nervous tension upon arrival at the track. On the way home, with Eddie behind the wheel again, Bruce would spend the time analysing his night's performance, scrutinising and examining every detail to find ways of improving before his next outing. Invariably, there would be a combination of British League matches, open meetings and other events four or five times per week even in that first season. The weary travellers may not arrive home until 2 a.m., and with Eddie dropped off at home, Bruce would roll up at his own house for the night. But next morning, there would be bikes and leathers to clean, while poor Eddie was back in work as well as having his mechanical jobs to do on the bikes at some point.

It's strange to think that as an American, Bruce came to Britain and found journey times across the country intolerably long. The difference is that his racing in the USA was concentrated almost exclusively in the state of California and he rarely had more than a couple of hours travel to get to any track. His friends and family back home found it hard to believe that he may travel four or five hours to a place like Exeter, only to find in April or October that the match had been cancelled due to rain, so he would turn round and head home again. At their suggestion of getting a hotel for the night, Bruce would have to point out that he might have another engagement a couple of miles from his home the following evening, so may as well get back and get some more sleep than usual in his own bed!

Preceding the World Championship disappointment in June, Bruce had enjoyed many highlights in the first few weeks and months of his British career. He had surprised another London crowd to score 10 points in a Volkswagen Grand Prix Qualifying Round at Wimbledon, but it would actually have been more had he been told before the meeting about Plough Lane's anomaly of having the start and finish lines in slightly different places along the home straight. He had led Peter Collins for four laps in his first race on the track, but eased up as they came off the last bend thinking he was home and dry, only to be overtaken with a few yards still remaining! He top-scored for the Heathens for the first time with 13 at Hull, a big track that he would grow to love against all expectations. His gating had begun to show signs of improvement when he finished fourth in the Olympique at Wolverhampton on a wet track with little chance to pass, but then he was forced to pull out of the Midland Riders Championship at Coventry with machine troubles. He was back at Wimbledon for a second appearance before the end of May, although disappointed in the Embassy Internationale, along with Cradley partner Steve Bastable. The pair had ridden for the Heathens at Halifax on the Bank Holiday morning, then travelled from Yorkshire to London in the afternoon. It was a sign of the fatigue that could so easily set in when faced with such a rigorous schedule that both riders topped the charts representing their club at The Shay, but both failed to make any impression at Plough Lane in the evening, with Bruce scoring just 3. In between the hustle and bustle of racing, Penhall had turned twenty-one-years old and received a heap of birthday cards and messages on his twenty-first, from his adoring new fans in Cradley Heath. It was another sign of things to come in the future, as his fan mail would eventually reach unimaginable proportions. At the time, he was overwhelmed and asked promoter McCormick how he could best express his thanks. 'Just keep on riding as you are', was the simple reply. A party was held a week later in the bar at Dudley Wood with some supporters snapping up a limited amount of tickets to attend.

With all the incredible highs, there came some inevitable lows, and it was the month of June in 1978 which bought misery in more ways than one. After the World Championship qualification debacle, Penhall was dealt another stroke of bad luck with injuries received as a result of a horrifying Dudley Wood crash. In the second leg of a Knock-Out Cup encounter against Reading, he was chasing Dave Jessup hard for the lead and reared awkwardly coming out of the fourth bend. Bruce smashed into the fence, which then sent both man and machine dangerously out of control and back across the track into the path of trailing riders. The Racers' Steve Clarke collided unavoidably with the carnage and suffered serious back injuries, while Bruce escaped with a dislocated ankle. The starting gate bore the brunt of Clarke's impact and was virtually demolished, leaving the remaining races to be started by just a green light, as he and Bruce were taken away to hospital by ambulance. From a positive point of view, it enforced a much-needed break in Penhall's schedule. Since arriving in the UK, his commitments both on and off track had built steadily, and although he loved it and wouldn't have wanted it any other way, the injury lay off provided time for reflection and recuperation. It certainly had the right effect, as he came back after two weeks out of the saddle, including a week away in Spain, looking more determined than ever. He rattled up six consecutive double-figure scores for Cradley during July, including his first paid maximum for the Heathens when he was unbeaten by an opponent in a thrilling and memorable encounter with Belle Vue at Dudley Wood. Two weeks later, he was given the role as captain for the first time, after former skipper Bruce Cribb had been transferred to Bristol and next in line Steve Bastable picked up an injury in the Golden Hammer. Penhall himself failed to live up to the huge weight of expectation on his shoulders in the Hammer, Cradley's new prestigious individual event. He didn't even manage a race win, albeit against a high-quality field, and it was his compatriot Scott Autrey, who took first place. Despite the contrasting performances by the Americans that night, Autrey had been forced to change his opinion of Penhall. The more experienced Yank had never expected Bruce to stick it out in England, and was widely believed to think of the young pretender as something of a spoilt Californian surfer. After his opening few months in Britain, Penhall had changed many opinions though, not least that of his recognised number-one comrade Autrey.

One problem that Bruce struggled to conquer in his first season, and to a lesser extent for some of the years which followed, was the challenge of attracting any significant sponsorship, or more precisely having to change the opinions of potential sponsors. He had been tagged with a label right from the first blaze of publicity surrounding his arrival, which hindered him, annoyed him and which he couldn't get rid of, and yet it is one that might be enjoyed in very different circumstances. He was frequently, yet inaccurately, referred to as a rich kid and even a dollar millionaire, and subsequently shunned by certain sponsors who thought their financial assistance may be more appreciated elsewhere. The source of the description hailed back to the family tragedy that Bruce had suffered in his teens. The family business, The Penhall Company, for which young Bruce had worked while just beginning to ply his trade on the speedway tracks, had been inherited by his brother, sister and himself after their parents' death. The decision was made at the time to sell the highly profitable company, but all money was placed into trust and tied up. Although his mother and father had made sure of leaving their children in a comfortable position, Bruce didn't come to England as a millionaire, and tried to make the point that if he had so much money at his disposal, he would probably be sailing in a yacht along the coast of a much sunnier island while sipping cocktails, rather than hauling himself and a pair of speedway bikes hundreds of miles per week around Britain in the cold and the rain. It was an unwanted image that was to stick with him though and potential sponsors who didn't know the full story understandably looked for another outlet. For Bruce, he simply had to get on with things and ride.

On the track, of course, he was able to create a much more desirable image, and it was one to which the Cradley supporters were growing increasingly accustomed to. It was one of success and entertainment, and one that they simply hadn't even imagined in their wildest dreams just a few years previously. Bruce was at the forefront; young, exciting, determined, good looking, approachable and incredibly, bearing in mind his limited experience in the British League, already being considered on the verge of greatness. It was a view compounded by the all-encompassing powerful displays that he churned out through a summer fortnight to brighten up the end of a wet and miserable speedway period. Rain had forced the postponement of an unusually high number of matches all over the country in the middle of 1978, the worst possible weather for a twenty-one-year-old in Britain, fresh from the Californian beaches. But with his golden tan rather more faded and his blonde hair noticeably darker without the bleaching sunshine, Bruce provided his own way of cheering up the faithful fans on the terraces. He had been keen from the beginning of his European adventure to attract bookings on the continent as well as just in Britain, and in August made his first two appearances in Sweden. His fourth and fifth-place finishes in the open meetings on his initial visit to the Scandinavian country came in a week where he also clocked up his first five-ride maximum for Cradley (in an away match at King's Lynn), and then won his first open meeting at Birmingham the following evening. It was a period where Bruce pinpoints that his confidence really came alive, and those who had sung his praises beforehand began to up the ante a little more by even tipping him as a potential world title candidate for the following season.

The Skol Masters Trophy, which was his first individual victory in Britain, was special for so many reasons. Bruce remembers it fondly as the first of all the scores of successes that would follow, but also recalls how 'awesome' it was to do it by beating Ole Olsen in their title-deciding final race, just a week before the Great Dane collected his third World Championship victory at Wembley. The travelling Cradley fans also recall the sweet taste of success, not just because it came at the home of their fierce local rivals Birmingham, but also because the Brummies' centre green presenter had tried to wind up the Heathens supporters all night, before they had truly enjoyed the last laugh. The icing on the cake was a £500 first prize, to which Bruce responded in the pits, 'Oh good, now I can afford to buy myself some new riding boots at last!' It was another stride forward in the progress of the affable American, and a significant one at that. He had proved, without any home-track knowledge or other unfair advantage, that he could beat the very best riders of the time. At the end of the gruelling run of matches, Bruce did not shirk his off-track responsibilities and rounded the busy schedule off with a guest appearance at a local scout group summer fete. Another gesture typical of the guy, who had also been found as guest of honour at Oldbury Cycle Speedway Club a couple of weeks previously and turned out in a charity cricket match just a few days later. The latter of these public engagement has been remembered for more notable reasons than a mere appearance. For Bruce had never seen, let alone played in a cricket match of any kind, and his Yankee naivety of the great English game was only overshadowed by the exhibition of his obvious sporting prowess. The game was jointly organised by Dan McCormick and was a testimonial event for West Indies opening batsman Ron Headley, who played for Worcestershire and lived in the West Midlands. After Penhall's team, featuring a couple of other speedway riders, including Bruce Cribb, had unspectacularly batted first, they took to the job of fielding against some accomplished players. McCormick vividly recalls the story of Bruce, fielding at square leg, after casting a keen eye on his opponents and their tactics. A few balls into the innings, Bruce saw his opportunity for a catch and leapt several feet in the air at full stretch to claim the ball, but before his feet touched back on the ground, he had somehow thrown it up again and caught it a second time, to the sheer amazement of both his teammates and opponents. When quizzed by Dan on what the heck he was doing, Bruce replied that he thought those were the rules of a catch, and everyone else had thrown the ball in the air (in celebration) after they had caught out a batsman!

As Cradley Heath neared the end of the season, Bruce was in more demand than ever ahead of his October departure for the California sun. Rumours were abounding that he might decide to stay in the USA after already now proving himself capable in Britain. They were all way off the mark and Bruce had pledged his future to Cradley in the British League on numerous occasions. He did admit to missing surfing and swimming in the sea, and suggested in conversation that it would have been nice to live around somewhere such as Cornwall or Poole on the South Coast, where he could be closer to the beach. It was, after all, one of the very reasons why his compatriot, Mike Curuso had made the switch from Hull in Yorkshire to ride for Poole Pirates. Unfortunately, Cradley fans – so desperate not to lose their new hero – managed to hear the twisted version of the story and news filtered through to a local radio phone-in that Penhall wanted to ride for Poole! Within minutes, phone lines to the radio station were hot, and the matter had to be quickly cleared up afterwards to prevent a mutiny, with the explanation that Bruce would have simply preferred to live on the coast, but knew it would not be logistically feasible due to Cradley's Midlands base. He certainly didn't wish to leave the club and there was never again a hint of him ever leaving for another British club! Needless to say, the Heathens fans breathed a huge sigh of relief. He soon went about demonstrating his love for the Dudley Wood circuit as his home track by demolishing the track record in a four-team tournament in early October. His time of 64.6 seconds knocked 0.8 seconds off the record that had stood at the beginning of the meeting. Elsewhere, he teamed up with Bastable in the British League Pairs final, forcing both riders to miss Cradley's away match at Sheffield on the same night. The pairs event was abandoned due to heavy fog before its scheduled finish, with Steve and Bruce tied for the lead with Coventry's pair of Ole Olsen and Mitch Shirra. The rather unsatisfactory conclusion was that the result should be declared and both Cradley and Coventry declared joint winners of the event. Although it was treated by many as something of a second-rate championship and received minimal credibility at the time, it was effectively the first piece of National silverware that

Bruce had helped the Heathens to claim. It capped a remarkable year where Bruce had achieved a phenomenal debut official average of 9.26 in the British League and 8.96 including all matches. It was a figure that arguably represents the very best opening season enjoyed by any newcomer to the top level of speedway in the UK. It was no wonder those Cradley fans didn't want him to leave!

One couldn't blame old Dan McCormick for the exceedingly smug grin he had at the time. Not only could he proudly boast of being the man who took the gamble to bring Penhall to the stage of the British League, but the words he had committed to print in his match day programme notes, a week *before* the Skol Masters Meeting, were beginning to appear prophetically true. Bruce had turned from untried novice to a genuine World Championship candidate in around six months. So no apologies should be required for reproducing the promoter's comments in full here, but it is hastily pointed out that they were written by McCormick in August 1978, in Bruce's first season, before he had won a single thing:

Bruce Penhall is the hardest trier you will ever see on a speedway bike. He doesn't know when to give in and doesn't know when to stop giving out. He is a hard and genuine competitor with solid ambition to become the greatest rider in the world. He has this determination. He has the ability and the class. He will make it.

But on the way to the top he will make more friends than any rider in the business because he has the attributes which make him an outstanding person in an activity where the very limits of gamesmanship are continually encroached. This is because he is a truly fine sportsman who would not, in any possible way, wish to triumph by use of doubtful or dangerous tactics. He is totally delighted every time he wins... and equally delighted for his opponent each time he is beaten.

He has never been known to make excuse for losing. Not for him the track was bad, or machinery failed, or the start was raggy, or indeed any of the usual excuses that are sometimes stressed, and he has suffered much frustration and plenty of plain bad luck. How refreshing and how revealing this attitude, which has now permeated right the way through the 'Heathen' camp, from Pekka to Steve and all the way back to the juniors creating an atmosphere unique to the Cradley pits and an example for all in speedway.

Bruce Penhall has shown us the way and has set this example which we are all pleased to follow. With such a spirit we can look forward in happy anticipation of growing success, confident we have learned to accept such success with dignity and regard for our opponents, and our defeats with dignity and regard for ourselves. Such is the lesson this young Californian has brought home to us.

We are delighted he is here and delighted he enjoys being here. We want for him the great success he truly deserves, and when it comes our celebration will be such that history will record the occasion. Good luck Bruce, from all of us, in all of speedway.

Bruce was still twenty-one-years old and he was still, by his own admission, learning his trade, but he was clearly destined for the very top.

SEVEN

FAREWELL, FOR NOW

You could forgive the Cradley fans for worrying that they may lose Bruce for some reason, whether it be to the delightful surroundings of his home in the USA or even more outrageously, to another British League club. The fact is that it was never likely to happen; Penhall was happy at Cradley and Cradley were more than happy with him. But in the case of supporters who had felt starved of such a rider for so long, and then received an initial glimpse, their defensive stance is understandable! If Bruce had any doubt whatsoever about the adoration bestowed upon him by his new set of followers, they made sure he would not be forgetting them in a hurry, before the star attraction boarded his plane for a few months in warmer pastures. He had been forced to leave the UK two weeks before the end of the season to return home for commitments in the US. The only home meetings he missed were a couple of farewell events, but he was able to bow out in magnificent style on an evening that became totally dedicated to his presence.

The Dudley Rotary Club International Best Pairs meeting was staged on Wednesday 18 October 1978, two days before Bruce was due to fly out of Heathrow. He was supposed to be paired with first Scott Autrey and then Steve Gresham in an American partnership, but both were unavailable for different reasons so Cradley's recent record signing, British junior Phil Collins, filled the role. Although Collins was already showing huge potential and would go on to enjoy a very successful career for club and country, he was still a young and raw talent in the company of some well-regarded opposition. Leading pairs throughout the meeting were the Heathens' other two heat-leaders, Steve Bastable and Alan Grahame, and another British duo of Gordon Kennett and Dave Morton. They would eventually finish level on points at the end of the twenty-one heats, but the night was all about Penhall. He scored a colossal individual total of 17 points, conceding just one defeat in six races to Australian Phil Crump. Collins could only manage to contribute a further 2 points to the pairing's final tally, and at one point even apologised to Bruce for not chipping in with anything more. The American assured him that he was doing fine and learning from his experience, and told him not to worry but to enjoy himself. By the completion of their fifth outing, Bruce had clocked up four race wins, each time receiving one of the sponsored prizes that rewarded the winner of each heat. So, in a marvellous gesture, he sent his partner for the night round to the start line to pick up the accolade instead, hence Collins walked away with the unexpected bonus of a microwave oven!

The outstanding memory for many Cradley fans in attendance that evening was the song played constantly over the public address system: 'You'll Never Walk Alone'. The presenters brilliantly captured the mood of the supporters, who had all become the most devoted Bruce Penhall fans and who all wanted him to know of the place which he filled in their hearts. There must have been over half-a-dozen airings of the anthem, designed to give Golden Boy Bruce the fitting send-off that his debut season deserved, and to ensure he left safe in the knowledge that several thousand Cradley fans would already be eagerly anticipating his return.

On a wider scale, his achievements were recognised when he was voted the inaugural 'Newcomer of the Year' by the newly formed Speedway Writers and Photographers' Association (SWAPA). The organisation was created to 'foster goodwill within the sport', open to all journalists working within speedway at the time, and they raised their profile within a month of institution by voting in a whole set of end-of-season accolades. Bruce ran away with the votes to win the newcomer prize, beating off token competition from Kenny Carter, Gary Guglielmi, Rudy Muts and Dave Shields. A staggering measure of his accomplishment was laid out in black and white with the published league rider averages. He finished in eighteenth place in the full list with the official figure of 9.26 from 29 league and cup matches. In comparison, the other pretenders to the newcomer of the year title, included Rudy Muts in seventy-second on 6.42, Gary

Guglielmi in eighty-eighth on 5.79 and Kenny Carter in ninety-fifth on 5.40.

The highlight of the close season and American retreat should have been the US qualifying round for the following year's World Championship. In yet another change of policy, the AMA decided that the best solution would be to stage the event in December when most of the European-based riders were back home. So the qualifying round for the Inter-Continental final of August 1979 was staged at the end of 1978, but that was only the beginning of the debacle surrounding the meeting. Scott Autrey and Mike Curuso withdrew from the final, completely in disagreement with the way the authorities were staging the event, and Autrey even went as far as threatening retirement due to the ongoing conflicts with the AMA. Bruce suggests that he 'begged and pleaded to be allowed to qualify through the British rounds instead' – a radical idea, which would have given him more hurdles to get through and arguably much tougher opposition, but his view was that at least it was fair. The staging was switched from Costa Mesa to Santa Ana – a venue far less popular with riders and fans alike, which resulted in an attendance of only 2,500, in comparison to the previous year's qualifier which had drawn a crowd of nearly 7,000.

When it came to the action on the track, things didn't get any better for Bruce, who was out to prove a point to those very officials who had overlooked him in the 1978 World Championship in favour of Steve Gresham. An engine failure in his first ride gave him an uphill task from the very beginning, but the real drama unfolded in his second ride, which pitched Penhall and Gresham against each other with Mike Bast also in the race. In a hard tussle, Bruce appeared to be dumped in the dirt by Gresham. Moreover, the American system of not stopping the race when a rider had fallen proved extremely costly. Gresham was subsequently excluded after the race had finished, with Penhall awarded a consolation third-place point, but his chances of qualification were already over. Under FIM rules, the race would have been rerun without Gresham and Bruce would have received a second chance.

'I remember not wanting to go back for the qualifier because they didn't have a proper track. We had to ride at the Santa Ana

Bowl which was a track that no-one from England had ridden on. I also remember Steve Gresham knocking me off and that was the end for me. It was a huge disappointment.'

Bruce was eliminated and out of the World Championship race for another year – before the year had even begun. The meeting was won by Bobby Schwartz, who ironically had also just signed a deal with Cradley Heath to join Bruce at Dudley Wood. Schwartz, nicknamed 'Boogaloo', was one of the next emergent group of Americans to head for British shores. Dan McCormick was keen to follow up his highly successful acquisition of the previous year, so he asked Bruce to help broker the deal that brought the second American into the Heathens' line-up. When Dan asked Bruce whether Schwartz would be able to get into the increasingly strong British League team at Dudley Wood, the reply was 'Dan, I'll have a job to beat him myself!'

The enormous disappointment over the US final qualifier was slightly softened with frequent droplets of good news that filtered through to Bruce from the UK. He spoke to his team manager McCormick on an almost weekly basis in the first few weeks of the winter and was kept informed of progress on team-building. He finished runner-up to Ole Olsen in *Speedway Star* magazine's poll for Personality of the Year, while at the same time votes were being cast by members of the speedway press to nominate which riders would compete in the Master of Speedway series for the season. Bruce's first season popularity was borne out with thirty-seven votes – only Olsen and Peter Collins received the backing of all forty-two participating members.

On the bike, Bruce got in plenty of winter practice in many different forms. It had begun with some rides at Costa Mesa and the other local speedway tracks and included the US Longtrack championship at Ascot. The half-mile circuit was completely different to any other Californian tracks and not just in terms of size. 'The track material was clay, very grippy and with loads of crap in it! There were huge car parts, spark plugs and whatever else. Ascot was notorious for that.' It was all taken in Bruce's stride though, as despite the grim recollection, he beat Shawn Moran for the longtrack title in November of 1978. After Christmas it was on to New Zealand for a short racing tour at tracks including Dunedin and Christchurch. He was involved with home favourite

Larry Ross in a series of fantastic races, some of which were played out in front of the movie cameras for *On Any Sunday II*, the sequel to a cult hit motorcycle documentary. The producers would continue to work with him later in the year. By March it was back home again, in time for the annual USA *v.* The Rest of the World, when Briggo and Mauger were bringing the troupe to face the Yanks again in California. Bruce scored 8 and 10 in the first two Tests; reasonable returns but not spectacular compared to Schwartz's top score of 16 for the hosts. Still, preparations for the looming second British season were going well and Bruce was enjoying the visit of Peter Collins, who was riding in The Rest of the World side. The pair took time out to have some fun with a couple of motocross bikes and took them out into the desert to blow away a few more cobwebs with a couple of other mechanics and friends, when disaster struck. Penhall was involved in a frightening accident that could have put an early end to his speedway racing career and even have caused a lot more serious damage: 'I had taken PC on a Mexico trip and we had been riding all day, for roughly about 250 miles. We'd just got into a small town called San Felipe when I was run over by a big truck! The driver was drunk and the truck had no brakes. I had made a safe turn into a petrol station and this huge truck just ran me over. I had my head underneath the truck and one of the wheels had gone over my shoulder. I was in a lot of pain, but we had a five-hour drive to get to the nearest civilised hospital. I had dislocated my shoulder, and in total it was out of joint for about seven hours before it was set back into place. I had numerous problems with it in that following season and after that I really limited my fun riding.' In fact, Bruce was lucky not to be killed as he slid in between the wheels of the Mexican cattle wagon. Peter Collins certainly feared the worst at the time and admitted that he was amazed to see his pal get up in one piece. Apart from the dislocated shoulder, Bruce got away with severe bruising but was forced to pull out of the remaining Test matches. He immediately promised to be fit for Cradley's first scheduled match of 1979 and was due to fly to the UK only a week later.

Dudley Wood was supposed to come alive to the sound of roaring motorbikes again on 17 March with a challenge match between two teams captained by Bruce and Steve Bastable.

However, the initial staging was postponed by a week due to heavy rain and snow. As McCormick took the unusual decision of calling it off three days in advance due to adverse weather forecasts, it allowed Bruce, Bobby Schwartz and Eddie Bull – who had taken a holiday in California – to delay their return slightly. They eventually flew into Heathrow airport to be greeted by some more terrible March weather: a typical introduction to Britain for Schwartz and an early reminder for Bruce about how cold and miserable conditions could be on the other side of the Atlantic. The season was preceded by *Speedway Star* publishing a Penhall portrait shot on their front cover, complete with partially unzipped leathers, gold necklace and of course the gleaming white smile. The Cradley fans welcomed him back and he responded by shrugging off the shoulder injury to open with 11 points from four rides in the rearranged challenge.

Picking up exactly where he left off in 1978, the early part of the 1979 season continued in style. Individually, Bruce shone with 11 points in the Midland Riders Championship semi-final at Leicester, fourth place in the Spring Classic at Wimbledon and second in the Olympique at Wolverhampton. He later also finished fourth in Cradley's Golden Hammer with an unusual 11-and-a-half points following a dead heat with Michael Lee. Instead of the coveted winners' trophy in the Dudley Wood meeting, Bruce received the 'Unluckiest Rider' award after a big engine failure while leading cost him enough points to have secured first place overall. He did also take the 'Rider of the Night' prize, which was little consolation when reflecting that if it wasn't for the bad luck, he would have been a clear winner. Much was made of the rivalry between Bruce and Scott Autrey when the pair were drawn to meet in Cradley's round of the Berger Grand Prix series. Autrey was not only the number one American, but had reached a career-high of third in the world and sat pretty on top of the league averages. The pair met in the first race with Bruce speeding to a convincing victory and going on to chalk up a 15-point maximum score as he secured his place in the GP final later in the year. On the team front, Cradley Heath were beginning to justify their media tag of the new 'glamour team'. Along with Penhall and Schwartz, all three British boys, Bastable, Grahame and Collins, were scoring well and another recent capture by the name of Erik Gundersen was settling in well at reserve. Gundersen, another World Champion of the future, would join Penhall before too long to form arguably the best top two in any team over the next three years. The young Dane had made a whistle-stop tour of England with fellow countryman and Cradley rider Kristian Praestbro, making a single appearance at Dudley Wood in the 1978 end-of-season challenge match that Bruce had missed. Just like Penhall he scored only one point from his first four rides on the tracks. And just like Penhall he would be a huge star of the future and go on to be one of the best riders in the world.

The all-round strength of the squad was something that helped to ease the pressure on all the riders, especially the new foreign recruits, but equally served to motivate them all and keep each team member on his toes. Crowds at Dudley Wood had increased by a staggering fifty per cent in two years and they had surpassed the five-figure barrier on a few occasions. Promoter McCormick had juggled his riders impeccably to squeeze them under the new team-strength limit of 50 points, and when the first-choice septet of 1979 were able to ride together for the first time against Wolves at the end of April, Bruce led the scoring with 10 and a bonus, in a 50-27 victory. They were beginning to show genuine title credentials and the two thrilling Americans were leading the charge. McCormick highlighted the philosophy behind his winning formula with the comment, 'We've got a fantastic bunch of great riders, good-looking guys and the fans love them'. It was an exciting time to be part of the Cradley Heath setup, both for the fans and the riders.

Even Bruce's problems attracting sponsorship began to show signs of receding, with a handsome cheque for £2,500 presented to him on the centre green of the track by Midlands company Oak Steels Limited, and further considerable support provided by a couple of Californian Tax Consultants, under the banner of D&J Racing. It was down to a combination of success on track and much hard work off the shale. 'I had to prove myself to corporate executives that I could benefit their company', says Bruce, and so that's just what he did.

International progress was not to be overlooked with the USA causing their first real upset in the World Team Championship. Even without the presence of Autrey, who was continuing his war against the nation's authorities, the Yanks finished second behind New Zealand, thus helping to eliminate home favourites England. Bruce was included in the four-man team, despite suffering from a bout of flu, and was joined by Schwartz, Gresham and Kelly Moran. From being unable to field a competitive team two years earlier, the Americans now had to leave out Ron Preston, who had joined Poole, and Dennis Sigalos. Bruce's childhood friend had also joined him in the UK by signing for Hull Vikings.

The USA's story of the season was reserved for the World Pairs Championship in Vojens, Denmark. After Bruce had been paired with Kelly Moran to successfully secure qualification from the semi-final in Yugoslavia, Moran picked up an injury in the week preceding the final and withdrew from the event. Steve Gresham stepped in as a late replacement but unfortunately found himself grounded in London due to a strike at Heathrow airport. Upon hearing the news that he was without a partner, Bruce spent several hours telephoning his contacts in order to arrange a second replacement. Despite persisting until the early hours of the morning, it was to no avail. Even his attempts to smooth the conflict between Scott Autrey and the AMA proved fruitless. 'I worked like hell to get a partner, and you would have thought that someone could have got to Vojens,' he said afterwards. It all meant that Penhall rode as the sole American in the 'Pairs' event, partnered by a Danish junior, whose scores did not count in the final tally. Bruce notched 14 points alone, while the Danish pairing won the meeting with 25 points on their home track. At the suggestion that it must have been difficult to find the motivation to ride once he knew he would effectively be on his own and with no chance of his country winning the meeting, Bruce responded, 'no, it wasn't difficult to get motivated at all. I simply tried to raise the flag as high as I could possibly fly it.'

The pairs farce was made all the more frustrating by the form of Bruce and Bobby Schwartz, riding together for Cradley. They were carving out an impressive reputation as a duo, and providing almost textbook examples of team-riding out on the track. This was emphasised no more so than in a televised pairs meeting, staged at Dudley Wood. The 'Courage ATV Pairs' meeting preceded a full Knock-Out Cup match between the Heathens and Leicester, but was used partly to court the attentions of the television public. There were no better personalities than Bruce and Bobby to lead the serenades. They lapped up the opportunity of riding side-by-side, constantly looking out for each other and blowing away the opposition throughout the qualifying stages of the meeting, but equally enjoyed the chance to look after the sponsors and television company. Presenter Gary Newbon interviewed Bruce and the Dane, Finn Thomsen, before the final deciding race. Thomsen wasn't keen to divulge any tactics about the race, but when Penhall was asked in turn whether he was confident enough to say how he and Schwartz would ride, he responded: 'I'm confident that we'll do alright. Our strategy is just to gas it. No two ways about it, just turn the gas on and go!' It was not actually the case, because, ever-mindful of his team-riding duties, Bruce would be looking behind for his partner at every single corner. The victory presentation for the Americans was held on the home straight of the track in front of a noisily cheering home-straight crowd. The fresh-faced boys provided the most natural subjects to be interviewed after their victory, playing perfectly into the hands of the eager TV crew. 'Thanks a lot to Courage for sponsoring this trophy and it's a great meeting. We'd like to have more television meetings,' said Bruce. Newbon duly reciprocated and then thanked them for their entertainment, and Schwartz rounded off the pleasantries by thanking the commentator and ATV, the television company. Pure sweetness and roses, and no doubt the TV producer's dream. Hardly surprising that McCormick staged a second pairs meeting later in the year, this time the Badge of Courage Best Pairs, and once again it was victory for the same American pairing.

If the two Yanks were getting along well, both with each other and with the Heathens supporters, then one man feeling the cold shoulder was the deposed terrace idol, Steve Bastable. Darling of the Dudley Wood faithful less than a year or two earlier, he was known to be rather disillusioned with the influx of foreigners, but remained captain of the side. That was until he broke his ankle and was forced into a two-month lay-off. The team could wish for no better replacement than Penhall to step into the skipper's boots. In June, just over a year after arriving in Britain, Bruce took over as captain of the Cradley Heath side and immediately led his new charges with a thrashing of local rivals Coventry. It was another significant step up the ladder, and a great honour to be chosen in the role.

Bastable returned as captain on 18 August, but the night ended sourly with a waterlogged track forcing the postponement of the meeting and an argument between Bastable and McCormick culminating in the skipper demanding a transfer. The move was granted, and despite Steve sticking around for another month while a deal was negotiated with interested neighbours Birmingham, the path was cleared for Penhall to resume as captain, this time on a permanent basis. Before the season was out, he would skipper the Heathens to home and away victories in the Knock-Out Cup final against Hull, when the team became the first opposition to win at the Boulevard since the legendary Ivan Mauger had joined the Vikings. In fact, Cradley went through the year's competition losing only once, by a single point at Wimbledon, and winning home and away against Leicester, Wolverhampton, Halifax and of course Hull. Bruce also inspired the club to victories in the Inter-League Cup and Dudley-Wolves Trophy, as their quest for major honours moved up another gear.

After taking over one of the worst teams in the league, straight-talking Dan McCormick had become the Heathens' very own Messiah, and turned his squad into a high-calibre set of riders who went within a whisker of winning the British League. At the same time, he had ruffled the feathers of many of his peers and colleagues with a no-nonsense publicity and hype manner. He may have failed to deliver his biggest promise of bringing the League title to Dudley Wood within three years, but the immense progress towards that holy grail was clear to see. Under Penhall's stewardship on track, Cradley finished in third place in the British League in 1979, meaning that the team had moved up two places each season since McCormick took over, which certainly boded well for the following year. The club won two KO Cup trophies and, as the rest of the speedway public were forced to realise, they had built up a mouth-watering stable of stars. On top of it all, team spirit within the camp was widely acknowledged as the best around. Bruce reflects on some of his teammates from the first two seasons: 'In the beginning there weren't too many problems with the other riders. Stevie B. was Cradley's favourite at the time, plus being a local it gave the fans something to grasp on to. Alan [Grahame] too was a favourite and we can't forget about Bruce Cribb. He was helpful to the team, but he wasn't the most consistent. My first few months I somewhat struggled with my twin-cam Jawas, so I decided to make the change to the Weslakes. That was the best decision I could have made and after the change, my scores increased in a big way! That is when the problems started with Stevie B. It wasn't like I wanted to come in and make waves; all I wanted to do was get valuable experience and always try my hardest. Stevie B was one of those riders who would have two good days of racing and two bad days, he was not very consistent and always seemed to blame it on his bikes. Alan was pretty consistent, but he was always going to be a 6-to-8-point rider, with the occasional 12-point night. Cribby, you would never know! He would have some good nights and a lot of bad nights because of engine failures. Perksy [Dave Perks] was great, I loved his personality. Kristian [Praestbro] was almost the perfect professional; his motorcycles were always perfect, but he lacked confidence at so many of the tracks and he would at times bring Erik [Gundersen] down with him, especially at places like Hull, Halifax and Exeter. He would also struggle at some of the small ones too. Erik was one of my really good mates, he was also there to win big races. I knew Erik would be a champion the day I saw him ride. I had always thought that somehow we had to get him away from Kristian because at the time he would brainwash Erik. Don't get me wrong, Kristian was a great guy but seemed to father Erik, and in the beginning Erik looked up to him in a big way. Erik had the talent and personality to take him to the top for a long time. The Cradley supporters adored him, as we all did.'

As the team was gradually moulded into shape, there were fewer and fewer signs of the Cradley side from the 1970s and an increasingly talented and glamorous feel for the 1980s. Bruce was the beginning of all that. Everything that he brought with him as a rider helped to transform the club around him, from the immaculately presented bikes and leathers, good looks and media-friendly personality to the on-track determination, the desire to succeed and the steadfast refusal to make any excuses for failure. Those that followed, including riders who would later become icons of the 1980s speedway scene such as Schwartz, Gundersen and Collins – and many more later, would all benefit from the standards set by Penhall.

Team spirit was always encouraged by Dan McCormick and the post-match relaxation on a Saturday night would usually end with a meal and some drinks at the nearby Kingfisher club and restaurant. Riders and mechanics would be invited – from both the home side and the opposition, and would often go on late into the night. 'What a great man Dan was! We used to have so much fun at the Kingfisher and he always threw great parties,' acclaims Bruce.

In fact, on occasions, the riders would still be together on a Sunday morning, when they would regroup for some organised water polo matches, either against each other or involving other local speedway colleagues. McCormick recalls one typical occasion when he was acting as referee, Birmingham rider Arthur Browning sneaked behind him and when Bruce gave him the nod, he pushed the promoter into the pool. Within seconds, there were dozens more bodies in the heated pool as everyone joined in the fun. Of Bruce's aquatic talent, his former promoter recalls, 'he was a great swimmer – he could cut through the water like a barracuda. Even if he had injuries that stopped him walking as fast as the other riders, they didn't stop him swimming!'

It was all in the days when a speedway rider's racing schedule was not necessarily as busy as it frequently is now, but it is hard to imagine any other club investing so much time and support in their riders and employees. It was a setup at Dudley Wood that would lay the foundations for the forthcoming years, and it became increasingly rare that anyone wanted to leave – least of all Bruce.

EIGHT

MASTER OF SPEEDWAY

Penhall's individual year in 1979 provided a significant breakthrough on the international stage, despite his World Championship disappointment. He was determined to justify his inclusion in the Master of Speedway series, after receiving such a relatively large number of votes for a rider who had so little previous international experience. It became a focus for his individual racing and he suggests that it was the most important event of his season. The leading lights behind the series were multi-World Champion Ole Olsen, and the Dane's personal manager Peter Adams, who was also team manager of Olsen's British club Coventry. At its height, the competition was seen as a genuine rival for the individual World Championship but at the other end of the popularity scale, it was frowned upon by promoters who saw it as another unwelcome distraction for their contracted club riders. Still in its relative infancy, the title had been won by Peter Collins in both 1977 and 1978, and was raced over a series of rounds where riders accumulated points, similar to a Grand Prix system. Bruce made his debut by being nominated for inclusion in the 1979 series and finished as runner-up in the first of three rounds, after losing a run-off to England's Michael Lee, narrowly missing out on the £3,000 winner's cheque. Reigning champion Collins was third at the Kumla track in Sweden. From there it was on to Bremen in Germany a few weeks later, where Bruce made his first appearance in the country. Before the meeting even started, he was offered the chance to compete in two lucrative meetings at nearby tracks later in the season, and by the end of his exciting performance on the night, several more offers had been received! Mike Lee's challenge fell by the wayside at the German venue and although Olsen won the round, it was the consistency of Collins and Penhall, finishing the night in second and third place respectively, who led the series overall. Going into the final round at Vojens, the two friends were tied on 22 points each, with Olsen and Lee next in line on 15. Crowds were very good for the meetings – 18,000 watched in Germany – and competition was fierce. The Bremen track record was broken in every one of the twenty-two heats, although Penhall clocked his overall result with five second-place returns and no heat victories. He was a great advocate of the series at this point and suggested that a separate round should be held in every speedway nation.

In the deciding meeting in Denmark, Bruce knew that he had to finish above Peter Collins to spring something of a shock overall victory, and a top-three finish would also guarantee that the rest of the field couldn't overhaul him. It was first blood to the Englishman as he defeated Penhall when the pair met in heat seven, but both rode out of their skin through the night, as they almost managed to outdo each other with every outing, charging stylishly from the back. A costly fall severely dented Collins' hopes in his penultimate ride though, and then it was left to Bruce to wrap-up proceedings by beating Ole Olsen in his own backyard in the very last heat. Commenting after the meeting, Bruce could not hide his elation at the series victory, despite not winning a single round. He saw the success as the most important of his career at that point and was immensely proud of his new title of 'Master of Speedway'.

It wasn't only the prestige of the success or even the fact that it made up for the world title disappointment that made it so fulfilling, but all the doors which were opened in terms of finance – beginning with the £10,000 first prize, sponsorship and bookings for open meetings right across the continent. Bruce was already in popular demand around Britain and probably one of the most sought-after names for any evening's programme of riders. Meetings were almost being arranged around Bruce Penhall; suddenly clubs wanted to stage challenge matches against an American Select – but only if Penhall was available to captain the side. He rode in pairs events, three and four-team tournaments under banners such as 'The Californians', 'The Yankees' or 'The American All-Stars' – everyone wanted a sunshine ray of the American razzmatazz brought by Penhall and his countrymen.

Bruce had earned a huge reputation for putting 'bums on seats' in any speedway stadium in the country, and now that reputation could begin to spread further afield. In fact, the title-clinching round-three performance came very shortly after a return to America where his international strides weren't going unnoticed. In a hectic schedule, Bruce had flown back to his homeland to compete in four meetings in about as many days. After heading the score charts in each, it was back onto a jumbo jet from Los Angeles to London, straight into a waiting car at Heathrow airport that whisked him to Reading's Smallmead stadium for a British League tie in Cradley colours. Once again it was three straight wins from his first three rides, in immaculate style on a bike ready and prepared by mechanic Eddie Bull, followed by a clean sweep in the evening's second-half individual races! On one hand this was a punishing timetable leading up to the 'biggest night of his season', but on the other it was a wonderful confidence boost. Penhall was certainly beginning to get his wish for more racing, and there were plenty more hours of air travel in store for the next few years.

Victory in the 'Masters' series was much sweeter given that it ended something of a jinx in Bruce's individual meetings during the season. His unfortunate luck had almost begun to affect him, following the Golden Hammer and a similar fate in the Midland Riders final when a loose plug lead had left him sitting motionless at the starting tapes, again costing him his chance of the title. 'Things always seem to go wrong at the crucial time, always in the big meetings' he had mused at the time. Despite feeling tremendous confidence in the Weslake manufactured bikes since his switch from Jawas, there had been a few niggling mechanical problems that hampered his big results. The doubts had been brought to the forefront of Bruce's mind in the middle of the year, not for the sake of his own performance, but with a totally unselfish worry about letting down someone else. Ever-willing to help out his friends and colleagues, Bruce was more than willing to answer an SOS from Peter Collins when PC suffered a spate of engine troubles of his own leading up to the Commonwealth final of the World Championship. Already out of the World title race, it was a chance for Bruce's bikes to play a part in the championship if not the man himself! And as the call came one Sunday morning only a few hours before Collins was due to line-up in the next round of his qualification battle, Bruce couldn't afford the time to worry about a reoccurrence of the gremlins. Mechanic Eddie Bull was summoned out of bed to clean and prepare the bikes that had been used in league action for Cradley the previous evening. 'I was delighted I was able to help him,' Bruce wrote in his regular newspaper column for the *Sandwell Evening Mail*, 'though I must be honest and admit that I was more nervous than if I had been riding myself! I was worried that my bike would let him down and he would miss out on the next stage. It would have been awful if that had happened.' As it turned out on the day, Collins made the qualification cut and Penhall's season seemed to just get better from then on.

Although Bruce would later spend many post-speedway years in the movie industry, he was able to sample a small taste as early as 1979 with the feature-length motorbike documentary *On Any Sunday 2*. It followed up a highly successful docu-film starring Steve McQueen, among others, and producers in the US were keen to capitalise by recording the sequel. Coincidentally, the producers were a duo called Dave Waldon and Jim Cavanagh, the same guys who had provided a small amount of sponsorship to Bruce and Bobby Schwartz that year as D&J Racing. Motorbike fans Waldon and Cavanagh put up the money for the project and invited Bruce to be one of the stars, alongside other legends including 'Superbike King' Kenny Roberts. The cameras followed Bruce around for hours and hours of footage throughout the 1979 season, beginning during his winter tour of New Zealand, and culminating in the Masters Series victory in Vojens in the summer. The huge majority of action caught on film would eventually be lost to the cutting-room floor before the Hollywood release in 1980, but some sensational action was encapsulated in a great American advert for speedway, which still retains cult status several decades later. One of the highlights of the filming for Bruce was a sequence for the opening shots of the movie, filmed on location in the famous sand dunes and desert of Glamis, near El Centro in California. Penhall, Roberts and off-road racer Malcolm Smith tear up and down the dunes in the stunning backdrop of endless sand and sun, as the narrator announces that 'on any Sunday almost anywhere, you'll find friends getting together to ride motorcycles, but these three are a little different!'

Penhall's form in both club and individual pursuits went from strength to strength in the latter part of 1979. He finished second in the *Daily Mirror* Berger Grand Prix behind fellow American Scott Autrey after the competition went right down to the wire despite eighteen qualifying rounds all around the UK. In a thrilling and heavily sponsored climax, Autrey needed to beat close rival John Davis in his final race to make sure of the title. However, if Davis had taken the victory then both would have joined Penhall on equal points. Although few of the Wimbledon crowd realised the rules at the time, there would have been no three-man run-off, but it would have been Penhall's fastest winning time that would have automatically earned him the crown and a £1,250 winner's cheque. Bruce had to be content with second place and then found himself with another near miss in the British League Riders Championship at Belle Vue on 20 October in front of a crowd of 20,000. The line-up for heat eighteen of the meeting in Manchester, consisted of Penhall alongside Ipswich veteran John Louis, both level on 11 points and both major players in the destination of the BLRC crown. Also at the start line were Peter Collins, just one point behind them, and Phil Crump just two adrift. Mathematically any of the four riders could have won the title at that stage, and when the tapes rose, it was Bruce who gated to lead into the first corner. Collins nudged briefly in front but was soon out of the reckoning as Louis, nearing the end of his distinguished career, surged into the reckoning and began a battle of wills with Penhall. Louis snatched the lead, but Penhall roared around his outside. On exactly the same spot, one lap later, Louis grabbed the lead back as Penhall slowed but as the pair crossed the line to enter the last lap it was Bruce again who swooped to hit the front for a third time. The stadium had erupted throughout the encounter and as the Cradley fans in the crowd thought the honours were seemingly pocketed, Penhall cruised into the last corner and suffered desperately for a single moment's lack of concentration. Louis dived underneath, forcing Penhall wide and gaining extra drive from his own machine. Bruce struggled to control his lifting front wheel as they hurtled towards the chequered flag and it was the

Englishman who stole the 3 points by nothing more than a metre or two.

This time, Bruce was devastated. He knew he had relinquished control of the race from a commanding position in the fourth lap, and should have been able to wrap up the proceedings. Maybe it was a reminder of his youth and relative inexperience against a rider sixteen years his senior. Such sparkling form had led supporters to an almost false sense of expectation so early and there was a tendency to take for granted the talents of the young man. Still, it was Bruce's nature to mentally punish himself for the slip up. He had looked every inch a winner, and received all the plaudits as most entertaining rider of the night – only one of his victories had been from the gate, while he worked typically hard from the back to win most of his other points. 'I am choked' was his immediate reaction afterwards. 'It has been the worst thing to happen this season and was as bad as going out of the World Championship last winter.' Defeats such as the BLRC were already rare in the Penhall camp, but still immensely difficult to take. Even after the adrenalin-fuelled wheel-to-wheel tussle and a highly creditable second place overall, Bruce would be slumped in his pits corner; head held in his hands. The smile on the rostrum was visibly forced even though many pundits were lavishing him with praise for the achievement. Despite having won the prestigious Laurels Classic at Wimbledon two days earlier, it was the bitter defeat of the League Riders final that would rule his mind. It may appear to an outsider that, despite being tremendously ambitious, Bruce was a touch too harsh on himself. What can be gleaned for certain is that it all contributed to the character of a rider who drove himself to the highest peaks of his sport, and anything less just had to be a disappointment.

Later in October, there was a significant victory that went a long way to make up for the Belle Vue setback. Dan McCormick had spent half the season campaigning for Bruce's nomination in the Golden Helmet match race series. Challengers were picked by committee, according to their British League form at the time, and consistent high scores had put the American in the frame on several occasions. Each month, a different name was announced and it seemed that Bruce would not get the chance to take over the reins from Peter Collins. The competition received an unexpected twist, however, when Collins was beaten by September challenger Phil Crump, bringing to an end a record-breaking two-year reign. Crump would get to hold the title for the shortest possible time though when Penhall received his long-awaited nomination in October, and as final challenger of the season, he duly delivered a convincing double victory to become the winter holder of the crown for 1979/80. Defeating Australian Crump 2-0 both home and away, Bruce became the first Cradley rider and the first American to claim the distinctive prize. What was all the more remarkable was that it came near the end of another very demanding schedule for the rider. Cradley Heath staged an unbelievable thirteen home matches during September and October alone, and the increasingly attractive team were also understandably popular guests to contest challenge matches around the country.

Bruce added to the gruelling timetable for himself, continuing his desire to race as much as possible. He only just made it to the first leg of the Knock-Out Cup final against Hull, a fixture on which the Cradley fans had placed enormous prominence. They had missed out on the league championship, but secured another vital improvement by finishing in third place. They had also beaten Kings Lynn to take the Inter-League Cup final, but the next best trophy to the league title itself was the Knock-Out Cup – and the Heathens had barely won anything at all in their thirty-year history. On the day of the first leg, Bruce had been grounded in Munich where fog had delayed his flight back to the UK after a meeting in the German city. He managed to get on a rearranged flight and landed at Heathrow airport just before 5.30 p.m. He was then picked up and chauffeured by Michael Lee, and arrived at Dudley Wood two hours later, just a few minutes before the start of the vital meeting. Wearing the number one race jacket, he was out on the track in the first heat, showing no signs of fatigue and defeating World Champion Ivan Mauger! Cradley won the meeting 62-46, and Bruce topped the score chart with 11 points.

If any Cradley fans had been worried by the events leading up to Penhall's timely arrival, then their nerves would have been rattled a great deal further by the proceedings surrounding the second leg at The Boulevard. The Heathens riders and management stormed out of the Vikings' home venue after the cup decider was abandoned due to rain with only seven races completed. The fury was stirred up by the nature of the call-off. Hull were already depleted by injuries and trailed Cradley by 23-19, despite not being beaten on their home circuit for almost two years prior to the occasion. Ivan Mauger complained to the referee that the conditions were dangerous for riders coming from behind, even though he had been overtaken by first Bobby Schwartz in heat one and then Penhall in his next outing. The Americans certainly had no problems in coming from the back, making light work of the flying shale. Both team promoters voted to continue the meeting, as did Bruce as the Heathens' captain, but Mauger voted against and the referee sided with the world champ, meaning that Hull's rapidly diminishing hopes of staying in the tie would be salvaged and the slate wiped clean for a rerun.

After McCormick blazed a trail of complaints and protests over the following days, even suggesting 'they can have the cup if that's their attitude', Cradley were forced to return north for a restaging. Team manager Bob Wasley was seething at the ruling, feeling that the team's best chance of overall victory had been taken away from them and that Hull would hold a strong psychological advantage. The Cradley riders however were eager for revenge. Bruce led the troops, with fellow American Schwartz backing up his attitude of 'bring 'em on and let's race!' Amid a multitude of mind games, Bruce recalls 'we just wanted to go there and win second time around. We were so fired up, we just went for it.' The course for the meeting was laid out in the first race with a maximum 5-1 return from the American pairing while Mauger trailed in an uncomfortable and uncharacteristic last place, dogged by machine trouble. The confidence of setting such a tone worked wonders as the rest of the team followed their captain's example and attacked the big Hull track, traditionally disliked by Americans who were used to the smaller ovals. 'Actually, Hull is one of our favourite tracks,' they announced together, undoubtedly unsettling the hosts further. The Heathens built up a steady lead before being pegged back in the middle of the meeting as the home side threatened a major revival. Halting any potential of a crack in confidence, it was again the team-riding American pairing who romped home in the twelfth race to put Cradley back in control on aggregate, sitting prettily on a

16-point lead from the first leg. With a couple of heats to spare, the destination of the cup was decided and the Midlanders clinched their first ever major honour. Bruce had one more ride and came out in the final race, again partnered by Schwartz. Ending in exactly the same fashion as they started, the Yanks scored another 5-1 giving victory on the night and thus inflicting Hull's first home defeat in two seasons. The Vikings were demoralised, they had the salt rubbed into their wounds and the Heathens hammered home their supremacy with both Penhall and Schwartz dropping just one point each to the opposition. Bruce was only beaten by his good friend Dennis Sigalos in the eighth race. Team-riding was once again provided in awesome abundance at The Boulevard between Cradley's American duo. One could only marvel at what the secret was and how Bruce and Bobby managed to pull each other around the track as if attached by some invisible elastic. Bruce has his thoughts on the key to their success: 'We never practised it or anything like that. Bobby is just totally unselfish in his riding, that's the most important thing. He loved the inside and I loved the outside, so that was always easily decided. He'd take the inside gate and I'd be out wide. He loved it and so did I. Bobby was also real good at blocking, a vital part of good team-riding when he was holding the inside, and he could slow everything down from there if he needed to. The biggest difference between us was I always wanted maximum points, whereas to Bobby, a bonus point [awarded for finishing directly behind a teammate] was as good as a point.' Commenting further on the way the boys' characters would shine through, he adds, 'We loved the cameras. We knew that to make money and to get notoriety, we had to get the masses to see what we did. We were brought up on televised sport. We knew that we had to take care of the fanfare and it was all part of being a showman, just like doing the wheelies. I have always enjoyed the fans, my father and mother have always taught me to be kind to others, have a great attitude and if nothing else that alone will carry you through life!'

As October drew to a close with the cup finals and the glut of individual events, Bruce was able to reflect on a very satisfying and successful year, despite the nightmare beginning caused by his exit of the World Championship race at the very first hurdle. He finished ninth overall in the British League averages on 10.02. He achieved a home average of 10.73 at Dudley Wood, which placed him fifth in that particular list and wore the number 1 race jacket from August, along with the captain's armband following the departure of Bastable. This time around, in the end-of-season polls, he was voted 'Overseas Rider of the Year' and 'Young Rider of the Year' by SWAPA. Overwhelmingly, he polled more votes for the Overseas award than any other rider in any of the seven nomination categories and then just edged out Kenny Carter by a handful of votes for the Youngster award. Cradley Heath won the 'Team of the Year' at a comfortable canter, and McCormick was handed 'Administrator of the Year' for his third season running. In *Speedway Star* magazine's readers poll, Bruce collected over half the total votes to be named as Personality of the Year ahead of Ivan Mauger in a distant second. Bruce became only the second different winner of the Master of Speedway title, and the first ever American to win the Golden Helmet match race title. He won the World Championship Grand Prix Qualifying Round at Dudley Wood with a faultless 15-point maximum, along with the various rostrum finishes in open events around the country, and together with Schwartz, was successful in the Badge of Courage Best Pairs Championship and the ATV Best Pairs Trophy, both also at Dudley Wood. Significantly, it wasn't just the big prizes for which Bruce put in the effort though. In the second half of the season, he had carved out an immaculate reputation of winning the modestly sponsored second-half events at Dudley Wood nearly every week.

With two years of British League racing and British living under his belt, he was rapidly becoming part of the fixtures and fittings around the Black Country. He even admits to being lured by some of the rather more British pastimes such as watching football, or soccer, as the man himself would suggest in his alluring Californian accent. Bruce was known to frequent more than one of the local clubs, including Aston Villa and West Bromwich Albion in some rare spare time, and is proud to proclaim the fact that he even went to Old Trafford once, home of Manchester United. Local speedway journalists Tom Johnson and Pat Foley were instrumental in introducing him to the English game, and although he enjoyed the experience it was baseball that ranked as one of the biggest attractions that Bruce missed about 'home'. A keen follower of the Anaheim Angels nowadays, he found it difficult to be completely detached from another of his childhood pastimes and couldn't find any following for the very American sport while residing in the UK. But if baseball had young Bruce beginning to ache for home, then only the taste of American food could go even further towards inducing a terrible homesickness. As many American speedway riders will confess, the taco is one of the Yanks' great alternatives to traditional British takeaways, and it is the taste of Mexico that brought the boys from across the pond back together in England. Dennis Sigalos, being the main culprit, would throw 'taco feasts'. Living near an American air base, he had plentiful access to the food, but whenever Bruce went back to the States, he would return with an overnight bag crammed full of tacos, seasoning and sauces to last for the next few weeks! The closest thing to his favourite American diners was the TGI Friday chain in Britain, where some of the US riders would get together and relax after competing against each other. But above all, more than the baseball and even more than the food, Bruce confesses that he simply missed the sun and the beach. And who could blame him?

There were mixed feelings when the beginning of November 1979 signalled the end of another British season. Bruce loved racing more than most things in life and wanted to be competing all the time. At least when the British clubs closed up for the cold winter, he had the consolation of returning home to the Californian sea, sand and sun. Never choosing to take it easy, there was still plenty of racing to pack in between November and March whether it was in the US, Australia or back in Britain for something such as an indoor meeting, even though most British-based riders would be filling their time well away from the shale. 'I didn't really have an off season, I was always Down Under, but if I did have the time I would go on a couple of Mexico rides. It's always fun to trail ride, however there was always the possibility of getting hurt as I did back at the beginning of 1979. I made the trip to Oz a few times, once with Ivan's troupe and the other times were with Boogaloo. We always had great times together but when the flag dropped, we were still always out to win!'

Just two weeks after the end of the British season came the American qualifying round for the 1980 World Championship.

There was yet another change in policy and venue. The meeting, scheduled even earlier than the previous year, was switched to the Anaheim football stadium where Bruce's Anaheim Angels baseball team now plays. Just a couple of miles from Disneyland, the meeting once again took on a 'Mickey Mouse' style of organisation. The stadium was in the middle of renovation to accommodate the Los Angeles Rams American Football team, who were preparing to move into the venue, and the speedway track was hastily built in less than a week. The event was part of a two-day double-header with the Anaheim Supercross racing in an attempt to draw a bigger crowd for the speedway, but the move backfired when the practising motocross riders tore up the track. One of the most important meetings in the American Speedway calendar was subsequently staged on a track resembling a ploughed field, and afterwards, Bruce was among the group of British-based Yanks who yet again had to field strong complaints to their own authorities. Earlier in the year, the riders had grouped together under the banner of the 'International American Riders Association' with senior figure Autrey elected as chairman and main spokesman, and they collectively submitted a very strongly worded written protest to the AMA about the dreadful conditions. Despite the now annual anger and controversy, there was a job to do and Bruce was out to make amends. Since his surprise qualification to the Inter-Continental round in 1977, he had missed out on nomination in 1978 and then unexpectedly failed to make the cut in Santa Ana for the 1979 championship season. With his sights set on the 1980 World final, Bruce overcame the appalling circumstances to take the top spot in the score chart and the first qualifying position for the next round. He was beaten just once on the night by Scott Autrey, who had decided to compete after withdrawing the previous year, and Autrey also won a run-off with Dennis Sigalos for the remaining place in the Inter-Continental final scheduled for just over eight months later! Thousands of dollars were lost again by the promoters of the meeting and the crowd was still a relatively disappointing 5,000. For the first time in years though, at least people perceived it as the 'right result' from a speedway point of view because the 'big two' of Autrey and Penhall lived to fight on the World Championship – which was judged to have been poorer for the absence of both of them throughout 1979. At last, America would have their best two riders representing them in the race for the biggest speedway prize of all and many knowledgeable folk suggested that an American winner was not many years away. The icing on the cake at Anaheim was the ridiculously large prize fund put up for the riders to try and encourage a competitive meeting. As the winner, Bruce earned a prize of $2,500 – more than the winner of the World final itself was due to receive the following September. Every one of the sixteen-strong field pocketed $46 per point, a truly huge amount in the sport in those days. But the money pot was still a distant second to the big stride that Bruce had taken towards his ultimate goal; he would begin the 1980 season just five rides away from World final qualification and was already being billed as one of the favourites.

NINE

'80s LEGEND

Bruce set himself a hectic schedule for the entire British winter at the end of 1979. He had returned to California at the beginning of November and in his first appearance on home shores, he finished second to Shawn Moran in the US Longtrack Championship at Ascot, before beginning preparations for the Anaheim World Championship Qualifier. After securing his place in the next round, he returned to the UK in December to compete indoors at the Wembley Arena, before he set off to spend Christmas in the States. On 1 January, Bruce joined Bobby Schwartz on their planned trip to Australia, where they were greeted by constant drizzle from the influence of a tropical cyclone. Adding to their troubles, as a Rest of the World select took on an unofficial Aussie side, were niggling mechanical problems for both riders, as well as fellow countryman Denny Pyeatt. In typical American style, the three of them shared around the working equipment they had and battled through for a team victory. Bruce was unbeaten in five rides to score a 15-point maximum. Before the end of the month, the boys were back in Britain again, competing in a second indoor event, this time at Birmingham's NEC Arena. Four meetings were staged over three days on a latex rubber surface, and then it was back to Australia to finish their tour down under. In February, the Sydney Showground staged a match between two sides nicknamed Penhall's Yankees and Sanders' Warratahs, the latter being captained by former Ipswich star Billy Sanders. Penhall and Sanders became good friends while racing together and on this particular occasion were able to serve up a tremendous feast of racing in a relatively short, six-race format. The pair faced each other no less than four times in the six races, as each team was made up of only three riders. Each encounter turned into an epic battle, but Bruce was unable to beat his opposite number to the chequered flag in any of them! There was great racing though as Sanders had to use his local track knowledge to come from behind almost every time, thrilling the crowd. A fortnight later, the promoters at Claremont and Bunbury took advantage of having Penhall and Schwartz in the country, along with Danes Ole Olsen and Hans Nielsen, to run a pairs event at each of their respective tracks. It was another opportunity to display their fine team-riding skills, but the Heathens duo were unable to slot into their usual routine on the big fast Aussie ovals. Rounding off the stay Down Under, Bruce joined a host of other big names in an individual open event under the banner of the 'World Championship Solo Challenge', where he bowed out in fine style. After just 2 points from three rides, he made a late surge up the score chart and qualified in the top eight for the semi-final stage. Sailing through to the final four, he went on to finish second overall behind Ivan Mauger. This meeting was staged at the beginning of March, but there was still time to pop back to the US before arriving in Britain again for Cradley Heath's 1980 season opener on 22 March. Even then, Bruce only made it just in time – flying into Heathrow on the day of the challenge match against a League Select and facing another motorway dash to arrive at Dudley Wood before 'tapes up'. After starring as top scorer with 11 points, he then missed the post-match second-half event to fly straight out of the country again, this time to Germany where he rode the following day. Bruce worked out that between November and March he had spent a total of around 150 hours in the air, as he commuted between the UK, USA and Australia, and he only had chance to enjoy less than two weeks in total at home in California. The busy winter would then simply extend into an even more demanding schedule for the European season. After two highly successful years in the UK, Bruce was now very much sought after by promoters everywhere, and there was nothing more that Bruce wanted to do than race – in essence, the perfect combination!

While Penhall was jet-setting around the world, his club Cradley and promoter Dan McCormick had endured a torrid time in trying to build a team for the 1980s that complied with the controversial maximum strength of 50 points. In short, the ruling by the BSPA meant that the Heathens must lose at least one, and more likely two, of their top riders to bring them under the imposed ceiling. It was an attempt to create a more level playing field across all league clubs, but to Cradley it was the break-up of McCormick's bold young team, and both management and supporters at Dudley Wood lobbied furiously to reverse the regulation. On a fleeting January visit to Britain, Bruce had backed a rider rotation scheme – or squad system – as one alternative suggestion. 'It will mean each rider in turn being left out of the team for one meeting in six but we could compensate any loss of earnings with guest and open bookings,' he argued. 'Riders with weekend commitments on the continent might even benefit from such a scheme. I think it's the ideal solution to keep riders together.' However, the plan was knocked on the head by the sport's General Council who told McCormick that it contravened the spirit of the rider control system. Cradley supporters collected 2,000 signatures on a petition against the limit, but to no avail, and the upshot was that Bobby Schwartz was forsaken from the 1980 septet, and later joined eventual league champions Reading. Schwartz was Bruce's good friend, countryman and the rider whom he had helped to bring over to England. They had lodged together for a while off-track and built up one of the best partnerships in the world on it. Along with the further omission of Kristian Praestbro, it was a bitter blow in the quest for club honours and the Heathens ultimately struggled to match the exploits of the previous season, despite the advancing leadership of Penhall.

The prospect of tough decisions on team-building had led to almost inevitable rumours that Bruce could be one of the riders on his way from Cradley, with no shortage of clubs that would have loved to have him as their own, and even the suggestion that he would not ride at all in the UK. 'I would never ride anywhere else in Britain other than Cradley,' the Heathens' hero had countered, 'it's a marvellous setup, the fans and officials are great – this place is priceless to me'. And his opinion was compounded by his unusual contract with the club. After his first year in 1978 when he set the British League alight, Bruce committed himself to a three-year deal with the Heathens, covering the seasons of 1979-81. Erik Gundersen and Phil Collins, it was revealed, were on similar deals that were extremely uncommon in the sport. Even twenty years on, it is rare for any rider to be offered a deal longer than one season. The terms of Penhall's agreement prevented any other club trying to lure him away from Dudley Wood, but allowed for renegotiation by either party after each completed season. It was the perfect arrangement for both rider and club, ensuring stability and security, and it added to the American's decision to become more settled in the Black Country. After a year of living in rented accommodation, in the close proximity of Bobby Schwartz, Bruce splashed out on buying his own house on the outskirts of Birmingham, in time for the 1980 British season. Tucked in among the golf courses and country clubs in the so-called stockbroker belt of the Midlands, it was a plush new pad for the rising star, who had become accustomed to some comfortable living during 1979. He had been residing in a 300-year old manor house on Dove Farm, owned by local businessman, racing car enthusiast and speedway sponsor Jeff May. While Bruce rented a room in the May family's huge residence, Schwartz lived in the cottage next to the main building, and both riders enjoyed the use of an onsite ultra-modern machine shop and garage, as well as the expert tuning advice on hand from May's mechanic. More importantly, with the new house in 1980, Bruce was putting down some roots and demonstrating that he wasn't going anywhere, at least for the time being.

Penhall's season got off to a flying start in March at Dudley Wood. While his schedule around Europe had been stepped up, his scores at Cradley's home track could match those of any club's top rider on their own patch. He started the season as an established team captain after taking over the role so competently halfway through 1979. The thought of this extra responsibility being any kind of burden is instantly dismissed: 'I was comfortable in the role and I was excited about it,' Bruce explains. 'I had the confidence in terms of the club, management and riders that I could be that guy. I was always on track anyway, patting guys on the back, congratulating them. It took a while to earn the respect of the other riders and there was a jealousy thing but that didn't bother me. "Throw more at me" was my philosophy. The team spirit was evident more and more and more! Kristian [Praestbro] was a bit negative, and Stevie B. could be negative – but they had both left by 1980. Dan gave me the opportunity to talk to the riders and everyone played their part.'

1.   Bruce made a name for himself – in more ways than one! Streaking in nothing more than helmet and boots one night at Bakersfield in the mid-1970s.

3.   *Right:* Signing his first Cradley Heath contract with Dan McCormick, in the bar at Dudley Wood.

2.   *Below:* Bruce looks over his shoulder during an early meeting in Costa Mesa, California.

4. *Left:* A rare picture of Bruce Penhall wearing the number seven race jacket, after only lasting one month in the reserve berth for Cradley.

5. *Below:* Battling to be captain – Bruce on the outside of Steve Bastable.

6. *Above:* Where did you get that hat? Larking around with fellow American Keith Chrisco.

8. *Below:* Cradley Heathens at the end of the 1970s. Bruce was already elevated to skipper and number one.

7. *Above:* First British trophy – the Skol Masters, after beating Ole Olsen (in the background) following a decisive final heat. 'Oh good, now I can afford to buy myself some new riding boots at last!'

9. Bruce and Bobby Schwartz, darlings of the Dudley Wood crowd in 1979, pictured with Penhall's Master of Speedway Trophy.

10. *Left:* Looking after the sponsors.

11. *Below:* On his way to another double-figure haul for the Heathens.

12. *Right:* Trying out a different pair of wheels outside the Jeff May residence, where Bruce and Bobby lodged in 1979.

13. *Below:* The master of the wheelie – but sometimes they just came without warning!

14.　Another wheelie
– this time indoors
during the winter.

15.　*Above, left:* Penhall and Gundersen, rather pleased with Cradley's Inter-League Cup victory.

16.　*Above, right:* Flying the flag for America at the 1980 Inter-Continental final.

17. *Above:* A tight corner ahead of King's Lynn's Michael Lee. 'I always knew that if I was leading him, and there were still three feet between me and the fence, Mike could come by me any time.'

18. *Right:* One for the ladies? Posing in his 'civvies'.

19. Bruce with the prestigious Golden Helmet.

20. As comfortable as always behind the microphone, being interviewed by Central Sports reporter Gary Newbon.

21. Flanked by Cradley teammate Phil Collins (left) and Alan Grahame, in opposition for England v. USA.

22. *Opposite:* A moment of concentration before USA take on England in an international Test match.

27. Proudly displaying a telegram on the centre green at Dudley Wood as part of the homecoming for Cradley's first world champion.

28. Bruce reads the telegram from then-President of the USA Ronald Reagan. Promoter Peter Adams, who arranged the memento, looks on.

30. One of the most famous rivalries in speedway – Bruce shakes hands with Kenny Carter before they do battle for the *Motor Cycle News* Golden Helmet. 'We both wanted the same thing and we both had our different ways of trying to accomplish it.'

31. *Above:* The bumps from his teammates for another maximum, away at Ipswich.

32. *Below:* Cradley Heath, 1981 League champions.

33. *Above:* The 1981 US National Champion. Bruce receives the champagne treatment on top of the rostrum from old adversary Mike Bast.

34. *Above:* Team USA in deep discussion as Bruce's mechanic, Jurgen Goldstein, stands guard in the foreground.

35. *Right:* The end is nigh and Bruce takes the microphone from stadium announcer Pat Foley to explain the reasons behind his immediate retirement to the Dudley Wood crowd.

36. The final meeting of Penhall's career and the defining moment of the 1982 World final. Bruce looks on as Kenny Carter is retrieved from under the fence of the LA Coliseum. Did he fall or was he pushed? *'I'm absolutely sure that I didn't hit Kenny when he went down. We know when we have hit another rider – you feel it happen.'*

37.   The 1982 world champion. Bruce turns from speedway rider to Hollywood actor, on an unforgettable night where the two worlds uniquely collided.

38.   A Cradley Heath reunion in 1988. Bruce joins Dan McCormick to turn out for Erik Gundersen's ten-year testimonial meeting.

39.   Back at Dudley Wood with the next generation. Bruce visits to watch Billy Hamill (left) and Greg Hancock, the new wave of Black Country Americans. 'I always told everybody else that Billy Hamill would be World Champion – before Greg was, but that Greg would probably outlast Billy, because of the difference in their style.'

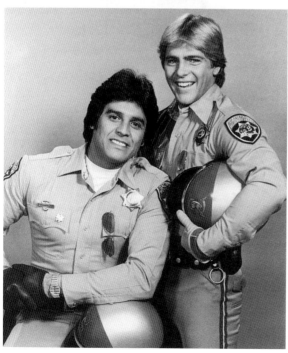

40.   At the beginning of a new career. Pictured with CHiPs co-star Erik Estrada.

Despite the team being weakened by imposed changes from the powers above, the blossoming talents of Gundersen, Phil Collins and Alan Grahame around skipper Bruce still made for an impressive top four. Cradley won most of their early matches and Penhall rarely achieved anything less than double figures. The Heathens beat all their local rivals in the Midland League competition and Bruce was unbeaten by the opposition when both Birmingham and Coventry came to visit in March. In the first six weeks of the season, Cradley contested twelve matches but only four of them were in League competition. There was a concern over the amount of relatively insignificant meetings being staged, especially when promoters around Europe were offering huge sums of money to riders in order to acquire their services for open meetings on the continent.

Bruce's opening weekend dash in and out of Dudley Wood for Saturday night, followed by a plane trip to Germany on Sunday became something of the norm. The quality of his club performances were never brought into question, although by the beginning of May, team manager Bob Wasley was already begging him to slow down and 'take things easy'. Specifically looking after Cradley's interests, as well as Bruce's, the manager was quoted by *Speedway Star*: 'Bruce is doing a lot of travelling about, jetting from one country to another and I am worried he will lose his edge as a result. You only have to ask Bruce to ride somewhere and ninety-nine per cent of the time he immediately accepts. Other tracks realise he is a big crowd-puller and obviously want him to take part in their open meetings but this should not be to the detriment of Cradley or the rider himself. Doctors should be given the power to say enough is enough. After all if a footballer is not one hundred per cent fit he doesn't play – and I think the same should apply to speedway. I would hate to see Bruce's high standards fall because of all this travelling. He has the ability to become World Champion and I hope he does it. I have just been trying to give him some fatherly advice.'

Bruce was unimpressed and responded that he felt fit and well and was not suffering from any ill effects because of his other commitments. He also criticised the amount of meaningless challenge matches staged by British clubs to fill blank race nights in the calendar, blaming them for the number of clashes and the sheer volume of fixtures: 'The money you get on the continental scene cannot be passed up. But in Britain there are quite a few meetings where we practically ride for nothing. Challenge matches are ridiculous. They are OK at the start of the season when everyone is a little cold. Maybe some of the other riders like a few extra meetings but I personally have that many meetings lined-up that I can do without them.'

The disagreement built up and was mirrored at other tracks around the UK. The suggestion was even made for British promoters to charge a fee to their continental counterparts, who were taking advantage of flying the top Americans over to mainland Europe, once they were based in Britain. Had they not been brought over from the States by their British club for no small cost, then European promoters wouldn't have looked twice at the much more pricey air fares. The squabble was joined when the American federation decided to raise their heads again. The AMA threatened to suspend all their Americans riding in Britain, unless the BSPA allowed them to make 'compulsory' returns to the States. The rule had been enforced from 1979 as the American authorities felt they were being robbed of their best assets by the British League. Despite not seeing eye to eye with the organisation, Bruce sympathised with their argument. He had stated after the 1979 Master of Speedway victory that he would be returning home more often in 1980 and wanted to promote the sport much more in the USA. The 'duty trips' brought big crowds to the small American circuits when the likes of Penhall, Autrey and Sigalos made their rare appearances on home shale. The plan was four or five trips per season, for around four or five days at a time, a request that Bruce saw as perfectly reasonable, although it raised concern among some Cradley supporters who once more felt their best asset being gradually prized away. In his newspaper column for the *Sandwell Mail*, Bruce refuted the claims that he would miss too many matches for the Heathens and suggested that good planning could ensure that the vast majority of his commitments could be fitted in around the British fixture list.

Another factor in Penhall's co-operation with the forces 'back home' was that he felt the AMA were finally starting to listen.

Harry Oxley had been more actively mediating between the riders and the authority. The 1979 US qualifying meeting had at least been run under FIM rules and there was more professionalism being introduced to the American circuit. Bruce's patriotism towards his country was such that he supported the view that British-based Yanks were needed in their homeland, because all the big stars were leaving the States destined for Europe and it was not good for the American product.

Putting the politics aside, Bruce was always able to focus his mind on racing once he lined his machine up at the starting tapes. His approach was to treat every race as a World final, and that would always be part of why supporters loved him. The huge amount of effort being ploughed into each outing maintained the admiration of the speedway public, and it also earned the anticipated results. Bruce was surfing a tremendous wave of success that was getting bigger each month and each year, and he wasn't about to jump off just yet. Pursuing individual glory, he narrowly missed out on Wimbledon's Embassy Internationale Trophy with the runner-up position behind Dave Jessup. He articulated his defeat to the Englishman's superior gating technique, explaining to the TV cameras that Jessup had been 'coming out of the start like a gang of bandits!' He'd also just missed out on a rostrum place in the *Daily Express* Spring Classic, despite going into his final race needing a win to earn the chance of a run-off for second place. But he was more successful with his opening defence of the prized Golden Helmet. After retaining the honour during the winter, Bruce was pitted against John Louis in April and comfortably disposed of his opponent before inflicting a similar result upon the May challenger, John Davis. Against Davis, Bruce did all the hard work in the first leg at Smallmead, notching a 2-0 victory over the home challenger. Not only that, but having just flown back in to England after a European commitment in Germany, he clocked two of the fastest times of the season around the Reading track, followed it with a 12-point maximum in the main event – the Racers' British League match against Cradley, and then became the first visiting rider to win the second-half support event at Smallmead! It summed up the flying form that he was in as the summer rolled on, and it was transferred to his club performances too, as the American radiated confidence. Bruce loved the success that he achieved in club colours as much as anything else and in a mid-season victory by the Heathens at Coventry live on television, he punched the air in delight for a whole lap of honour after his winning final race, whipping the travelling Cradley hordes into a frenzy. The Bees had suffered only one home defeat in the previous five years, so it was no small feat. Not surprisingly he was still in jubilant mood when interviewed afterwards by TV presenter Gary Newbon. He wore a grin from ear to ear as well as a playful pin badge reading 'News Flash – Gary Newbon promoted to Crossroads' that was immediately spotted by the TV crew. 'Just a little inside joke to rib you a little bit,' Penhall cordially teased the presenter with on screen. 'We like to have you on a little bit, Gary!'

There were still some British tracks for Bruce yet to visit and National League Glasgow were the recipients of the full natural charm offensive in June. With the Heathens taking a strong side to contest an Inter-League Cup match, Bruce was invited onto a local radio station during the day of the encounter to add to the build up for the Second Division club. Naturally, the local crowd turned out in good force for speedway's star turn. The first talking point of the action that followed later in the evening was a rare individual defeat at the hands of local boy Steve Lawson – who would be called upon to guest for Cradley in place of Penhall a few weeks afterwards – but then it was three straight victories in commanding and impressive style. Bruce proved as polite, accommodating and articulate off the track as he was stunning and exciting on it, delighting dozens of waiting autograph hunters after the match and leaving the Scottish fans talking about his appearance for weeks afterwards. Penhall-mania was now sweeping the speedway public in the UK, almost like Beatlemania had struck the pop world a couple of decades earlier. By mid-1980, his Stourbridge-based fan club boasted over 2,000 members from around the world, a figure which most other riders would never even dream of reaching. On his fantastic unprecedented support, Bruce suggests: 'The fans and fan mail was something that no-one could ever imagine. This was another reason why I always wanted to race in England. The supporters were incredible. The horns, banners and flags – this was something I had never experienced in my life. Again, I get back to the fact that my parents always told me to have a good attitude, be respectful, try your hardest and great things will come. They were so true!' The next couple of months brought a mixture of highs and lows and some unaccustomed experiences to add to the increasing tapestry of the season. Bruce was still able to put off worries about the next hurdle of his World Championship qualification, even though he had secured his place in August's Inter-Continental Round all those months earlier in Anaheim. He had decided to try his hand at the much faster Longtrack racing after conversations with the likes of Peter Collins and a promising young English rider by the name of Simon Wigg. Picking up useful contacts around Europe, it was relatively easy to get fixed up with the necessary opportunities and Bruce won his first qualifying round of the Longtrack World Championship trail in West Germany, the day after his twenty-third birthday, despite feeling the effects of a recent bout of flu. He was soon booked up virtually every weekend of the summer to fly out of the UK on a Sunday morning after Cradley's Saturday night home match, competing in either speedway, longtrack or even the other popular variant of grass-track racing: 'I don't think I was ever real good on the longtrack. I was always dragging into the start and never quite had worked it out. If I made a start I could go as fast as anyone, but I just didn't make starts in longtrack and that's what hurt me more than anything. I wasn't afraid to go but if I missed the start, it was pretty much all over.

'Grass-track was pretty fun, but I was a little leery of it. Most of the open races that I would be included in, I was racing against guys like George Hack, and these guys were absolutely out of their mind. They were so fast and if you got in their way, they were gonna take you with 'em no matter what! Even though we made very good start money – I made huge amounts of start money – I knew that my bread and butter really was speedway. I would try and I would try, and I didn't have problems with the rough tracks, but for one, I never really trained much on the grass – or ever – there was only a practice day and that was the only practice you got. The same with longtrack, but speedway I practised and I practised and I knew it well. I didn't know grass-track well and I didn't know longtrack well. So I somewhat struggled from time to time. I had some good meetings, but the chances of those were between slim and nil!'

In another break of routine, on one of the imposed trips back to the USA, he fared less favourably and ended up on the wrong end of a nasty collision with Steve Columbo. As a rider in such complete control of his machine, it was extremely rare for Penhall to pick up many injuries, but by competing in such a sheer volume of races in an undeniably dangerous sport, it was equally inevitable that there would be some instances. Trying to make up ground from thirty yards in a handicap race at Santa Barbara, Bruce had just caught up with race-leader Columbo, only to see his opponent pirouette his machine right in front of him. Columbo's bike shot up into the air and hit Bruce full in the face, knocking him unconscious. Thanks to his face mask and helmet, he escaped any serious injury, and in the spirit of any hardened speedway rider, he was back in action two days later at Costa Mesa!

Upon his return to Britain, he was able to take a rare day off to join Peter Collins in the pits for the Commonwealth final again, also keeping a close eye on the form of the qualifiers who would be joining him in the next round. Even when not racing, Bruce just had to be trackside! He also brought back from America a personal recommendation for the Heathens' next possible US signing. He had spotted a couple of young riders named Keith Chrisco and Lance King, and Dan McCormick was quick to follow-up the advice of his captain by getting in touch with them both. King would visit the UK at Cradley's expense but would have to wait another couple of years to sign for the club because he was under the required age of eighteen, necessary for an international license, while Chrisco would later join Birmingham.

The Golden Hammer again eluded Bruce, as he chalked up the awards this time for 'Top Heathen' and as usual 'Most Exciting Rider' for his 10 points, and he also lost his grip on the Golden Helmet in July to Hans Nielsen. He then agonisingly finished second to Nielsen in the 1980 series of the Master of Speedway, losing his defence of another title to the same man. Penhall had received unanimous backing to defend the crown with all SWAPA members voting for his inclusion. After the competition had been mooted as a threat to the World Championship, the series unfortunately never built on its initial impact and by the third season was already faltering, not least because British promoters were not offering their backing. The worldwide impact was reduced somewhat and the calendar included rounds in West Germany, Sweden and Denmark. Things went from bad to worse for organisers when the second round in Linkopping, Sweden was abandoned due to rain halfway through, with the result being declared void. So only two meetings contributed to the overall standings and Nielsen had won them both to be crowned a slightly hollow victory. Bruce finished second behind the Dane in Germany and third in Denmark, which gave him an equally trivial second place overall. He was involved in an exciting climax on both occasions, however, splitting the Danish compatriots Nielsen and Olsen in a three-man run-off in round one, then defeating Peter Collins for the third place in round two.

Another minor disappointment was Bruce's premature end to the *Daily Mirror* Berger Grand Prix, as he eventually finished eighth in the overall standings after missing out on the final due to injury. He had been the leading points scorer from the qualifiers and red-hot favourite to win the event. The consolation came from a magnificent evening at Birmingham in round three. The track record, which had previously stood for twenty-five months, was lowered no fewer than eight separate times during the night. Bruce lowered the fastest time in progressive stages in each of his first three races, eventually bringing it under the magic minute mark for the first time. After the culmination of the series was the more significant concern that he was being plagued by one persistent injury, which initially threatened to play havoc with his schedule of club, country and individual obligations. It was the direct consequence of his lucky escape from underneath the Mexican cattle truck, but began to reoccur unpredictably, each time leaving him temporarily unable to hold onto his bike. 'Yes, the nagging shoulder!' he recalls now. 'There were several times that my shoulder would pop out of the socket in the middle of the turn. At first it was very painful but after six or seven times, it had stretched so much that I could pop it back in myself coming out of the corners! I can remember it coming out in Italy, and it would not go back in so Ronnie Preston had to set it for me on the infield of the track. The track workers around could not believe their eyes. In fact there were a few of us that had the same injury, including Siggy. I remember I had to set his shoulder at the hotel prior to a meeting once. He was taking a nap beforehand, turned over and it popped out. It wouldn't go back in its socket, just like mine in Italy, so I went over to his room and set it for him!'

TEN

TEAM USA

When Bruce had arrived in the UK in 1978, he became one of just three or four American riders competing regularly in the highly regarded British League. By mid-1980, it was little short of an exodus of the best US talent flocking to European shores to further their speedway careers, and the British promoters were falling over themselves to snap them up. The cream of these imports were beginning to show that they could go all the way to becoming true world-class riders, and collectively the USA began to establish itself as a dominant force in the sport once more. There had not been an American World Speedway Champion since Jack Milne in 1937, and since the rebirth of oval racing in Britain after the Second World War, there was almost a complete dearth of talent from across the Atlantic. With the promise of young riders such as Shawn and Kelly Moran, Dennis Sigalos, John Cook and Bobby Schwartz, it was easy to look upon Penhall, along with the equally established Autrey and Gresham, as the elder statesmen. This was easily compounded by the fact that Bruce certainly did a great deal to pave the way for his compatriots to make the big step up to European racing. Riders in the States saw the success that he enjoyed in 1978 and 1979, and likewise promoters in the UK saw the potential to further their teams and their attendances by searching for 'the next Bruce Penhall'. While few, if any, lived up to that billing, the Americans forged a reputation for being flamboyant and exciting on the track, while living a happy-go-lucky party life behind the scenes. Though not always strictly accurate, it had its obvious appeal to the paying public, and whatever anyone's opinion, speedway folk had to start taking notice of Team USA in the 1980s.

The riders themselves were acutely aware of their increasing power and presence, and they knew that together they would have a collective influence against the decisions of the AMA. Once more, Harry Oxley – Costa Mesa's 'Godfather', from Bruce's early days – also played his part. The alliance formed by the British-based Yanks would grow ever-stronger as more riders joined UK clubs, while Oxley could see the potential in harnessing the talent of his young troops to push American speedway further. An international Test series was arranged for 1980 between England and the USA, to be staged on British soil, and Oxley was named as joint-team manager of the Americans. The notion of such an event would have been laughed at as little as three years earlier, but the US contingent could now boast not only enough riders to make up an eight-man Test match squad, but in their own minds they even fancied their chances of giving the hosts a run for their money.

'The Test matches were a blast. We were pretty short-handed for riders in that first year, but there was so much team spirit among the Americans. We didn't really get to spend much time together, because we were so spread out, riding for our British League tracks. So when we were together, it was like 'old home week' and all we wanted to do was to kick their [England's] ass.'

The team proudly lined up behind captain Scott Autrey for their team photo, decked out in matching Team USA hooded sweatshirts and baseball caps. It was the first meaningful series to be staged between the two nations. The only other time they had met in similar international circumstances was almost thirty years earlier in 1951. On that occasion however, the England team was selected only from Third Division tracks, while the Yanks had unlimited selection amongst their minimal rider resources. Incidentally, England still managed to win that series by three Tests to two. In 1980, Scott Autrey was chosen as captain, while he and Penhall looked on paper to be the best that the 'visiting nation' had to offer. The question was whether Schwartz, Sigalos and the rest could provide enough backup to match a mighty England squad. The Americans simply marched into the May event bold and brash and threatened a serious upset. Some British promoters were less enthusiastic about the visitors' chances and there were even suggestions that England could field a weakened team as the series was 'only against America'. Any doubts about a mismatch were wiped away in the First Test, widely remembered as one of the finest Test matches in history. Wimbledon played host to the opening clash and the racing was top class. The result went to the wire and in the end the two sides could not be separated, a last-ditch England 4-2 forcing a 54-54 draw, after the lead had changed hands several times throughout eighteen heats of hard-fought nail-biting action. It may not have been outright victory for Bruce and the boys, but they had shown that they would be no pushover and the next stop was the Second Test, just two days later at Cradley Heath.

Bruce and Bobby Schwartz had renewed their on-track acquaintance at Wimbledon. Schwartz had been in fine form for his new club Reading, and the duo were paired together at numbers one and two in the team to maximise the effect of their telepathic team-riding partnership. Their combined score of 21 points at Wimbledon was pleasing, but no-one knew the Dudley Wood circuit like these boys. Moreover, the track was widely accepted to be most suited to the USA out of all five venues, but this series was not about to be decided by previous form. Bruce led the way and, looking as dominant as ever, he took three straight victories. While he was first past the tapes in three out of the first seven heats, however, his partner Schwartz was not on the pace, chipping in with only a couple of third places. Penhall clocked up 15 points to lead the USA scoring, but while his team could not offer sufficient back-up, the England team flexed their muscles and won the match 62-46.

An England victory in the Third Test at Hull would have put them in a virtually unassailable position. The Americans decided it was time to turn on the style, and turn up the heat. Bruce arrived at The Boulevard early and began the mind games by setting up shop in the 'home' area of the pits. It was the flame needed to light the blue touch paper and the competition between the two nations erupted.

Bruce remembers it with a smile: 'Yes, there were some off-track tactics going on and I can say that I was the one that started this little battle. When we arrived at Hull, I was the first one there. I could see that Ian Thomas or Brian Larner had somewhat jacked up the visiting pits or deliberately tossed loads of crap on our side, so I simply told my team to pit on England's side. You should have seen the look on Ian Thomas' face when I told him we would not move until they made the USA side a little more presentable. Ian was very upset with me, but it didn't bother me at all. In fact, it bothered the English boys because they couldn't set up until things were sorted.' Futile attempts to persuade the Yanks to move along led to some angry confrontations between riders and officials before the two teams took to the track. The result was a 61–47 victory to level the series at 1–1 after three rounds, with the first round tied. Dennis Sigalos led the rout with 15 points on his home club track and both Penhall and Autrey contributed 14 each. No-one matched the large narrow Boulevard track to the Americans' style, but a few of the crowd on that day were reminded of just what Penhall and Schwartz were capable of, recalling their performance in Cradley colours when the previous season's Knock-Out Cup was at stake. Three maximum heat advantages from the pair made up for a shaky opening when they were pegged back by a brief early England threat.

A week's break followed in which Harry Oxley returned to the States, leaving John Scott as USA team manager, and Bruce celebrated his twenty-third birthday by winning the Longtrack qualifier in Germany. Oxley was bullish about his country's chances, suggesting that they now held the upper hand and, in contrast, England managers Eric Boocock and Ian Thomas were facing criticism from all quarters on their choice of riders, venues and tactics. Penhall underlined his continuing form with 11 and 12 points respectively in away matches for Cradley at Wimbledon and Reading, dropping just one point in his eight races.

The England managers thought they could pull out a trick of their own preceding the Fourth Test, countering what they saw as underhand tactics by the Americans over the pits debacle at Hull. Boocock and Thomas ordered barrowloads of extra shale to be added to the Poole track, a reported twenty tonnes in all. They had allegedly pinpointed the fast starting of the American top three and planned to aid the exciting dashing-from-the-back style of their own Peter and Les Collins, Chris Morton and Michael Lee. On the night, the whole plan backfired horribly as it was the Yanks who settled best on the deep, wet surface and they proved more willing and committed to get stuck in and take their chances. In fact, they had played right into Bruce's hands. Although he had mastered the start in the first Tests, he revelled in the extra grip provided and was more than happy to rely on attacking from the back and his love for racing past his opponents. Right from the first heat, Schwartz made a good getaway, but Penhall blasted past Les Collins to join his partner and on his way sprayed an ample amount of the extra second-bend dirt right across the bows of the home pairing. While everyone else was getting covered in dirt, America's most dynamic duo were splendidly clean as they cruised side by side, with matching 'Bel-Ray' sponsored stripes down each outside leg of their vibrant leathers. 'I don't know what they were thinking down at Poole when they dumped loads of dirt on the track. Everyone knew the Yanks loved dirt on the track! For me, that was one of the best Test matches ever. The team spirit was unreal, and the Yanks just loved to ride against the English Boys.'

An even bigger victory than the previous test ensued, eventually ending up at 63-44 to the visitors. Penhall was more apt than anyone in adapting to the conditions with his best score of the series, 16. Bruce and Bobby were the real powerhouse partnership, going one better than their Hull return, with four maximum heat victories from their six rides. They missed out on a fifth when Schwartz fell while leading. Typically, he was looking around for his teammate, but momentarily lost control. Bruce was beaten just once by an England rider when Dave Jessup spoiled his paid maximum in their final race. In a complete turnaround however, it was now the USA who had forged into an unassailable series position. Trailing 2-1, and remembering the drawn Test at Wimbledon, England could only level the series with a Fifth and final Test victory at Swindon.

Far from the earlier expectations of an England whitewash, the home contingent were now left with discussions as to what would happen, should they be victorious in the last Test and salvage a tie. Would a draw be declared? A sixth and deciding test arranged? Or even a race-off between the top rider from each country? The Americans let them talk and subsequently rendered all the debate academic by sweeping up for their third successive triumph and a 3-1 overall victory. Again they grabbed the home pit area, and to make matters worse for their opponents, the Blundsdon crowd seemed to be far more supportive of the stylish, exciting new imports who were gracing their local clubs, rather than displaying the expected patriotism to back the Brits. An angry John Davis summed up the feeling in the England camp, commenting 'You would have thought we were racing in America instead of England'. Following an injury to Ron Preston in the previous test, USA were down to just eight remaining fit Americans in Britain, but once again it was Penhall and Schwartz who kicked off proceedings with a first race 5-1 and the Yanks never looked back.

Penhall's overall record in the series from five matches, was 30 rides, 72 points plus 2 bonus, which gave him the highest six-ride average in either squad of 14.80. He was the only rider in either squad to score double figures in every test and, as a pair, Bruce and Bobby conceded a heat advantage to the Englishmen on only six occasions out of their 30 outings. They scored ten 5-1s, five 4-2s and nine 3-3s.

In between the Fourth and Fifth Tests, both England and the USA were involved in the first qualifying round of the World Team Cup. It was a chance for the Americans to capitalise further on their growing collective talent and edge further up the international rankings. Although making steady progress in the competition over the three previous years, they had yet to make a real impact, but were buoyed by the timing of their first qualifier. The team of Penhall, Schwartz, Sigalos and Autrey had spent plenty of time together during the Test series, and felt on a high. At King's Lynn they were able to ease through to the next round, finishing in second place behind England but ahead of both Australia and reigning champions New Zealand. Bruce scored 9 and then improved further with a magnificent 11 in the following Inter-Continental round in Vojens, two months later. Again England were victors, but this time the Americans pushed them close and the two teams were separated by just a point in the final analysis. The final was staged in front of 55,000 people at Wroclaw in Poland, but the home nation were never realistically in with any chance. Neither were the Czech team, who would only once manage to get a rider into the first two finishing places of any race. That left England and the United States to renew their rivalry and battle out the top two places. With Ron Preston added to the previous quartet as reserve, the worst that the Americans felt they could achieve was second place, having done the hard work by ensuring their safe passage to the final itself. Bruce warmed up with some fine domestic displays in Britain, scoring 14 points at Ipswich immediately after equalling his best tally so far for Cradley with 17 points in a Knock-Out Cup victory at Birmingham.

On the flat, wide Polish track it was England who were more fired up and out to avenge their Test series defeat. The Brits roared to a comfortable World Team Cup victory as the USA failed to provide enough strength in depth to climb above second place. Nevertheless, it was a feat not to be understated and their first appearance in the final was worthy of a creditable runners-up medal. In the final breakdown, England provided ten winners out of the sixteen races. One rider had put up a sterling fight though and was undoubtedly the individual star of the night. Bruce was unbeaten, clinching a 12-point maximum, and claiming victories in four of those six heats in which England did not triumph. Although not winning the trophy, the Yanks cemented their status as a recognised force in World events. Considering they had not even entered the competition a few years earlier, the stars and stripes were now pinned to second place in the history books and ahead of some very well-established speedway countries of the time including Sweden, Denmark and Poland.

Bruce returned to the UK from World Team Cup duty and just about had the chance to change his clothes before switching planes to head home to the States for his brother's wedding. After a few admittedly 'boozy days and nights' of family celebrations, the return flight to Heathrow was dogged with problems. Engine failure led to an unscheduled stop in Kansas City, which at least allowed him an extra few hours sleep. However, it also meant touching down four hours late at 3.30 p.m. with yet another motorway rush to reach Dudley Wood for a double-header, including the second leg of the Knock-Out Cup tie against Birmingham. As ever, refusing to let any jet lag get the better of him, he clocked up 23 points from nine rides during the evening. He even scorched to a paid maximum against the Brummies, inspiring Cradley to a 22-point aggregate victory. The very next night, the team went to Coventry and Bruce went one better to score a full maximum, then it was off to Hackney the night after for four more unbeaten rides. Exhaustion finally began to set in with the fourth match in as many nights as he scored just 7 at home against Halifax, but he picked up the pace again with 9 the night after in the return fixture at The Shay! All in all, five nights, six matches and three consecutive maximums. World Team Cup heroics suddenly seemed so long ago.

The World Pairs competition did not offer such rewards for the USA as the team championship, and they found themselves eliminated from the semi-finals. Sweden pipped Penhall and Autrey to the last qualifying place by a single point, but Bruce was philosophical. At least he had a partner this year!

ELEVEN

WORLD FINAL AT LAST

By the first weekend in August, Bruce's long wait was over. Since his ill-fated appearance in the 1977 Inter-Continental final, it had been three years before he felt that he had the chance to redeem himself. The penultimate round of the 1980 World Championship was at the same London White City venue as 1977, and rather than a rookie rank outsider, Penhall was a clear favourite to qualify for his first final this time and many pundits' tip for at least a rostrum finish. However, his familiarity with the track was minimal and his experience of this advanced stage of the sport's ultimate prize was even less. In his favour was a huge determination to make it through, and that was the attitude with which he arrived at the meeting.

Two race wins from his first two outings were the perfect start and put Penhall clear at the top of the early leaderboard. The 6 points he had already gained were almost enough to hit the target that was expected to ensure safe passage to the final in Gothenburg, but the crusade took a hefty dent in his next ride with third place behind two good friends, Billy Sanders and Peter Collins – enough for Sanders and Finn Kai Niemi to match his overall tally. The pressure began to mount, especially as Bruce had been followed around all day by Barry Briggs, who was interviewing and commentating for a special US television broadcast for CBS. His fourth ride became crucial; a win would not only put him through but also in with a chance of the title, whereas an unthinkable last place would leave any hopes of qualification resting perilously on the very last heat of the event. Up against fellow meeting leader Niemi, Bruce made no mistakes and led from start to finish for the vital 3 points and an enormous sigh of relief. He went into his final ride on 10 points with World final qualification already ensured, but now needing one more victory to be the first American ever to be crowned Inter-Continental Champion. Lining up on his outside were three riders all on 5 points, all needing at least first or second to join him in qualifying for the showpiece in Sweden; Ivan Mauger, six-times champion at forty years old wore the blue helmet colour; Scott Autrey, the established American whose reign as top Yank was being threatened by Penhall; and Hans Nielsen, the young Dane who had wrestled Bruce's Golden Helmet title away from him earlier in the season. Sometimes speedway just writes its own script and no-one is even capable of imagining a better scenario. This wasn't the first time and certainly wouldn't be the last time that such a dramatic or ironic ending would be thrown up in an individual meeting.

On this occasion, Bruce made it to the first turn in front with three riders chasing desperately around the outside. From nearest the perimeter fence, it was Nielsen who produced the speed to go around Penhall as they raced into the back straight. Second place for BP would mean a run-off with Chris Morton for the title, Nielsen was doing enough to send himself through to Gothenburg, but Autrey barged underneath Mauger into third and set his sights on second place. As they all went into the last lap, Penhall went wide to attack Nielsen, Autrey aimed for the gap up the inside and there was little to choose between all three. One last effort around the very last bend rocketed Penhall up almost alongside Nielsen, with Autrey at full stretch to plug the exposed gap on the inside. It was victory for the Dane by no more than the length of a wheel, or if you believe the exaggeration of that commentator Dave Lanning, a mere tyre width! Bruce subsequently lost the run-off, but was delighted to qualify for his first final, especially as the big names of Olsen, Mauger and Autrey all failed to make the cut. He was promptly drawn out of the hat first to be given the number one race jacket and riding position in the final, and with previous contenders fallen by the wayside, he was immediately installed as 5-2 favourite to win by the bookmakers. The weight of expectation was amplified again, but 'one thing is for sure,' he told reporters, 'nobody will be trying harder than me in Gothenburg'.

Making the last sixteen was the major achievement Bruce had targeted for the season, but just like waiting for a bus, no sooner had he qualified for one World final but within the space of a week, he made it into another. Returning to Germany, he took fifth spot in his World Longtrack semi final in Jubek, coincidentally finishing with the same points total as Chris Morton once more. However, he was involved in a high-speed crash with Larry Ross in the first bend of their first race, which resulted in a badly gashed knee as well as rib and back injuries. Ross had fallen directly in front of Penhall and, as he tried to avoid the New Zealander, the rider behind them both slammed straight into Bruce. BP was carried from the track on a stretcher, but refused to be taken to hospital until he had ensured his qualification from the meeting! 'The track was slick that day and the accident happened as we went into turn three, I think. Larry Ross turned around backwards in front of me and all three of us were collected into the fence – it took them about an hour to repair it afterwards. I knew I had some internal injuries which were hurting really bad and I felt something trickling down from my knee. When we came into the pits and got my leathers down, we could see that my kneecap was opened up all the way across. I needed one more heat to secure a place in the final, so I went out and did it. My mechanic had to lift me off the bike because it hurt so much inside.

'They put me into an ambulance and took me off to hospital, but we were out in the middle of nowhere – typical for some of the German longtracks. When we arrived, it was one of the scariest things of my life. We pulled up and two guys opened the back doors to get me out. They looked like they had been up for four days straight on a drinking binge. I was told that they used these people for volunteer work at the weekends, but I had no idea of the extent of my injuries and was thinking "where the hell have they taken me?" I had hit my head and I was feeling kind of groggy and it really scared me. But when they got me inside, I had four or five doctors go over me and I can honestly say I was given the best emergency surgery I have ever had in any hospital, and I've been to a few hospitals in my time. The kneecap was split open so bad, but they stitched it up something fantastic; when it healed you could hardly even see that a scar was there. They sorted me out and had me back at the track to collect my equipment before the meeting had even finished!'

Bruce missed two Cradley matches with the knee damage and the more serious internal injuries, after being ordered to rest for at least a week. Returning after the brief lay off, he only managed two matches before aggravating the old shoulder injury against King's Lynn at Dudley Wood. After two race wins, he fell awkwardly in his third ride and bravely attempted to ride in his final outing against the advice of the track doctor, but was forced to retire after a couple of laps. He missed the second–half event completely and put himself out of the saddle again, worryingly less than a fortnight before the World final itself.

The turmoil of the injuries somewhat still managed to pale into insignificance compared to off–track developments at Cradley. Promoter Dan McCormick had taken over the reigns at nearby Birmingham, and on the suggestion that this would surely cause a conflict of interests, he promptly resigned from his duties at Dudley Wood to make a clean break. As the man who brought Bruce to England, treated him so well and gave him the responsibility of team captain, McCormick had been a major influence on his career. Heathens fans, reeling from the news that they had lost their leader, must have been rather relieved when Bruce stepped out before the match against Birmingham and pledged his allegiance to the club, even without McCormick at the helm. After losing teammate and compatriot Schwartz at the beginning of the season, the loss of his mentor and manager completed a double blow. Cradley were left in the hands of Bob Wasley, who continued as team manager, and Derek Pugh, who became sole promoter. On Wasley, Bruce is totally complimentary, and on the loss of Dan, he still believes that there was never any way he would have followed him out of the door. 'Bob was a truly great friend of mine. We spent many lunch times eating together as his garage had been just a block away from my house in those days. He helped me a great deal and he was a good team manager. Dan was the showman, but every single thing he told me he would do, he did it. The Pughs [Derek, and wife Norah] bought me into the office after he left and said that everything would be going on as normal, there would be no change in things for the team. But I had to wonder at first – would the riders stay together? Would Erik stay or go? As for me, I was a Cradley rider and that was it. Yes, Dan brought me over, he took that first step and showed the faith in me, but it was the supporters that took me into their arms and nurtured me. Even though I liked Dan, I felt strongly that Cradley was my home.'

The season to date had been almost as successful as the previous one. While the league position was slightly inferior, the Heathens had achieved home and away victories over Wolverhampton in the Dudley-Wolves Trophy, led by another Penhall maximum. Making Monmore Green a happy place to visit, they had also won the Inter-League Four-Team Tournament final when Bruce won the final race to snatch victory. It was the first time Cradley had been in front throughout the event, as King Lynn had led for the whole meeting after winning their semi-final ahead of the Heathens, but the captain clinched it when it mattered. Domestic individual pursuits for Penhall had continued through the summer with second place in the Midland Riders final at Coventry behind Scott Autrey. He had beaten his elder compatriot in the semi-final at Dudley Wood with another brilliant maximum, but it was almost as if Autrey was out to prove that he wasn't giving up the mantle of top American quite so easily. To hammer home the point, the long-serving Exeter rider took the honours at another Midlands venue, winning the Golden Gauntlets Open at Leicester. Bruce lost a run-off for third place, to – who else? – Chris Morton.

Not for the first time, minor injuries turned out to be something of a blessing in disguise, giving Bruce a brief respite from his schedule which otherwise, he was unlikely to have taken. Recovering from the knocks, he returned to action for Cradley with just enough time to clock up one more maximum, with 12 points in a hammering of Sheffield at Dudley Wood. The talk of the terraces that night was all about the World final one week later. Penhall had beaten all the major contenders on plenty of occasions during the season. Cradley fans were not used to having any home interest in the big event of the year and their number-one American idol was the first real hope of individual silverware for nearly thirty years. Bruce was interviewed and explained that he realised this was his big chance after some bitter disappointments in the previous years.

By the time he reached the Ullevi Stadium in Gothenburg, Sweden, he was being tipped by many to feature in the top three, despite being aged just twenty-three, and being up against the record that no rider had ever won the title at the first attempt. Around 1,000 Cradley fans travelled to Sweden, and several of the Penhall family made the trip to Europe. Among relatives and friends in the crowd were sister Connie and brother-in-law Mark Cherry, plus brother Jerry and his fiancée Carrie. Following the successful transmission of the Inter-Continental final, CBS did another TV special on Bruce's World final debut. Camera crews followed him relentlessly throughout the evening. The pressure was huge, and proved to be even bigger than Bruce Penhall had previously experienced. At the practice session two days prior to the big event, he was asked what his game plan was for the race. 'I'm not going to have one,' he replied. 'I'm just going to try and relax. I've never experienced a World final before so I don't know what to expect.' But relaxing was much easier said than done. He was tense and nervous throughout, and never the loose, laid-back rider that most fans had come to expect. Crucially, there was a disagreement between Bruce and Eddie Bull over a mechanical issue. He had previously used a side-mounted carburettor, but during the official practice, had tried out a centre-mounted version. Eddie thought he was better on the new model, but Bruce overruled him, suggesting he was equally as fast on either, but that the side-mount would get him out of the starts quicker.

After winning his first heat, Penhall failed to win another one. He couldn't contain eventual champion Michael Lee in their second race, as the Englishman took advantage of a slight gap coming out of the bend, and barged through on the inside of the third lap, almost knocking Penhall completely off balance. Lee later described it as his hardest and most enjoyable race on his way to the title. Any hopes of glory for Bruce were dashed by the end of his third, when he made a slow start and couldn't get past Peter Collins or Egon Muller ahead of him. The track was hard and slick, which didn't make for close racing and even his chances of a rostrum place were out of the window when he was taken wide by Kai Niemi in the first turn and ended with a second consecutive third place.

Two points from his fifth and final ride gave him nine in total and a very creditable fifth place from his debut appearance, but that wasn't enough for Bruce, who felt strongly that he had let people down, as he was expected to do better. He felt that he'd had a great year and should have won it. He was almost in tears when interviewed in front of the camera after the meeting, but ended with the words 'I'll be here again next year'. In the pits area afterwards, he could no longer contain his agony. Incredibly upset at the perceived failure, he sat on his toolbox and cried; devastated. 'Hindsight gives you 20/20 vision,' he says now on reflection. 'I guess you could say that the pressure and the cameras were a factor. It was a learning curve for me, but I was always able to block that stuff out. I had been in some pretty intense, pressure-cooker meetings before and the TV cameras didn't bother me all that much either. I was not the sort of person to say "Oh my god, national TV is here." I can't just blame it on the motors either – I just didn't ride brilliantly. I had some good heats and I had some terrible heats. It tore me apart though, because I wanted it so bad; that was the reason. You can be the best rider in the world, you can have the best equipment, but if you don't want it enough, you won't win it. And I knew I wanted it from the very first time I started out riding. After all the problems I had in 1978 and 1979 with the qualifying and the AMA, I had got there and I'd been having a great year and I didn't win it, and it just hurt so much because of how much I wanted it.' He went home to California feeling 'choked', and admits that he sat around doing nothing for a few days, feeling sorry for himself. He couldn't get his mind back into gear by the time the World Longtrack final came around just over a week later. Bruce delivered one of his worst ever performances. He failed to score a single point in Schessel, West Germany, as home riders took all the rostrum positions; Karl Maier leading the way from Egon Muller and Josef Aigner. It stands out because Bruce so rarely ever posted a zero score in any meeting, anywhere! 'I remember that day. It poured down with rain, even though it had been dry in practice. It was as wet as can be, and I was just in a totally different ball game. I had not been great in practice anyway, and in the meeting the clutch was pulling me into the tapes. In longtrack you need absolutely maximum revs; if you have low revs, you're history. The conditions hurt me too though. Longtrack was never my priority at any rate and I never had great longtrack bikes. I had some flashes of brilliance when conditions were right, I have to say that. I made great money out of it and enjoyed it on occasions, but I never lost any sleep over it. My priority was speedway.'

A combination of World finals, the World Team Cup and a return to California meant that Penhall's matches for Cradley in September were thin on the ground, but a maximum against Leicester at home in the Midland Cup semi-final saw him welcomed just as enthusiastically as ever by the Heathens fans. It was a pick-me-up that Bruce could hardly have appreciated more, and he followed it with a mammoth 31-point haul from his only other two Cradley appearances of the month. The remaining focus of the British season was to end on a high for the club. Despite McCormick's departure, the Heathens qualified for both the Midland Cup and Knock-Out Cup in October. Against Coventry in their first appearance in the regional championship, Bruce was unbeaten at Brandon, leading his team to a 40-38 upset in the first leg. It was enough groundwork for the Heathens to complete an aggregate victory a week later at Dudley Wood without Bruce, who returned once more to his homeland. Although missing the second leg against the Bees, and the first leg of the Knock-Out Cup against Belle Vue, it was an opportunity and an unexpected bonus that Penhall had been unable to refuse. For the first time, foreign-based riders were invited to compete in the US National final. This was separate to the American qualifying round for the World Championship and was traditionally only open to those riders regularly competing in the US. However, as so many stars had left for Europe, the competition would have been seriously devalued had it been missing around ten of its best riders.

Not everyone would have chosen to miss their British League fixtures to fly halfway around the world for one appearance, but it was a title and a target that had previously eluded Penhall. The chance to make up for the World final was attractive, as was the opportunity to go one better than his last shot at the National Championship when he finished second in 1977.

Although seeded into the final along with Scott Autrey, Bruce flew back early to fit in some extra practice on the tight Costa Mesa track, determined not to make the mistake of losing out to the local boys because of their superior familiarity with the circuit. The preparation proved worthwhile, as he scorched to an unbeaten performance in front of a capacity crowd, and finished a great 4 points clear of nearest rival Alan Christian. The new title had a nice ring to it: Bruce Penhall, US National Champion.

Two trophies were left up for grabs in the UK, one team and one individual. In the first, Bruce had to settle for second place – runner-up again in the British League Riders Championship to Les Collins. His challenge came just too late in the meeting after amassing only 3 points from his first two rides. Larry Ross headed home a complete American trio in heat three as Penhall split his fellow countrymen Autrey and Sigalos, but then Kenny Carter was inches ahead of Bruce as the pair crossed the line in heat seven. After that it was three straight wins, including a crucial heat twenty when he needed victory to ensure second place overall, and champion-elect Collins was kept behind, albeit securing the point to stay ahead of Penhall and claim the title. So, it was down to the team prize if 1980 was to be rounded off with some more success. There were no mistakes this time and if anything, Penhall's club form had outshone his individual performances during most of the season. He raced to his thirteenth full maximum of the season for Cradley, in fifty appearances. The Heathens pulled back a 26-point deficit from the first leg, when Penhall was missing, as they mauled a weakened Belle Vue team in soggy conditions at Dudley Wood. In an inspirational partnership, Bruce combined four times with Alan Grahame for 5-1 maximum returns. The trophy collection for the season now comprised the Knock-Out Cup, Midland Cup, Inter-League Four-Team Tournament and Dudley-Wolves Trophy. Fifth place in the British League was highly creditable, but some fans pinpointed Penhall's absences as one reason why the position wasn't higher. What is clear is that, with an official league average of 10.35, he was undoubtedly the master of many team victories. Even more remarkable was his away figure of 10.46 – 0.09 higher than his overall average and 0.22 above his home figure of 10.24. To achieve a more consistent figure away from home than around the familiarities of his home circuit was a true measure of Penhall's broad capabilities.

He was voted SWAPA Overseas Rider of the Year once again – the second successive season that Bruce won this category and again dominated the voting, amassing twenty-seven of the forty-eight votes and beating second-placed Bo Petersen who mustered sixteen. He almost inevitably took the honours in the inaugural allocation of a Personality of the Year Award, pipping commentator and then-Reading Chief Executive Dave Lanning by two votes. Also in 1980, Bruce's name was attached to a book, *Bruce Penhall's Stars and Bikes*, a measure of his immense popularity and pulling power even in just his third season of racing in Britain. Produced in partnership with then-Leicester manager Martin Rogers, the intention was to 'illustrate something of Penhall himself, and something of the world in which he lives and competes,' although much of the content was devoted to various riders and speedway events from the preceding season.

The rearrangement of the Knock-Out Cup final second leg meant that Bruce had to delay his final return home in 1980. When he did catch a flight back to Los Angeles, one of the first priorities was medical consultation on his troublesome injured shoulder, which had dogged his season. He competed in the annual US Longtrack championship, which was staged over two separate events – a qualifying meeting and a final. After being head and shoulders above most of the qualifying field, the shoulder gave way in the last race. In the final later in the week, Bruce persevered and finished fourth overall, behind Shawn Moran, John Cook and the young prospect rapidly being referred to as a Penhall protégé, Lance King. Cradley were still seeking the services of King after Bruce's initial recommendation, but he wasn't eligible for an international move until his eighteenth birthday in August 1981.

After an appearance in a 'Superbikers' event with Michael Lee, which featured many of the USA's top motorcycle racers, Bruce succumbed to an operation on the shoulder. He finished as the top-ranked speedway rider in the televised competition that drew a viewing audience of 75 million people, but then it was time for a long overdue, well-earned rest. The operation was performed by some of America's top surgeons at the time. A piece of bone was taken from his back to lengthen and strengthen the shoulder joint, and the procedure was completed with the insertion of a two-inch steel screw. Deciding to skip his usual winter tour of Australia and New Zealand after that, he instead soaked up the Californian sunshine and took time out to make a proper recovery. 'I spent some time in serious rehabilitation with a very good physiotherapist. We didn't just work the shoulder but the entire body. There was a top American Football coach who helped me learn a lot about my body and about nutrition. At the end of it, I felt as fit as I had ever done in my life. It was one of the best things I could have done, and I have not had one problem with the shoulder ever since.'

The ultimate result was that Bruce felt perfectly conditioned and ready to embark on a huge, huge season.

TWELVE

GLORY YEAR

1981 was Penhall's year. After the winter of recuperation, the season warmed up with a planned series of matches in California between USA 'Home' and USA 'Overseas' teams. Bruce joined some of his fellow British League compatriots, including Bobby Schwartz and Dennis Sigalos, to take on the American-based Yanks at Costa Mesa, Ventura and San Bernadino. Although the second meeting was cancelled due to rain, the overseas select were victorious in each of the others. For Bruce, it was a steady competitive racing comeback to ease back into the groove, with modest scores of 7 and 8 points respectively. His only racing of the previous few weeks had been at a couple of local training tracks. He had spent some time at the motorplex, Saddleback Park, which featured a motocross track, flat track and speedway.

He flew back into the UK on 17 March, although Cradley's opening meeting was cancelled – as was the tradition – due to more bad weather. It gave him a few extra days to settle and prepare for the beginning of an enormous British season. The Heathens' management vacancy had been filled by Peter Adams, who moved directly from the helm at nearby Coventry. As well as taking over Dan McCormick's former promoting position, Adams also appointed himself as team manager, allowing Bob Wasley to leave the club. He had previously managed Ole Olsen while with the Bees and had a hand in running the Master of Speedway Championship. Many questioned his move across the Midlands and plenty suggested that a decline would be imminent without Olsen at his side. By March, Adams had already been forced to make his mark on the team, by squeezing the septet under the 50-points limit. The top four of Penhall, Gundersen, Collins and Grahame had been kept firmly together from the previous season and were joined by Aussie Dave Shields and another Dane, Bent

Rasmussen. Still unable to bring in Lance King for another few months at least, the final team spot was filled first by veteran Arnold Haley in the twilight of his career, and later another Australian, John McNeill.

As far as Bruce was concerned, there was an immediately more professional approach instilled by Peter Adams. As their relationship developed, Adams would work closely as Bruce's advisor as well, and deserves huge credit. It could not be any more forthcoming from Penhall himself. 'Pete Adams was, in my estimation, the best team manager speedway ever had. He was the best manager I ever had as well! He was a numbers guy – a brilliant numbers guy. Every step he took was calculated. Dan [McCormick] was flamboyant and he had a brilliant mind, but not quite so calculated. Bob [Wasley] was a good manager, but Pete was a *brilliant* team manager.'

There was another less publicised change to the Penhall back-up team for the 1981 season, with a new mechanic joining the ranks. Mike Tzouanakis, better known as 'Mikey T', was a friend and colleague from Indiana, whom he had met at the tracks in California. Mikey had previously been mechanic for Gene Woods in the States and he moved to the UK with Bruce in March, lived and travelled with him and took over all duties such as routine machine upkeep and repairs, cleaning and washing the bikes, and general mechanical preparation. 'Mikey was a massive boost for me. He was meticulous, he had the same personality as me. We are still great friends to this day.'

Eddie Bull was still very closely involved and his relationship with Bruce had continued to develop over the previous three years. However, Eddie gradually became more focused on engine work, and after the closure of the motorcycle shop where he worked, began to take on work from other riders, specifically just for engine tuning. Bruce was the main priority and Eddie would still travel to the important meetings at Penhall's side, but from 1981, he also worked closely with Cradley's other rising star, Erik Gundersen. As everyone at the highest level tried to keep pace with the cutting edge of technology at the time, Eddie played a hugely important role in the mechanical side of Bruce's racing. He would also still play an equally important role balancing his state of mind and mental approach to the sport. As various other influences came and disappeared, Eddie Bull was one of very few people who was an integral part of Penhall's life in British and world speedway, from start to finish.

In 1980, another mechanic had been taken on to lighten the burden on Eddie's duties. Paul Frisby worked alongside the pair for the majority of that season, but his role was filled by Mikey T in 1981, and Mikey would stay on until the end of Bruce's career. The support team that Bruce required to fulfil his racing schedule at the absolute pinnacle of the sport cannot be underestimated. While Eddie and Mikey provided the bulk of the technical expertise in England, Bruce also had the help of Jurgen Goldstein in Germany and Spike Creith in the USA. By 1981, his stable of machinery comprised a staggering twenty – twenty-five speedway bikes. Jurgen was taken on to take care of the continental affairs, and would meet Bruce at the airport, drive him to the track and have the bikes ready to race. He was also previously responsible for the machinery of Peter Collins and Ivan Mauger, who had similar arrangements for their regular European excursions. Spike was a laid-back character who ran a motorcycle shop in California and acted as mechanic for the bikes that were kept in the States. Everyone played their part and played a vital role in allowing Bruce to do what he did best.

Mechanically and technologically, Penhall and his team had come a long way since his arrival in the Black Country with Mark Cherry and just two bikes at the beginning of 1978. But Bruce is quick to point out that to achieve the ultimate goals, so much more must fit into place. It is this crucial philosophy that was the essence of his whole approach. 'The entire combination has to be right – mechanic, girlfriend, training, diet; it all has to be right. It comes down to "How much do you want it?" – even things like the travel, you must be conditioned if you're going to stay healthy. I tell all the kids I help now that this whole combination must be fitting together to achieve the ultimate success.'

Training is one example where Bruce further illustrates his unquestionable commitment to the goal. Taking advantage of a sponsored gym membership, he developed a routine of running, lifting weights plus hand-eye co-ordination exercises such as sessions punching the speed-bag. He was keen to increase his stamina to assist both his racing and the intense amount of travelling. In some of his earlier days riding for Cradley, he would train every day. It is a lifestyle at which many of his peers would have winced with the thought, but one with similarities to the highly professional approach of modern international footballers and athletes. If dedication was to play a part in achieving the ultimate success, then there was no way that Bruce would be lacking in that area. In fact, all of the pieces of the required combination for success, which he believes have to slot together like an intricate jigsaw, were just about clicking into place for Bruce as the 1981 season began.

When the tapes eventually went up at Dudley Wood at the end of March, Cradley's number one was out of the traps like a greyhound. His scoring for the Heathens began with a paid 13 return and in April he followed it with five totals of 14 or more from his eight meetings. At Sheffield in the League Cup, Bruce scored the only 18-point full maximum in his domestic career, and hence his biggest ever score for Cradley. The required six rides to achieve the full house were a rare occurrence in the early eighties, compared to more frequent instances of the feat two decades later. Penhall was certainly flashing the warning signs to his rivals at the top of the World Championship pecking order. With the American qualifying round scheduled for May – as opposed to being raced seven or eight months in advance as per the previous season, his form was peaking nicely. At the very beginning of April he had gone straight to the top of the British League averages, thanks to an early 15-point maximum at Birmingham, although he had to miss an early clash with Belle Vue due to his first compulsory season return to the States – just a month after landing back in Britain. Bruce's performances were topped with his elevation to captain of the USA Test team, replacing Scott Autrey who was stepping down, and he was also elected by his fellow countrymen as chairman of the International American Riders Association. Charged with the job of representing the British-based Yanks in their continuing quest for a reasonable deal with their governing body, he was naturally pleased and proud to take on the role, not to mention a natural candidate for the post. John Scott, the man who would assist Bruce in looking after the US riders' interests as well as gradually becoming more active as official team manager, was also delighted with the choice of his troops. He suggested that Bruce possessed exactly the right administration abilities to match his skill on the track. Cradley's club captain was now also skipper of the States and he would continue to lead by example. On track, the USA took on England for the second successive season, opening with defeat by the home nation at Belle Vue in Manchester. Off the track, Bruce continued to be as amiable and affable as ever, and managed to increase his popularity with Midlands supporters still further with an appearance in a charity soccer match between speedway riders and the sport's journalists. A 1,000-strong crowd watched in Oldbury, a few miles from the Cradley track, as he tried to convert his recent experiences of watching England's first sport into plying his new skills on the field. It's fair to say it wasn't the most natural thing for a Californian surfer and speedway rider, but Bruce predictably joined in the fun anyway.

A multitude of vital meetings flowed thick and fast in late spring with an unfortunately timed bout of flu striking several of the Cradley team, although it didn't prevent Bruce from fulfilling his domestic and international commitments. The England v. USA Test series dominated the end of April and the beginning of May, culminating with the final Test at Cradley Heath on Bruce's birthday. The presentation of a cake on the centre green couldn't compensate for the Americans slipping to a 4-1 overall defeat, unable to live up to their heroics of 1980. England thoroughly exacted their revenge under new manager Len Silver, the man who was to prepare the track for the World final later in the year. The hosts were rampant in the early tests, going 3-0 up with victories at Poole and Swindon, to add to the Belle Vue opener. The sole American success came against a weakened English side at Ipswich, in a meeting abandoned with the result declared valid after sixteen of the eighteen heats. Battling in vain, Bruce scored 61 points overall plus 4 bonus from 30 rides which put him a long way clear at the top of the Yanks' statistics once again, with a match average of 13.00. Taking his skipper's role seriously, he quietly felt that some of his teammates did not have a professional enough approach and was somewhat let down by certain members not being properly prepared.

In the week following the England defeats, a diluted American squad travelled without the services of British-based Cook,

Autrey, Sigalos and Gresham to give the younger emerging talents a chance to compete under the guidance of 'old' masters Penhall, Schwartz and the Moran brothers. Although also losing the series 2-1, it was a valuable experience in leading his troops for Bruce, who was striving to coax the best out of the ever-increasing number of riders providing competition to the top few Yanks on the international scene. 'There was also the problem of riders having commitments to their British League clubs. Some riders had problems with injuries and with bikes not being prepared. The decision to leave some guys behind was taken, even though they would have had to go if selected. There were still so many problems at that time with riders leaving their British clubs, especially on a Saturday night. So, a couple of guys backed out but Sweden were not really that strong then either. It was not like having to ride against England.'

Elsewhere, the USA did ease through to the next qualifying round of the World Team Cup, finishing second to England at a desperately muddy Reading, while Penhall continued his extracurricular pursuit of Longtrack success during the same week by making the grade at a qualifying round in Esbjerg, Denmark. He was selected to partner Bobby Schwartz in the World Pairs semi-final, which was staged at Treviso on the Venetian Riviera, but he and Boogaloo had to fly straight to Italy from Los Angeles after competing in the American final. Sandwiched between the USA's team and pairs championship events was the most important qualifier of all – the first step on the road to Bruce's goal of becoming 1981 World Champion. Meticulous planning seemed to have left nothing to chance, with confidence high following the superb domestic form and mechanic Mikey sent out to California two weeks in advance with a pair of bikes to set up. Disaster very nearly struck at the last minute though, as the van carrying the race machinery and equipment broke down en route to the final at the LA Coliseum. 'That's the sort of thing that can play with your mind and mentally break you down. I was pretty calm though, because I was full of confidence at that time. I was already having an unbelievable year, I was just in that state of mind. I felt that I just couldn't get beaten that season. I think Mikey and Jurgen were in the van and we were in contact with them. They said they would be a little late, but after I spoke to them I was OK, I knew they would be there.' The bikes and mechanics eventually arrived at the track just thirty minutes before the first race but Bruce settled quickly into the journey towards the 1981 World final. The meeting was staged for the first time at the Los Angeles Coliseum, solely because it was to be the venue for the 1982 World final and FIM rules stated that a meeting must be raced in the stadium before the big night. For promoters Harry Oxley, Barry Briggs and Ivan Mauger, it was an expensive burden, while for Penhall and his contemporaries, it was the first hurdle on the way to all of their greatest ambitions. A temporary 400-yard track was laid, which by its size alone was more suited to the European-based riders, and three of the favourites were pitched together as early as the fifth race. Penhall lined up against Dennis Sigalos and Scott Autrey, but unbelievably only he would complete the four eventful laps to win the race. Behind him, first Autrey's machine gave up the ghost and then that of Sigalos – the latter pushing his ailing bike over the line for a valuable point. From there it was plain sailing and Bruce scorched to an unbeaten, unchallenged and uncompromising 15-point maximum. Sigalos beat Kelly Moran in a run-off for second place and Autrey stole the fourth and final qualifying place. Extra slots had been allocated to the round as from there, the riders would join their British and Australasian counterparts in the Overseas final – introduced for the first time as an extra stepping stone before the Inter-Continental round where the Scandinavians were added to the mix.

'I loved the track and it was great knowing that would be the track for the 1982 World final too. The American final was always the toughest of them all for the guys because we knew there were so few slots available, but it was a totally new track so it was as neutral as it could be. I felt so comfortable knowing that and it was pretty satisfying to win it.'

After the luxury of a few days in California it was off to Italy, where Schwartz improved upon his disappointing American final exit to reignite the pairs partnership with Penhall. Only Denmark headed the US pairing, as they ensured qualification for the final in Poland, but they did make tough work of it after tying for second place with both Australia and the former Czechoslovakia.

Only two of the three nations could join the Danes in qualification, so a single rider was nominated from each country to contest an 'all or nothing' race-off. Bruce duly defeated Ales Dryml and Billy Sanders to see the Yanks through.

Two crucial meetings within seven days on opposite sides of the world had seen him progress to the next round in separate World Championship events, pairs and individual. Unfortunately the USA missed out on qualifying for the final round of the other event, the team championship, as they were defeated at King's Lynn in the penultimate stage. A tight tussle was fought throughout the meeting between the Americans, the Danes and the Brits with only 2 points separating all three before the last two races. Bruce had set a new track record in getting his country off to a flying start, but they couldn't quite maintain the pace. Any ambitious dreams of an international 'treble' crumbled in the final stages with the Yanks picking up only one more point thanks to Penhall, who completed a total of 9 in the last race.

If the USA were to claim their first ever team gold medal in a World Championship, then all the pressure was now resting on Penhall and Schwartz in the pairs competition. Boogaloo had been chosen as the number two, despite his American final showing, as he was one of the top-scoring British League Statesiders at the time. Interestingly, the decision was made by the riders themselves. 'The International Riders Association would get together before every big meeting and we would discuss who would be riding. We would look at where we were riding, who we were riding against, all those things. It was easier for the team cup or the Test matches because there were more places, whereas the pairs were just about the two of us. I was nominated and then it was about who would be the number two. Bobby was going good at the time and we could do things together on the track that nobody else could do as a pairing. So we discussed it, and it was always clear cut, it never had to come down to a vote, but if it did the guys would accept the decision. We would just talk about it and we were so tired of the AMA choosing, we pretty much wanted to eliminate them from the equation. After all, it was our livelihoods, we knew best and they were out of touch.

'We also had John Scott there as our team manager, who was a great guy, but he mainly acted as a mediator to pass the paper back and forth between us and the AMA. Lucky enough really, there never was a big problem. The only possible issue then was with Scott Autrey. He was still the pioneer, but by that time he wasn't scoring the points that some of the rest of the guys were every week. He soon settled down and became one of our group too.' There was little time for any nerves to set in about the importance of the occasion, as it came in the middle of June, only a fortnight after they had qualified from the semi-final. Held in Katowice in front of an intimidating 70,000 strong East European crowd, the event was fiercely contested on a huge sweeping track almost twice the size of a typical American circuit. By now, Bruce and Bobby were used to riding together on virtually any variation of speedway oval, and were drawn fittingly at riding numbers one and two, putting them out in the spitting cauldron of an atmosphere from the very first heat. It was a fine start with a 5-1 maximum over New Zealand, despite pressure from Larry Ross, with a winning time some three seconds long of the track record, showing the emphasis on looking out for each other, rather than each concentrating on their own game. Just like at Cradley Heath two years earlier, the pair demonstrated from the outset the very definition of team riding, following on from their textbook deliverance of the art from the British domestic open events. They made their task much more difficult in their next two outings, when firstly Penhall's engine ground his bike to a halt in heat four against the out-of-contention West Germany pairing and then they surprisingly gave away points to the Czechoslovakian pairing of Ales Dryml and Jan Verner in heat eight. Another victory was earned in heat eleven to bring the Americans back into the chase by scoring a second maximum advantage, this time over the much-fancied Danish duo, and thus effectively ruling them out of the reckoning. Ole Olsen had dived between the Yanks coming out of the first turn, with Penhall outside and Schwartz inside. Schwartz quickly battled through on the next bend to join his partner, with Penhall riding calmly wide to leave plenty of room in return.

Going into their final heat against Poland, the USA led the overall score chart, but New Zealand had clawed themselves back into contention after their opening-heat defeat and lay just 3 points behind. The Poles themselves were even more of a threat, having another ride still to come against Denmark and sitting 5 adrift. Zenon Plech shot from the gate and pulled clear of the Yanks, but left his partner Edward Jancarz back in fourth. Bruce and Bobby intelligently defended their middle positions and took an equal share of the race points, leaving the home nation needing nothing less than a 5-1 advantage over the Danes just to force a tie. Anything less would leave Penhall and Schwartz as World Pairs Champions for their country. Bruce's regular adversary of 1980, Hans Nielsen, was the man to pop out of the gate in that decisive race, silencing the huge Polish crowd and crossing the finish line in front to cue rapturous celebrations by the American contingent in the pits. The USA thoroughly deserved their valiant victory on the night with the ability to come from the back proving to be their most extensive weapon. Schwartz finished with 9 points and Penhall 14, with their total of 23 leaving them just 1 clear of New Zealand and 2 ahead of the Poles. 'Our team riding was just awesome and we did some pretty blatant blocking, but I always had all the confidence in the world in Bobby. He would go from inside to out just to block – all legally – and he wouldn't care who he was keeping behind him. He still reminds me that I blew a motor that night, and that kept the pressure on a little more than it should have been towards the end. I remember standing alongside that fence [watching the final decisive race unfold between Poland and Denmark] and I had Bobby alongside me. I had so much adrenalin inside me when they crossed the line I literally lifted him clean over my shoulder! We had such a blast! After the meeting though, they just opened up the pits gate and everyone piled in. The fans just engulfed us and I'd say they were about seventy-five per cent Polish, but they were just clambering for autographs and souvenirs. We couldn't even see our toolboxes right beneath us. Bobby actually became a little claustrophobic because it was just a sea of people. He was shouting "gimme some room" and we felt like we could hardly breathe, but it was a great feeling that night.'

Now the United States were very much back on the speedway map. With a dozen riders quickly following Penhall's path to the British League, the successive Test series against England and rapidly advancing progress in all of the international competitions, they had made their collective presence felt. Such a significant stride was the gold medal in their pockets however, that it turned the victorious pair of Californians into heroes. But with that in the bag, the attention for Bruce could be turned towards individual glory.

THIRTEEN

THE YANK VERSUS THE YORKSHIREMAN

London's White City stadium was the venue for the Overseas final of the World Individual Championship in July. It was the first of two 'Overseas' rounds in two years in which Penhall would compete, and neither would leave him with particularly pleasant memories. In 1981 it was the day where a bitter rivalry with England's fiery Yorkshireman Kenny Carter really exploded into public view, when Carter angrily accused Penhall of deliberately riding him into the fence. Both riders were seen as two of the greatest prospects in the sport for the years ahead, and they had both performed to incredibly high standards in reaching the highest echelon of domestic and international racing in a short space of time. Their clash was not until their final race of the afternoon, by which time tension across the field of riders had reached passionate extremes, with so much at stake.

Bruce had already experienced a lively afternoon. A mechanical glitch caused him to slip from second to last in his opening ride as he lost thirty yards on his opponents in the first lap, before spectacularly managing to climb back up to second again, missing out on victory by a matter of inches. A ding-dong battle with Dave Jessup ensued in a tough uncompromising second race before he made a flying start in his third, only to find reigning World Champion Michael Lee virtually glued to his back wheel for three laps. It was nothing compared to the excitement lapped up by the fans in the eighteenth heat. Penhall came to the tapes with 10 hard-earned points to his name and a real chance of lifting the title. Carter had collected a less impressive 6 and was battling for mere qualification. The Halifax favourite was frantically waving away the distraction of a photographer from the side of the track just before the tapes went up and when they finally did, he first clashed dangerously with Chris Morton as the pair clattered helmets in their dash to the first corner. Penhall was able to pull clear but Carter had the run around the outside, along the back straight and edged ahead. Kenny cut back across Bruce and the pair got caught up with each other, bikes locked together with Bruce completely unable to turn. The bikes straightened up across the bend, with Carter being led unavoidably into the fence and both riders unceremoniously hitting the deck. The Englishman picked himself up, shaking his head and pointing his finger accusingly at his rival, while Bruce looked up to see his exclusion light illuminated to signal his expulsion from the race. He rushed straight off the track, freeing himself from his helmet on the way to confront the referee, who declared 'foul and dangerous riding' as his rationale for the decision. Unable to change the opinion of the official, Bruce returned to the open arena, mystified by the verdict and laying the blame firmly with his adversary. In exceptionally dramatic fashion, he was interviewed immediately for the television cameras, claiming the decision was totally unfair. 'Kenny dropped it on me and I had nowhere to go,' he told Gary Newbon, trying to keep his emotions in check, as each of the crowd made their own choice of hero and villain. In stark contrast, Carter was also interviewed over the public address system and accused Bruce of deliberately knocking him off. It was this outburst that chiefly upset Bruce and his supporters more than the episode itself, as well as Cradley team manager, Peter Adams. Penhall later admitted the incident was technically his fault and that the referee was probably right to exclude him according to the letter of the law, but insisted there was nothing deliberate, furthermore suggesting that there was simply nothing he could do to avoid it.

'You have to go and speak with the referee, if nothing more than to just vent your feelings, even in vain. The decision was the decision and they wouldn't change their minds. You can't kick the bike and you can't shout at the mechanics because it's not their fault. I've seen all the top riders on the phone to the referee though, even those who are usually quiet and laid back.'

It was typical of Carter's personality to controversially speak his mind in front of anyone who would listen and not just privately to the referee, and Adams blasted his style in return, questioning his eloquence and maturity. Penhall's reputation, his manager retorted, was one of the fairest and cleanest in the sport. Journalist Tom Johnson described Carter's verbal attack as unwarranted and ill-advised, even in the heat of the moment, and suddenly everyone seemed to have an opinion on the matter. Penhall and Carter, two riders who could not have been any more different in their character, manner and background, were swiftly elevated to gladiatorial status. Few people realised at the time that a turbulent history between them had been bubbling under the surface for nearly three years. The first confrontation between the pair had unfolded at Cradley Heath much earlier in August of 1978, Bruce's debut season. Carter had not even contested the British League tie between the Heathens and Halifax at Dudley Wood, but was named as a non-riding number eight in the Dukes squad, and received his chance in the second race of the 'Star of the Night' support event. Bruce had scored 10 points in the main event, during a good run of form, but the bold young Northerner was keen to make his mark as he tried to force his way into the limelight.

'Our problems did start that night at Cradley during the second half. I will never forget what happened. It was in one of the heat races. Kenny was leading and I was right behind him but on the inside. As I was coming out of turn two, he was in the middle of the turn; he looked over at me, stuck his foot out and pulled it down hard on me as I was about to pass him. He deliberately left me no room, forced me onto the concrete kerb and I went down. I was really hacked off and I had a few words with him, but he clearly didn't care at all. So that is how it all started.' To compound matters, it was Bruce who was excluded that night at Dudley Wood too. On that occasion, it was him furiously gesticulating across the centre green, and from then on the feud simply grew. It became a vendetta where neither rider wanted to lose and Carter became public enemy number one in the Midlands.

The upshot of the Overseas final fiasco was that .Penhall's exclusion ruled out his chance of equalling Dave Jessup's top score and a shot at first place on the rostrum. While he was forced to settle for third place, Carter picked up 2 points in the restaging of heat eighteen, which was enough to clinch the very last qualifying position in the Inter-Continental final less than a fortnight later. Needless to say, the press made a meal of the battle between the two leading characters in the build-up to the next round at Vojens, but a class line-up were also fighting equally hard for one of eleven places in the biggest night of all at Wembley. While Bruce and Kenny were the centre of attention, everyone forgot to check the weather forecast in Denmark, and rather than the pair going head-to-head for a second round, it was a deluge of rain that took centre stage instead. The star-studded line-up was widely regarded as better than the World final itself and whatever happened, there would be some high-profile casualties from the championship race. Cradley fans were hoping that the list would not include Penhall or their other favourite son, Erik Gundersen. The Heathens' increasingly potent top two rode in a Knock-Out Cup quarter-final match for their club at Ipswich on a Thursday night and then flew out together the next morning as favourites to be among the top ten. So eagerly anticipating the outcome of the meeting were the Heathens faithful that Peter Adams arranged for a live telephone link-up to Vojens, in order to relay results to the crowd who were packed into Dudley Wood for a Saturday night four-team tournament meeting while the top stars were away. A score chart and agenda of heats was even included in the evening's race-night programme as the stadium became the first place in country to be updated with proceedings from Scandinavia.

On a pair of super-tuned Eddie Bull engines, Penhall and Gundersen got off to a flying start despite difficult track conditions early on, each winning their opening races to join Carter and Hans Nielsen at the head of the field. Then came the rain. Just as Bruce rode back into the pits after a victorious heat four, the heavens opened and literally flooded the Danish track. Conditions became atrocious and the riders voted overwhelmingly 14-2 in favour of abandoning the event, or at the very least postponing for twenty-four hours. However, referee Roman Cheladze came down on the side of the two, Ole Olsen – who was coincidentally not just competing in the meeting, but promoting it at his own track – and Nielsen. After a delay of over ninety minutes amid protests, flaring arguments and pure chaos, the Polish official gave his ultimatum, demanding that the riders return to the track or face being eliminated from the competition. Twenty-one thousand people had reacted so irately at the sequence of events that all available police had been called from two neighbourhoods to restrain then. A couple of thousand more had sat patiently in the Dudley Wood bar long after the close of Cradley's meeting, waiting for news. 'It never failed to rain at Vojens! When it was dry, and it rarely was, Vojens was one of my favourite tracks. I'd had one of my best meetings there in the Master of Speedway, and just like in the American final, I just don't think I could have been beaten at all. The rain was a hindrance, but I was so confident. It didn't bother me that it was Ole's track either. I don't care how he prepared the track, even if he did it to his liking, it still might not be enough on the night. You never know what could happen, and a lot of other things can go wrong for any rider.' Penhall and Gundersen eventually rolled out onto the track in heat six to face each other almost two hours after their previous outings and, unaffected by the melodrama, they finished first and second to relegate Olsen and Dennis Sigalos into the minor placings. It was Bruce who remained unbeaten, and although it was already getting dark, amid all the troubles his winning time was only around a second slower than times in the earlier races. He continued the record against Carter in his third race by making an electric start, riding a brave first lap to stay on the outside of his adversary and then gradually pulled away, leaving no-one any chance of overtaking due to the flying mud. It was the same story in his fourth and fifth races, as big names such as Ivan Mauger and fellow Yanks Sigalos and Kelly Moran all failed to make the cut. Penhall had reeled off another immaculate 15-point maximum. While others had been completely fazed by the off-track wrangling and on-track conditions, Penhall stood head and shoulders above them. He had never looked in danger of dropping a single point, leading every race from start to finish. As the rest skated around hopelessly, Bruce ended up with the only pair of clean leathers in the stadium, and became the first name in the line-up for the World final.

In a TV interview the following week, Bruce openly criticised the referee and expressed a desire that it be made mandatory for all referees to speak English. He cited the fact that the referee in question was Polish and communication between riders and the official was made through a Danish interpreter, who himself wanted the meeting to continue! No-one really knew what the other party was saying, except of course the interpreter. 'The hardest thing of all in a situation like that is translation,' he says now. 'If you had a problem, it was your prerogative to speak to the referee. I thought that we could even have had two referees for big meetings like that, even if it held things up a bit. It was the same in the Overseas final at White City; those meetings were like a pressure cooker. There was so much at stake and I'm not talking money because the international qualifiers didn't pay jack anyway. It was the round and the one which was coming next, it was all about getting through. As racers, because of the pressure, what took place on the track could sometimes differ to what the referee could see. They were such huge decisions though, they could affect not just your season, but your whole career. If something like that happens and you end up out of the competition it can affect you mentally, you might just think "what the hell with this sport" and pack it all in. Two referees could at least discuss a situation and it wouldn't come down to one guy.'

Bruce's next appearance at Dudley Wood in front of his home fans was for the Golden Hammer, a meeting in which he still had not performed well and still hadn't been dealt any luck. That all seemed set to change on the first weekend in August 1981, when the Cradley Heath fans, who were already clamouring for seats at Wembley the following month, welcomed back the top two finishers from the Inter-Continental final. Bruce and Erik received a great reception, and they each made great starts to their programmes races in Cradley's now prestigious and highly rated showpiece meeting. After all the riders had completed three races each, Bruce sat on top of the pile along with Chris Morton, both yet to drop a point, on 9 apiece; Gundersen was next in line, with 7 to his name. Bruce was looking untouchable, reeling off three straight wins, collecting a curious selection of sponsored prizes along the way, comprising a car stereo, a crash helmet and an antique stool, and leaving Kenny Carter at the back when the pair met in a much-hyped encounter. The event was building towards a stirring finale with him due to meet Morton in the very last race of the competition, with Michael Lee and Kelly Moran thrown in for good measure. So what else could happen at the height of the British summer? A downpour of torrential rain. Two races were completed after the programmed interval before the officials were forced to call a halt to proceedings, just after Morton had spun around in last place in his fourth race. Bruce was left as leading scorer, the only man to remain unbeaten, but the abandonment meant that no result was declared and the meeting never restaged. The Hammer would still elude his grasp. 'It really bothered me that I never won the Golden Hammer in front of the Cradley fans. That and the British League Riders Championship were the ones which I never quite managed. Something always went wrong, but it also has to be said that Cradley was one of the most neutral tracks around, not like Hull or Exeter where home riders had a big advantage in the open meetings. The Hammer also always attracted the best riders, so the line-up was always first class. I would have really liked to win it although I'd rather give that up than a World Championship or one of the qualifying rounds!'

Despite the neutrality of Cradley's racetrack, which was widely acknowledged by many visiting teams as one of the country's best-prepared and fairest speedway circuits, the Heathens had managed to build up an extremely healthy run of victories that had taken them to the top of the British League. In fact the team had gone on a streak of uninterrupted league victories from 13 June, when they lost at Swindon, and were not defeated again until October, shattering the previous record run. The top four of Penhall, Gundersen, Grahame and Collins were all on flying form, but none more so than Bruce, chosen as Coral's national rider of the month for June. A country mile clear at the top of the league averages, he blazed an unbeatable trail through all his opposition for the rest of the summer. Starting with a new Dudley Wood track record of 62.9 against Coventry in the first heat of the first meeting in July, he collected a staggering nine maximums in the next eleven meetings up until the middle of August. During the sequence, he lined up in forty-six races for the Heathens and won forty-two of them, losing twice to Michael Lee at King's Lynn, once at home to Les Collins and spending the other race shepherding home his partner, Bent Rasmussen, ahead of Scott Autrey for a home 5-1. At the very height of both Penhall's and Cradley's remarkable string of results was a most satisfying victory away from home at Brandon, over arch-rivals Coventry. It was not just a victory, however, but an absolute mauling of the Bees, led by four unblemished wins by Bruce. In a top-of-the-table clash, where ATV commentator Dave Lanning suggested the Heathens may be let down by the weak tail end of their team, they romped to an unprecedented 52-26 triumph, doubling the paltry total of the hosts and completely surpassing the narrow victory achieved on the same shale in the previous season.

It was no wonder that sponsors were now falling over themselves to clamber onto the Bruce Penhall bandwagon. He was *the* rider to be associated with. Top of the league averages, leading his team to the top of the league table; favourite to win the World final that he had just qualified for and already both American and Inter-Continental champion. He was taking in open meeting bookings across the country as the demand for punters to see Penhall at their track went ballistic. Naturally, the requests came in from Europe and the USA as well, and any company able to get their name or logo emblazoned somewhere across his person or equipment, would receive almost guaranteed gleaming exposure. Coupled with Bruce's determination to sell himself and hard work in proving his worth to any interested sponsors, it made for a complete turnaround in comparison to his first UK season. Now, it hardly mattered how potential sponsors viewed his supposed background, because they would be simply foolish to pass up the opportunity of being associated with the glamour and success that was attributed to him. 'I got over my initial problems in trying to attract sponsors simply by proving myself and establishing myself. Then, it didn't matter about the rumours. Companies wanted the publicity and they would have been crazy not to. Some firms had been with me from the start though. Bel-Ray [manufacturers of motor cycle oil] was a huge sponsor of mine. Wild West Stores were big but only in the States, whereas Bel-Ray on the other hand were going international when I moved to the UK and my contract with them required me to wear mostly all Bel-Ray logos. All but one of my initial sponsors stayed with me throughout the rest of my career. Scott goggles was the only one that I had changed. They were with me until the end of the 1981 season, before I switched and signed with Oakley.' A particularly interesting deal was struck with sports clothing company Offshore, which had bonus payments built in for TV and media appearances. At the end of the contract, later in his career, when the final bill was submitted to the company, it added up to an enormous figure of around $500,000, following around 150 television appearances featuring the Offshore logo. The company couldn't believe it and admitted that never in their wildest dreams had they imagined that Bruce could sell himself, the sport and their logo as much and as successfully as he did. All of the television tape recordings were submitted to prove the figures, but Bruce and his team declined to charge the full amount, eventually settling on a tiny fraction of what he would have been technically entitled to receive.

Peter Adams helped to forge further sponsorship links for the 1981 season, beginning with a lucrative tie-up with Pirelli tyres in Italy, where Bruce received free tyres from the company for the whole season. Other deals received far more publicity at the time but paid nothing, including an over-hyped arrangement with a local Western Clothing store. It was widely reported that the company paid up to £25,000, including an £18,000 Chevrolet travel cruiser motor-home in exchange for logo advertising and personal appearances. In actual fact, Bruce received nothing but a few items of clothing, despite sticking to the agreed appearances that had him photographed with fans in his cowboy hat in a local park and riding horseback in a wild west re-enactment show. 'I had a great relationship with Pirelli and was delighted to switch to their tyres as I had not really been sponsored by Dunlop before, but had been using their brand. There was nothing delivered from the cowboy place, certainly no travel cruiser. There were rumours that it paid millions, but it paid nothing. If I had a dollar for every guy that promised money I would be a frickin' millionaire. That's pretty common in the race industry though and you get used to it.'

Without the pledged super mode of transport, there was the consolation of a sponsored Volvo from a dealership in Stourbridge, which not only sufficed, but still rated as a pretty good deal for a speedway rider at the time. It was enough to replace an old BMW provided by Dan McCormick for his first season, which was 'nice and big but had lots of trouble overheating!' Riders were more likely then to arrive at the track with a bike either strapped to the back of their car or on a trailer towed behind. Bruce was ahead of the game when he swapped the Volvo for a transit van, via a short spell behind the wheel of a Citroen Safari. The van was able to accommodate four bikes and some limited sleeping quarters to take some of the discomfort out of the travel routine.

By late summer, Bruce already had his name pinned to a bevy of titles and awards for 1981 and had appeared here, there and everywhere that had a speedway track. He was the winner of the Yorkshire Television Trophy at Hull and the Blue Riband at Poole, adding the Brandonapolis at Coventry later in the year. He had finished second in Ipswich's Star of Anglia and third in Hackney's Superama, but also thrilled the crowds back at Hackney in August for the Thames Sport Riders Championship, significant as the first live televised speedway on ITV. His showmanship was on display from the very beginning, pulling wheelies and entertaining both on and off track. He almost seemed to embellish a close battle with Malcolm Simmons in the final just for the cameras, as he chased inside and out before passing the Englishman, and then broke into another wheelie display for the last two laps. Upon leaving the track, he parked his bike just inside the pit gate and swapped his helmet for his baseball cap, to be immediately interviewed for the TV cameras. It's the sort of thing both riders and the viewing public may take for granted now, but something that Bruce performed with great aplomb in the days where it was far from normal for cameras and microphones to be thrust in a rider's face within seconds of leaving the shale. Spreading the speedway gospel, Bruce was to be found on the Isle of Man, far more famous for its TT races than anything else on two wheels. Coinciding with the renowned motorcycle festival, Barry Briggs had organised an 'International Grasstrack Spectacular', so Bruce swapped the shale for the 'King George V' playing fields on the island and turned in his usual attention-grabbing performance.

Inevitably, there were one or two pursuits of glory that fell by the wayside among the multitude of other titles being chased. Bruce finished ninth in his World Longtrack semi-final on 2 August at Pfarrkirchen, to qualify only as reserve for the final. Along with former teammate Steve Bastable, he was not called upon before or during the final in Yugoslavia, so both remained outside the final sixteen. The Master of Speedway series went from bad to worse with a fast-dwindling reputation after it was reduced to just two scheduled rounds, following the eventual completion of just two in 1980. This time both were held in West

Germany with the rest of Europe following Britain's early lead in shunning any association with the competition. Hans Nielsen again took the title with Penhall second – an exact repeat of the top two from the previous season. Two fourth places for Bruce even denied him a position on the rostrum in either of the two rounds, but still proved consistent enough to head off the rest of the challengers behind Nielsen, including third-overall Bobby Schwartz.

The setbacks, if they could even be described as such, were certainly insignificant in the grand plan of 1981. Bruce Penhall was the speedway rider that everyone was talking about – and not just in closed speedway circles. In a time of sporting recession, Penhall was spreading the speedway bug far and wide. Speedway fans had someone to really rave about to their friends; anyone who knew anything about the sport knew about Bruce Penhall, and there were plenty of folk who knew nothing about speedway and still recognised the name of Bruce Penhall! There was just one outstanding article on the agenda that would really cement his burgeoning recognition and reputation: the individual championship of the world.

FOURTEEN

ON TOP OF THE WORLD

Bruce had barely put a wheel wrong during the entire season before 5 September 1981, but past form counted for nothing when the tapes went up on a World final. Sixteen riders qualified through their own merits and had five rides for their shot at becoming champion. One hiccup and any hopes were probably out of the window for another year.

Bruce travelled to London with Peter Adams and such was the enormous buzz about the showpiece meeting that even the official practice was covered by both BBC and ATV news. They featured racing sequences and interviews with Bruce, by then the bookmakers' favourite at 7-2. He was in constant demand for newspaper and television interviews, and conducted himself as admirably as ever while under the unrelenting media surveillance. He reiterated his commitment to the promise he had made to his parents; confident that he had what it took, but modest at the same time, publicly rating his own chances 'as good as anyone else's'. The rest of the speedway world had no reason to hold back. He was outstanding favourite among all punters, none more so than the thousands of Cradley fans who had booked their tickets for the Empire Stadium.

When the big day came, expectancy levels simply soared sky high. A group of around thirty family and friends flew from California, which brought about the first signs of any nerves as Bruce flapped and flustered, trying to allocate everyone their seats in the stands. His American girlfriend at the time, Jodi – a tennis scholarship student from Texas University, joined his big brother Jerry and his wife. There was sister Connie and her husband Mark, who accompanied Bruce to England in 1978, his aunt and uncle who had taken the family under their wing after the death of their mother and father, plus Bruce's cousins and other friends including US mechanic Spike. In charge of the bikes for the event would be both Jurgen and Mikey, along with Steady Eddie Bull. Pete Adams would be at Bruce's side for the entirety and had his own ideas about how to prepare for the meeting. Adams had noticed that his rider always performed better when he was tired, arriving back in England for example after a busy weekend racing on the continent and late-night flights, only to score an inspired maximum at Birmingham on a Monday evening. So, after breakfast on the morning of the final, he packed Bruce and Jodi into a taxi and led them into the city. The three of them toured London under a blazing hot sun, as speedway fans from across the country gradually poured into the capital. After being kept at the dinner table until 10.30 p.m. the previous night, and being indulged in a rare bottle of wine, Bruce and his girlfriend found themselves being marched around Piccadilly Circus, the Houses of Parliament and all the major tourist attractions. In one of few moments for reflection during the whirlwind day, he nervously nibbled through his lunch in a West End restaurant, with his mind clearly elsewhere. By the afternoon he admits to being completely shattered and severely cursing his manager, but it was just as Adams had planned. 'It's true. I will always remember coming home from the Continent on the Monday completely shattered, and always having a good night at either Birmingham or Reading. If I had a little time off, I would always get so worked up that I would be trying too hard in the first couple of heats.'

By the time Bruce reached the stadium again late in the afternoon, he was focused and ready. He was the first rider changed and set about his sequence of warm-up exercises, while the frenzy of the World final began to build. Adams was never far away, meticulously marking out the programme and always cleverly aware of every possible pitfall and permutation. The mechanical team quietly and efficiently went about their business, and critically, Bruce knew he could place complete faith in his entire back-up team. Although no-one knew it at the time, the meeting would be the last ever World final at Wembley, often considered speedway's spiritual home. Bruce had some idea what to expect from the atmosphere, having been to the last three finals in London, but still took Adams' early advice to take a walk down the famous tunnel towards the track, and acclimatise to the surroundings with a reported 92,000 people cramming in behind the Twin Towers. Some reports suggested that there were in the region of a staggering 10,000 Cradley fans present, and it was quite easy to believe it whenever Bruce, or fellow Heathen Erik Gundersen, emerged into view. Any sight of Penhall in particular at the end of the tunnel, either before or during the meeting itself, would trigger a huge wave of camera flashes and by the time the riders were brought out on parade, the noise of the cheers and air horns was positively deafening. The heat of the balmy day was increased another notch when the television crews from both Britain and the USA set up their high-power lights along the pits tunnel, and there was no let-up from either group in shoving a microphone under the nose of any rider. Australian referee Sam Bass briefed the riders beforehand and assured them that his day job as a senior police detective was ample preparation to deal with any protesting riders, or anyone delaying the start after a single warning. The time had finally arrived for racing.

When the meeting was underway, Bruce watched the first two races before making his bow in the third heat. As all four riders sat astride their bikes on the edge of the track before being pushed away, he found himself with close friend and reigning champion Mike Lee on his right-hand side, and with Cradley teammate and another pal Erik Gundersen on his left. Heathens supporters were more determined than ever to let their riders know just how well supported they were, and the club's top two didn't disappoint, flying from the tapes into the lead. Penhall was away first, and Gundersen gradually closed the gap behind him after Lee had hit problems. The Dane was never more than a couple of bike lengths away as he pushed his senior teammate all the way to the line in a time just 0.1 seconds outside the three-year-old track record. As they crossed the line to the frantic flag-waving of extrovert start marshal Paul Johnson, the biggest cheer of the night so far erupted around every corner of the arena. With one race down and four to go, the job was only about to get harder. Bruce thought the tension would be at its greatest in the early stages, but soon realised that it was increasing ferociously as the night went on. Gundersen went one better than his first race by winning heat six in a time that successfully lowered the track record, and Penhall was next on stage. It was the first of two of

PENHALL - WORLD SPEEDWAY CHAMPION

the most memorable races in World final history, as the young American faced up to the wily old master of Wembley, Ole Olsen, champion in the previous two Empire Stadium finals. This time from the start it was Olsen who led, while Bruce barged unceremoniously past the other Dane, Hans Nielsen, to give chase as they rounded the first and second bend. Attacking the inside line on the first lap, he hounded his adversary, rearing on the second lap and then drifting further wide to try the outside. Olsen glanced over his shoulder and blocked every move. The pair both went wide on the third lap, but Penhall chopped back inside, right underneath Olsen and pulled almost level. He stayed within a bike length and pushed hard again on the inside of the next bend, but again found no room for manoeuvre. Both riders drifted wide again and infamously hit exactly the same patch of dirt, which forced each of their front wheels inadvertently into the air in perfect unison. Penhall was so close he looked like Olsen's shadow. He stuck with the inside until halfway down the back straight of the final lap, then changed the line of pursuit and swung outside yet again; forcing his wheels in line in the dirt, he came from nowhere to hurtle past his opponent and steal victory right on the line, by no more than the width of a wheel. The noise had erupted once more during the race as the whole stadium rose to their feet. Flags, programmes and scarves were waved frantically in appreciation, in every row and every section of the huge stands. The record crowd had received their money's worth already, and they were barely halfway through.

Back in the pits, Penhall was hardly off his bike before being accosted by CBS reporter Andrew Marriott for the American TV crew, and then it was the turn of British ATV interviewer Gary Newbon, for the *World of Sport* programme that was broadcast later that evening. It was a cauldron of immense pressure, but Bruce had learnt how to handle it now. 'He [Olsen] had me covered every which way,' he told Newbon with a satisfied smile. 'I had to shut off, otherwise I would have hit him… then I had a nice long drive right across the finish line.'

Heat nine was his next outing and a showdown with the similarly unbeaten Dave Jessup. A tremendous start propelled Bruce into the lead, with Jessup constantly breathing down his neck, gradually making up ground through the race and moving right up onto his tail by the time they passed the flag which indicated the last lap. The crowd roared louder every time Jessup seemed to get close, almost as if to warn Bruce that his opponent was closing in. As everyone collectively held their breath for the final bend finale, Penhall briefly locked up and Jessup, trying to find the extra drive needed to see him level, had to turn sharply mid-bend to avoid the danger of slamming into Bruce, which in turned snapped a small component of the Englishman's bike, causing him to grind to a heartbreaking premature halt. The heat victory was Penhall's.

At the interval stage, as the golden boy strolled around the pits trying to stay calm, he knew the job was only half complete, but everyone sensed it had to be the American's night. He was performing with the conviction of a man who knew it was his meeting, his season, his title. More significantly, his opponents were one by one ruling themselves out of the reckoning, often by succumbing to cruel misfortune. Jessup was the first, then Gundersen suffered mechanical gremlins, but Penhall simply got on with his own hard work and scored the points he needed. Perhaps the most critical of all the night's disasters unfolded after the break in heat fifteen, and as Bruce watched Kenny Carter pull up in with an engine failure, thus wrecking the Englishman's chances, it was understandable that he punched the air with a mixture of delight and sheer relief. It wasn't all down to good luck though. Immediately before Carter's hopes had been crushed, Penhall had produced the second of his compelling battles to overhaul Tommy Knudsen in heat fourteen, and if the Olsen tussle had been impressive, then this one claimed every superlative the journalists could dream up in the days and weeks that followed. As if to anticipate what lay ahead, some of the stadium lights curiously went out beforehand, dimming the glare and brilliantly setting the scene for unintentional dramatic effect. And right from the first corner it was amazing stuff; Penhall bolted from the outside lane for the second successive time while Knudsen coasted right across from inside to out in order to block his charge from the right. Penhall spotted the move early and changed his attack to cut sharply down on the inside, ahead of the Dane, but amazingly Knudsen used the drive from out wide to shoot underneath Bruce again, taking him completely by surprise as they both powered out of the second bend. Gasps by the crowd were matched by the disbelief emanating from every inch of Penhall's body language. As the Dane went by, all Bruce could do was hang on to his machine for dear life. 'I couldn't believe it when he went by me,' he confessed immediately afterwards, followed quickly by the pronouncement of, 'shoot, I'd better start working harder than this because he was pulling on me a little bit'. And pull away Knudsen did, first a couple of bike lengths, then a few more, as Bruce struggled momentarily to get to grips with the situation, before deciding it was time to reel in the young pretender. By the middle of lap two, he gained the lost ground, looked inquiringly outside, and tried to go wide but checked his move as his front wheel rose almost uncontrollably. Time was running out as they tore into the last lap. In hot pursuit, it was the wide line again, edging neck-and-neck along the back straight for the final time. Knudsen's elbow extended over Penhall's left arm. Bruce kept the throttle open a split-second longer to give himself extra space around the third and fourth bends, and then wrestled with the bike to straighten it up, racing to the line, past his opponent once again, this time with merely an inch or two to spare. He instantly knew he'd won it, punching the air with delight. Knudsen gave a similar but reserved and submissive punch, with no real conviction. Still, the crowd had to wait with baited breath for the 'photo finish' and the subsequent verdict of the result, and you can bet that not a single programme was filled in before the referee's official decision was broadcast, sparking rapturous cheers and applause. So, did Bruce feel at the time that he had done enough? 'I knew that I had passed him, but I knew that it was very, very close and could have gone the other way. I even felt that I had it more comfortably than I actually did. I thought it was at least a half a wheel, so it was definitely closer than I thought it was, but I knew I'd won it and that's why the fist went in the air. But you never know what it looks like from where the referee is sitting, they may see it differently. The referee has to call it the way they see it, they don't have the benefit of a television replay. Luckily, the decision was right and was backed up by the TV cameras. Tommy didn't punch the air like I did, but the Danes never celebrated. They were never the ones to raise their fists in the air when they crossed the line. They never did the wheelies until we started doing them.' It added up to four wins out of four for Bruce, and with his closest rivals dropping points elsewhere, it left him needing just one point – third place – from his fifth and final ride to be crowned Champion of the World. The wait was excruciating as he was forced to sit in the pits from the conclusion of heat fourteen until the last race of the night, heat twenty, where he would line up outside Kenny Carter. Bobby Schwartz came down from the stands to sit at the side of his buddy and Bruce sat for part of the time, fighting off the anxiety, with his leathers pulled down and tied around his waist, chest exposed and a damp, clean white towel around his bronzed shoulders. A calm exterior masked the mounting pressure, which eventually crept its way into his pensive expression.

Further down the brightly illuminated tunnel, in the bustling warren of a pits area, an unnerving commotion was evolving out of sight. While routinely draining the oil out of the bike into a catch-pan, one of the mechanics, Mikey, found what he thought were traces of metal in the oil of Bruce's best bike, which could potentially have caused the machine to seize. As it later turned out, the foreign bodies were just sawdust shavings that had blown into the container from the floor of the tunnel, but it was enough for Eddie Bull and Peter Adams to agree that the second-choice bike would have to be used in the final race. It was the sort of upset that can throw a rider's focus way off beam at such a crucial time and an already over-eager Bruce had to concentrate his mind on the task ahead. Adams advised him to take it easy and not to do 'anything stupid', especially anxious that Carter should be a given a wide berth considering the recent history of the bitter rivals. A solitary point seemed like an easy catch after four straight wins, but the concerns about the bike, the fact that Carter could not be trusted and the simply huge amount at stake over the mere sixty seconds of racing made it anything but straightforward.

It had been a dazzling performance and four more sensible laps would change Penhall's life. No American rider had topped the speedway world since Jack Milne was champion forty-four years earlier, and Milne himself watched from the Wembley stands, after flying in especially to see his achievement potentially equalled. Not a day had passed during the preceding season without Bruce thinking about the forthcoming World final and as he lined-up for that crucial last race, he had to put everything else out of focus, apart from those four circuits of the hallowed Wembley shale. The tapes went up and Carter gated well from the inside. Penhall stayed level with him around the bend, keeping out of the path of flying dirt behind the Yorkshireman's back wheel, and then he sat back. No extra effort was wasted; it was a composed, level-headed race, staying inside, almost cruising. With two riders safely behind him, Bruce just made sure Carter knew he was there, but never made any serious challenge for the lead. He looked back over his right shoulder as they approached the yellow and black flag, and took a long, deep breath. One lap later, he was pulling the customary wheelie over the finish line and the celebrations broke out like never before.

Cynics may state that had Carter not stopped in his penultimate heat and gone on to pass the race leader Dave Jessup (who also subsequently stopped again with another mechanical failure), then Carter would have suffered only one defeat and faced Penhall in a run-off for the title. However, if Penhall had gone into that final race of the night needing to beat his arch rival to ensure outright victory, it's a mighty brave soul who would suggest that the Yorkshireman could have fended off the challenge, especially considering Bruce's earlier exploits from the back against Olsen and Knudsen. In that instant, it mattered not one iota. The stadium stewards had struggled all evening to keep the Cradley supporters in their seats, and they could do little to stop many jubilant fans streaming from certain quarters to congratulate the hero they simply adored. The first rider to shake Bruce's hand was Carter, who slowed down and offered his praise as they glided around into the back straight. Then it was third-placed rider in heat twenty, Jiri Stancl, who Bruce nearly clattered into immediately afterwards, as he was so caught up in undoing his cut-out cord while the Czech had pulled up just ahead of him. From the pit crew, it was Adams who reached him first. Almost lifting the rider from his the bike, the pair threw their arms around each other in an emotional embrace. He walked Bruce backwards down the track, before Stancl broke up the back-slapping to add his further congratulations. Next out was Mikey T., joined by fellow mechanic Jurgen, Harry Oxley and Bobby Schwartz, as the whole group bounced up and down, wrapped together in celebration. Erik Gundersen joined them and dragged Bruce away for a euphoric hug of his own, before the supporters who had run from all directions took over and simply hoisted Bruce onto their shoulders. The mass of people were surrounded by press photographers and carried Bruce triumphantly towards the pits, his arms held aloft with the noise hitting new highs. The American flag was handed up to the new champ, as was the all-important baseball cap to display the sponsors' logos.

Out of sight, the group eventually reached the pits tunnel for an emotive greeting by all the hysterical family and friends, who too had rushed from their seats in the stand. Even Ivan Mauger, who had acted as Kenny Carter's mechanic and advisor, shook Bruce by the hand and declared 'Well done Brucie, that's just what we needed!', referring to the sport's increasing desperation for a charismatic and professional ambassador as World Champion. At last the wish had now been granted and it thrust the articulate Penhall as close as he had ever been to being speechless behind a microphone. Gathering his thoughts, he told Gary Newbon, 'my dream and my ambition finally came true. I'm World Champion and nobody can take it away,' adding in a stadium interview to the ecstatic crowd, 'my parents rode every race with me'.

When the initial euphoria passed, the post-meeting merriment ensued with a BSPA reception dinner at the Wembley Conference Centre. Naturally, the new World Champion was guest of honour, and he talked to guests and sponsors as well as supporters. After a toast by BSPA President Jack Fearnley, the first words of his victory speech were, 'I can't believe it!' Despite admitting to having had a few drinks by that point – notably champagne gulped down like lemonade – he still managed to eloquently and articulately thank all those who needed thanking and graciously accept the mantle of the 'best rider in the world' with characteristic composure. At 2 a.m., he strolled back to the hotel in the company of friends and spent the next few hours partying in the SWAPA lounge, with press and journalists. He was still accepting requests for autographs when dawn broke the next morning.

Sleep was something that did not come with much regularity for a while, but Bruce always wanted to be a great ambassador, and relished the opportunities that came his way to publicize the sport. Most tracks in Britain had struggled financially in 1981 and many lost money. Speedway worldwide was in need of a boost and Penhall was the man to provide it. He immediately took the sport to unimaginable new audiences, such as an appearance on the *Merv Griffin Show* on American TV Channel KT TV in Hollywood, alongside Joan Collins, Beach Boys singer Mike Love and comedian Jerry Van Dyke. The show went out to 48 million people in eleven countries!

For his return to Dudley Wood one week after the final, Peter Adams arranged for a telegram to be sent from then-US President Ronald Reagan. The incredible accolade was rushed through much quicker than usual, after constant badgering of the White House office by the Cradley promoter. A process that would normally have taken two to three weeks after the words had been scrawled by the man at the top, was eventually reduced to less than seven days as the note arrived at Dudley Wood at 7 p.m. on the Friday night, twenty-four hours before Bruce's 'homecoming'. It read in part, 'You have brought great honor to yourself and to your country. I have the greatest admiration for any sportsman whom has the dedication to become a champion.' It hardly mattered that the scheduled Heathens match against King's Lynn was postponed due to rain, as Bruce was flown in by helicopter and received the framed message on the centre green, in front of hordes of well-wishing supporters.

He flew back to Los Angeles soon after and rode in meetings around California, which brought in huge attendances. His appearance eclipsed all other racing activity on each occasion as the Americans turned out to salute one of their own, including a 9,000 capacity crowd at Costa Mesa. Bobby Schwartz made the trip at the same time, but neither Bruce nor Bobby had a successful time on the Orange County track. Utterly distracted by such overwhelming treatment from all the fans, Bruce simply couldn't concentrate on his racing and bounced off the fence at the back of the pack in the hotly contested handicap heats. It was quite the opposite to a 15-point maximum that won him the Californian State Championship at San Bernadino, on another appearance a couple of days earlier, but equally understandable. Meanwhile, the plaudits for the world title continued to pile up, with a personal presentation from the California State Governor, to add to the letter of congratulations received on the other side of the Atlantic from the Mayor of Dudley. Hundreds more letters, cards and gifts poured in from all over the world, and sponsors Offshore took out an advertisement in *Speedway Star* magazine that read 'Congratulations Bruce, 1981 World Champion. God Bless America.Your father and mother would have been so proud.' The accolades were finally topped with one more unbelievable tribute when the Mayor of Costa Mesa declared a 'Bruce Penhall Day' on Friday 25 September! Not only was a dream fulfilled, but the whirlwind series of events sparked by that so-memorable night at Wembley turned out to be infinitely more than even Bruce had dared to dream.

FIFTEEN

BRITISH LEAGUE CHAMPIONS

The reverberations following the universally popular World Championship victory were such that it would have been easy to forget that the end of the season was still several weeks away, and moreover, Cradley were still blazing a virtually invincible trail towards the British League title. The Heathens' incredible run of victories was still in full swing when they visited bottom-of-the-table Wimbledon, on the first day of October, with the opportunity to wrap up the championship leaving half a dozen matches to spare.

Hundreds of fans travelled back to London for another anticipated night of glory in the capital and they were joined by the local television news crews for the planned celebrations. The evening started badly for Bruce as he was passed in both of his first two races by home riders, before restoring order with a victory in his third. By then there was still little separating the teams and when he partnered Alan Grahame in the last race of the night, the scores were tied at 35-35. Despite a win for Bruce, his teammate trailed in last after throwing everything at the Dons pairing, so the champagne had to be put on ice – although not literally. Still a point short of the target that would mathematically clinch the club's first ever league trophy, the riders cracked open the bubbly anyway, eager not to waste the bottles that had been transported with them from the Midlands. And they didn't have to wait long before the corks were popping again with good reason, as three days later the season's efforts were justly rewarded away at Eastbourne, when the twenty-fifth success in twenty-seven matches secured the points required. Again it was Penhall in the final race, but this time a 4-point cushion meant that his victory was enough to deny the home side any share of the spoils. The transformation had been irrefutably completed; the already superbly supported club that Bruce had joined in 1978 that had virtually no honours in a dusty unoccupied trophy cabinet, now boasted the world individual crown and the domestic league championship. The history books would forever recognise both Bruce Penhall and Cradley Heath.

Along with the glory and approbation for Bruce came a merciless demand, which took him back and forth across the world and as he bowed to his own altruistic sense of duty, and ultimately left him in a state of complete exhaustion. Following the league clincher on the South Coast, he flew to the States for the defence of his US National Championship on the back of a month's relentless race meetings, interviews, and public appearances. Two days before the event at Costa Mesa, the mental strain of the preceding weeks caught up with him in a shocking moment, when he dramatically collapsed while out shopping and was rushed by ambulance into hospital for exploratory tests. There were suggestions of food poisoning, dehydration and fatigue, plus more worryingly a lump found in his stomach. Refusing to miss the National final, and wanting to prove that his 1980 victory was no fluke, he delayed any further procedures until after the demanding closing stages of the season, suggesting the problem could have been the legacy of a heavy fall earlier in the season. He turned up at Costa Mesa after two days confined to bed and unsurprisingly lost his first race to old adversary Mike Bast. However, despite taking oxygen during races, he then rode through the pain to miraculously win all his remaining outings and claim the title with 14 points. 'I did get food poisoning and I was hospitalised. The main problem was that I was just so drained from the World final and everything, but it was also food poisoning. The reason they put me into hospital was so they could put me on IV and get some fluids back into me. A lot of people thought it was a way to psyche out Mike Bast but it honestly wasn't. I was literally in the hospital the night before the National final and I was real sick. The next day I was released and I felt good; I was a little tired, but that was to my advantage because that's when I performed better again.

'After Wembley, I had pretty well accomplished everything I had dreamt of, you know, and I had given everything I had to give. So for a short time after the Nationals, I felt I had to pull back a little bit. Everything wasn't as important, whereas normally every meeting was equally important. I was on this roller-coaster ride for a while and my high was so high, I just needed to come down from it all. It pretty much kicked my ass for a while! Not just for a couple of days, but it lasted for like a month. I was tired.

'You want to peak at exactly the right moment, emotionally, physically, all of it, and that's exactly what I was able to do. I peaked at the absolute right time. I could have peaked a couple of days earlier and been a little bit less aware on the day, and that timing had a hell of a lot to do with Pete Adams. He got me really so focused, he was perfectly well aware of what I was capable of. Physically was never a problem for me, and really emotionally it wasn't either, but one can only do so much. I think even Pete was surprised at what I could accomplish interview-wise. There were college people who wanted an interview for an assignment for their teacher, and I would do them. I treated everyone as important as each other. So when you throw on the fact that you have about a thousand interviews, it all took its toll on me. I was literally done – you could have put a fork in me, I was done.'

Unfortunately the illness and fatigue blighted the remainder of the campaign as Bruce did his best to divide his attentions between more individual pursuits, Cradley commitments and international engagements. On his return from the USA, he rode at Dudley Wood against Coventry in the Midland Cup, just a few hours after landing in Britain, but was too tired to take in as much of the league-winning celebrations as he would have liked. The same evening heralded a long-awaited tilt at the Golden Helmet match race championship, but it was an unsuccessful outcome against – who else? – Kenny Carter. The system saw the Helmet being contested once a month by the current holder and a nominated challenger. The fact that Bruce had been overlooked as the August challenger to Gordon Kennett had upset many folk in the Black Country, including most of all Heathens promoter Peter Adams. It was in fact Carter who was selected and who indeed went on to beat Kennett to become the new holder. After the World final, the authorities had no excuse but to nominate Bruce as the challenger to Carter's first Helmet defence. However, Bruce had initially been unable to fit the required dates into his enormous schedule. Coupled with the problem that both Cradley and Carter's Halifax both raced on a Saturday night, the pair never met in September, hence the contest was carried over into October, allowing the tension and the hype to build that little bit more. By then Carter was the new public enemy number one around Dudley Wood, after firstly the Overseas final fiasco and then a non-appearance when Halifax visited Cradley for a league match in September. Everyone was still talking about the increasing Penhall and Carter rivalry and the apparent animosity between the two. But with Bruce jet lagged, exhausted and far from fully fit, he conceded a 2-1 defeat and knew it wasn't his best. Despite making the gate in every race in the second leg just four days later, Bruce only hung onto his lead once and again Carter stole a 2-1 victory to comfortably fend off the overseas challenge on aggregate. It was the closest Bruce came to getting his hands on the Golden Helmet in 1981, which he had last held at the beginning of 1980.

Incredibly, in the space of those four days between the two legs, there was the prestigious British League Riders Championship and the deciding match of the Midland Cup between the Heathens and the Bees. Bruce never really got started in the big finish to the domestic calendar. The season had finally caught up on him and the gruelling timetable combined with the after-effects of the illness left him floundering. Mustering only 8 points in the BLRC, his disappointing tally placed him well down the order as Carter took that title too. It seemed mighty strange at the time to see a Penhall performance in any individual meeting that had not merited a double-figure score. And after being forced to settle for the runners–up position in the two previous seasons, the Riders' final was to remain an extremely rare example of a title that eluded the Californian. With Bruce below par, Cradley also had to concede the Midland Cup to their neighbours Coventry, but the importance had paled in comparison to their existing success in 1981.

The season indisputably belonged to Bruce Penhall and Cradley Heath. The fact was recognised far and wide, illustrated when Bruce and his team were presented to the fans attending West Bromwich Albion's football league match against Southampton, who duly gave the unlikely local visitors a rapturous ovation. After the match, Bruce chatted amicably for half an hour with England player Kevin Keegan about their contrasting sporting experiences at the highest level.

Although an open-top bus tour was arranged for the club to show off their silverware around the streets of Dudley, Bruce missed the occasion. He returned home to the States five days before planned, although after his commitments had originally been due to be completed. Cradley's season was programmed to end on 24 October, but Peter Adams decided to extend it to take advantage of the buzz surrounding Penhall's World Championship victory. Bruce had also been invited to compete in several meetings in the US around the same time, where there was a similar fervour. He naturally felt equally devoted to fans on both sides of the ocean, leaving himself in a difficult position, not for the first time. In addition to the town parade and a civic reception, he missed three challenge matches for Cradley, as he opted to soak up the interest in the States, while his fellow league champions basked in their own new-found glory. In his absence, it was no surprise that Bruce reeled in a clutch of prizes, awarded for his exploits both on and off track during the year. He took the major SWAPA award for the first time, marching away every bit as emphatically as you would imagine with the 'Rider of the Year' honour. In addition came the 'Personality of the Year' for the second successive season and 'Overseas Rider of the Year' for the third successive time in the annual speedway writers and photographers awards. Cradley received the 'Team of the Year' and Peter Adams completed the haul by bringing the 'Administrator of the Year' title back to Cradley Heath after a season's absence. Considering that Bruce was ineligible for the British Rider, Newcomer and Young Rider of the Year Awards, it was basically a clean sweep of all the rest on offer. To begin to illustrate the huge impact Penhall's charming personality had on the seventy or so voting SWAPA members, consider the results in the 'Personality of the Year' category, where he clocked up more than twice as many as all his competitors put together. First place Bruce Penhall had forty-five votes, second place John Cook had five votes. It capped the season that represented the real breakthrough from a mere world superstar to the unquestionable champion of the speedway world. The very height of success was achieved on that night at Wembley with the coveted and craved individual crown.

But, if that victory was the huge sparkling diamond of Bruce's season, then glittering on either side of it were the World Pairs title with America's name on it for the very first time, and the British League success, also achieved for the first time ever by Cradley Heath. On the way to the world title, Penhall won the American final and the Inter-Continental final rounds, and finished third in his only other qualifying obstacle, the Overseas final, after the controversial exclusion. He held top spot in the British League averages, almost from start to finish, and by the end of the season was the only rider to have obtained a figure over 11.00 CMA, a truly outstanding feat that has been only sporadically repeated ever since. Before 5 September, he had promised to win the world title. After that night, he vowed to be the exemplary ambassador the sport was crying out for. And he certainly didn't let people down in terms of publicising the sport whenever and wherever it was possible. It was typical of Bruce to always make sure there was time for every adoring young fan with an autograph book; always provide some words for every TV and newspaper reporter; and always conduct himself as the model professional sportsman no matter what the pressures at the time. Voted 'Mister Speedway' by *Speedway Star* magazine readers, he lived up to the mantle by becoming synonymous with the name of the sport in corners which seem so inconceivable now. From appearances on Saturday morning UK television with the zany *TISWAS* programme and in youngsters' magazine *Look-In*, to being awarded his own column in the *Daily Mirror* national newspaper and receiving a feature in the *TV Times* magazine that launched the following season's *World of Sport* coverage. Penhall was the face of speedway and the sport could not have dreamt of a better image to project.

By the time the winter approached, anyone might have expected Bruce to be more than ready for a rest, but after the inactivity of the previous close-season, any relaxation was furthest from his mind. After a short time back in California and a trip right across the world to attend the FIM congress in Tokyo, he took in another annual indoor meeting at the Wembley Arena before heading off to Australia and New Zealand as would always be his preference. The Lada Indoor International proved as challenging as ever and a 3-point return showed that Bruce couldn't quite turn his hand to every type of racing. He did impress with his dancing during the Andy Peebles Radio 1 roadshow disco at the event, but was happy to be back on a bike for another annual appearance in America's Superbikers competition. Kenny Carter joined him as speedway's two representatives but Bruce's standing earned him a £3,000 bike built especially for him to ride in the televised event. He explains: 'Superbikers involved all the top motorcycle riders from across the world. They would take a little piece of speedway, a little road racing and a little motocross, then combine it into one race which was televised on ABC's sports spectacular. I was invited to ride in it, but I struggled.'

Despite a range of activity on two wheels, it was nice to return to some conventional speedway in the trip Down Under after Christmas. The 1982 calendars had barely been hung on the wall before Bruce and Bobby Schwartz were in action in a best pairs meeting in Adelaide on New Year's Day. The reliable old partnership mesmerised the Aussie fans as their team riding took them to victory ahead of Shawn Moran and John Boulger, John Cook and Phil Crump. It was the first of two pairs victories with a significant individual event sandwiched in between. 'Solo racing' often played second fiddle for the Australians to sidecars, midget racing and other motor sports, but it received a huge shot in the arm at Claremont in Perth where Bruce produced some vintage races in a twelve-heat individual event. He finished third overall, despite winning all but one of his rides in a much better effort than his first visit to the track a few years earlier, where he had failed to score!

While all was going well in the Southern Hemisphere, back in England, where Bruce's house was being looked after in his absence, there was news of a problem that took a while to filter through to him. A burst pipe had created six inches of water spreading across the entire ground floor. Fortunately there was only limited damage. However, a different kind of problem had already been prompting him to consider moving away from the area to a more remote property. 'I had thought about going out in the countryside but I didn't get as far as putting the house on the market. One of the reasons for thinking of a move was because the fans had found out where I lived. Mikey would be out in the workshop and people would drive by, usually girl fans. He had this rubber mallet that he would hit the side of the house with, so that

I could run and take cover, hoping that people would think that I wasn't there! It started to happen real often, even late at night so it became a little bothersome. That made me think of getting a place out in the country, but it didn't actually happen. I stayed where I was until the end of 1982 and then I sold the house to Rick Miller [another young American recommended by Bruce, who signed for Coventry in the British League].'

As the start of the 1982 season edged closer, Bruce moved on to New Zealand, but had still not agreed a new contract with Cradley after the expiry of his previous three-year deal. For the first time, he was negotiating as the World Champion and was seeking the due recognition of his incredible exploits over the preceding twelve months. Also for the first time, the negotiations were left in the hands of his new manager, Jeff Imediato, after Bruce had turned to various outside influences to handle more of his affairs. His racing had always provided him with a bursting schedule, but with the added attention piled on him thanks to his incredible success, he felt that he needed someone else to take the pressure off. As with his first ever contract with Cradley Heath, Bruce saw his job as a speedway rider and he wanted to concentrate on 'putting his backside on the motorcycle and doing what he could do best – racing'. With an average of five meetings per week during the season, plus interviews, personal appearances, flights and travel to be organised and tickets to be booked, he sought assistance. 'I was with a guy called Alan Seymour for a while, really more friends than anything, but Alan was the one who set up the Offshore sponsorship deal. He helped out a lot before the World Championship, then we felt that someone needed to take it on as a full-time job. That's when I signed with a guy called Jeff Imediato to handle all the deals.

'I was racing and he was wanting to manage and he was a hustler. I could tell in the first hour when I spoke to him – I could pretty much feel people out and could tell whether they were flakes or not, with the amount of promoters I'd met over my time – and he seemed pretty genuine, and he was. I won the championship and he was all over me.

'I told him I would put my trust in him and he said in return that things weren't going to be easy, and that there would be a lot of pissed-off people. We linked up with the Mark McCormack company, not as a management deal, but more as a talent agency, and it was Jeff who set that up. Things didn't work out with them, and then we ended up signing for the William Morris Agency instead, and they handled all my publicity. That came right after the 1981 World final.'

In the British press, Peter Adams admitted some concerns over how much longer he expected Bruce to be in British speedway, since he had begun to receive a variety of offers from film and television companies, courtesy of his new advisers. The Heathens supremo was worried that his number-one rider would sooner or later receive an offer outside speedway that he simply couldn't refuse. Bruce publicly said that he would stay at Cradley for the rest of his career, but Adams pointed out that he didn't know how long that career would be. On Australian television, Bruce added to the headlines with a sensational interview, allegedly claiming that he may have considered giving up the sport after Wembley, if the 1982 final had not been in the United States. He also confessed to some acting classes in America and tests for the soap opera *Love Boat*, scripts from *Dynasty*, plus the first mention of a possible guest appearance in highly rated motorcycle cop show *CHiPs*. Moreover, it was reported that Bruce would be quitting the sport at end of the 1982 season. Trying to clear up the escalating rumours in the speedway world, Bruce was later quoted in the press as saying that he 'did want to pursue an acting career, but it would simply be whenever the right offer came along, maybe two or three years down the line'. He 'didn't say that he would definitely be quitting at end of 1982, but would have to make the decision eventually, because film company insurers would not cover him riding motorbikes'. He acknowledged, just as he had always done, that he couldn't ride motorbikes forever, and wanted to have something in place to move on to afterwards.

On reflection now, Bruce admits that 'the way Hollywood worked was they used you as a sort of vehicle to get to other people. They would say that you had all these other offers, and most of it is fabricated. What is not fabricated is the fact that I was pretty well coming to the end of what I wanted to accomplish in speedway. Don't get me wrong though, we did have a lot of offers on the table at that time.'

Meanwhile, it was new manager Imediato who took on the responsibility of discussions over a new deal with Cradley. The presence of a brash, big-talking American marketing agent did not at all impress the Heathens' promoters. One person that could have handled the negotiations,' Bruce points out, 'was Dan McCormick. But Dan was out of the picture, so it fell to Pete Adams and Derek Pugh. They were old school, and were like "wow what's happening? Has the fame gone to his head or what?" They laid the blame with me and it did ruffle a lot of feathers, but we held out.'I had someone who was fully in charge of my business affairs and I put all of my trust into that person. The thing was they thought they knew a lot more about it than me, in terms of how much I was worth – but I could always undersell myself better than anyone, because I loved to ride speedway so much. You see it all the time with any sort of sports person or actor, it's the agents who go after the promoters for more money, because they want the most for their 'principal', as they call it; for their athlete. I had to put my trust into him and let him do all the negotiating. The speedway people didn't like that, especially Cradley because as riders, we're a lot softer than what an agent is. They can get a lot more out of a deal because we love what we do so much. At times, we would be ready to pay them [the promoters] to do what we were doing!

'It was not that I didn't want to ride, because I did – I just wanted to be paid properly for it. That was the season where you're supposed to capitalise on becoming World Champion, and I knew that if I didn't agree with Cradley, no other club could afford the transfer fee. And they all knew that, everybody else knew that too. Of course I never, ever wanted to leave Cradley. I didn't have another club that I would even consider. We might have talked about a few other clubs, because of the hype, to get to the promoters, and then the fans would get to hear about that because of the press. The promoters would leak it out and so would agents, because they want to get the hype going for their rider, but you have to hope that the fans don't turn on the rider because they think he's this and he's that and that he's just being a greedy git!'

After landing at Heathrow only the day before the Heathens' opening match of the season, a Premiership encounter with Ipswich, and facing intense questioning on his future by the British press, including two television interviews, he was not his usual immaculate self at a foggy Foxhall stadium. Under the scrutiny of his fans and still without being under contract, he scored 8 points. Fighting off accusations of betrayal and greed proved almost as hard as fighting off the British weather after months in Australia and USA. Fortunately, the latter problem was aided by some ingenious battery-operated gloves and legwarmers, that only Bruce could carry off with any credibility!

In between the two legs of the encounter against the Witches, the two parties sat down for dinner and talked from 7 p.m. until 2 a.m., but still couldn't reach an agreement. The second leg was even billed by the press as Penhall's potential farewell to British speedway, with the rider threatening to return to the States if a deal was not struck. Peter Adams suggested that Bruce's original terms in the negotiations simply 'didn't bear looking at' and even his 'rock-bottom price was still thousands of pounds above what Cradley could afford'. Eventually, Wally Mawdsley was brought in as a mediator from the BSPA, and a deal was finally struck just in time for Bruce to take his place at number one in the first league match of the season against Wimbledon at Dudley Wood. By the end of the night, an emphatic 12-point maximum was enough to dispel any lingering bitterness about the whole saga, and a collective sigh of relief echoed around the town of Cradley Heath!

After February had been spent in New Zealand, with Bruce trying to get on with the racing amid all of the rumours and gossip surrounding his contract talks, he had returned to the States for a couple of weeks back home. While nearing the end of their trip Down Under however, he and Bobby Schwartz made the acquaintance of some unlikely fellow tourists. British punk rock band The Clash, were on tour and happened to be on the same plane as the American duo during a flight between islands. With Bruce as genial as usual, and Boogaloo always quick to find a friend anywhere, the whole group struck up an improbable association. Lead singer Joe Strummer and drummer Nicky 'Topper' Headon invited Bruce and Bobby to watch the band play live in Australia. Quick to accept and make the most of the chance encounter, the boys not only ended up watching them belt out some of their hits, such as 'London Calling', but also managed to get themselves invited up onto the stage during the performance!

'We sat on the speakers on the floor, while they were playing in the concert' Bruce recalls vividly. 'We got to know them pretty well, and after that they would come to the speedway at Wimbledon and watch us when we were in town. Bobby was always getting to know these kind of guys, and when we spoke to them in New Zealand that time, they just said come on over, and so we sat on the speakers! They brought us up on stage in Australia and let us watch. I'm still a huge Clash fan now!'

Some racing in California at the beginning of March was then combined with some quality time with the family. Nearly 10,000 people saw Bruce race to victory at Costa Mesa, but then Mike Bast stole his thunder by winning the Spring Classic at San Bernadino. He was due to fly to England on 17 March, but delayed the flight by two days to stay with his sister Connie, who endured a difficult labour with her first child.

'There was no way I could leave her side until everything was alright' he said. 'She's been through hell with me and my racing since our parents were killed and it was a wrench to leave them when I did. I wanted to be there and support her, and I felt that was more important than to do a practice day at Cradley.' Proving to be the proudest uncle, Bruce eventually left with a delightful memento, which would stay with him wherever he went, as a peculiar accessory of his racing gear. 'From then on I had a little diaper pin that I wore on my leathers forever. There was a little lapel on the inside of the leathers, which covered the zipper, and it stayed fastened in there. It couldn't actually be seen unless my zipper was down. My sister brought that for me and it was a nice reminder of home.'

Once the contract dispute was resolved, any thoughts of Bruce being lost to speedway were shelved, for what the fans and promoters hoped to be at least another twelve months. It turned out to be not nearly as long, but his popularity and appeal were soon back in abundance in between. The new management at National League club Long Eaton invited him to officially open a new era at their Station Road venue. He was introduced to an appreciative crowd, rode a demonstration lap and then cut straight through the starting tapes as a novel alternative to a big pair of scissors. With only one defeat in his next four matches for Cradley, including away excursions to Hackney, Sheffield and Birmingham, it seemed like everything was back to normal.

SIXTEEN

THE PRICE OF PATRIOTISM

After a third successive unbeaten home score in Cradley's League Cup campaign, Bruce had to make his first scheduled trip back to the States in the middle of April. Although having been in the UK for less than a month, he had agreed to become involved in an organised training school for eight-to-ten-year-old young riders in California. He was initially due to return from the trip in time for a much-hyped Heathens' clash with Halifax, who were becoming huge rivals on and off the track – thanks largely to the raging hostilities between Penhall and Carter, and fuelled by the media and both sets of supporters. Due to the timing of the training school, and subsequent flights back to Britain, Bruce quickly realised that he would definitely not be able to return in time for Cradley's home leg on Saturday 17 April, and would struggle to make it for the Sunday afternoon second leg in Yorkshire. Eager to capitalise on the World Champion's huge billing, the Dukes management put back the start time to Sunday evening, in order to allow him more time to travel from Heathrow up the motorway to The Shay stadium.

The extra few hours were never likely to make enough difference however, and trying to fit as much into his schedule as possible while flying in and out of Los Angeles for such a short time, Bruce decided in consultation with the AMA, that the requirements of the training school would necessitate him staying in California for the entire weekend. The American authorities sent a telex message to the BSPA in England confirming the arrangements and validating that the reason for the extended stay was due to his compulsory commitment in his home nation. The message was relayed to Cradley boss Peter Adams, and the BSPA duly granted a guest facility for the Heathens to cover for the absence of their number one. Fellow American Shawn Moran was booked to step into Penhall's place for the away trip to Halifax and an announcement was made at Dudley Wood during the first leg that Penhall would not be back in time for the following day's encounter. However, the message never officially reached Dukes, and when they discovered that Bruce would not be available for the match, they complained bitterly both to the match referee and much more publicly in the media.

Meanwhile, Bruce was incredibly well received by adoring American fans in a track appearance at Costa Mesa's weekly race meeting, beating Mike Bast in a specially billed match race that drew a large crowd. He also pulled off 'the impossible' at the tiny oval, passing the entire field around the outside – a feat almost unheard of at Costa Mesa, thus bringing the spectators to their feet in rapturous appreciation! With the trip home seemingly a successful venture for everyone, he was as surprised as anyone to arrive back on British shores to find a storm of controversy brewing over his non-appearance at The Shay, and moreover, that he was being fiercely criticised by some sections of the press for letting people down and setting a poor example. He hit back with the argument that people were all too easily ignoring the unpublicised things he had done, and was continuing to do, for the sport on both sides of the Atlantic, but felt stung by the stern condemnation.

Unfortunately, almost simultaneous to the Halifax dispute came another bigger row over the England *v.* USA Test series, which ran from the end of April into the beginning of May. The five Tests, coupled with a four-nations tournament planned for later in the season, meant that Bruce would have to miss a total of four lucrative continental bookings on Sunday afternoons, in order to take his place in the Yanks team. This meant a substantial loss of earnings, but was traded against the appeal of riding for his country. By way of compensation, Bruce knew that, as reigning World Champion, he was now entitled to an appearance fee for competing in the Tests, which would go a little way to making up for the start money that he would miss in Germany. The Test series did not have any official international status as per the World Team Cup or World Pairs Championships, where he had previously ridden at a loss, but because a USA team was on track, he was naturally expected to ride. However, the BSPA initially expected him to do so at the standard rate, and when Bruce's advisors cited his entitlement to the additional payment, which amounted to £1,500, the promoters refused to comply. A stand-off ensued and both the national and trade press made a meal of the episode, accusing Penhall of greediness and self-interest; once again he was hammered by the media who he had always gone so far out of his way to accommodate. One claim which hurt him the most was that of a lack of patriotism; the suggestion that he was simply putting his own finances before the honour of riding for his country.

'The bottom line was that it was contracted in the rule book that, once you won the World Championship, you were entitled to so much appearance money. And that's basically what I was asking for – what was in the rulebook at the time. And no more. I didn't feel that I should have been treated any differently, but it wasn't as if I was just riding for America, I was riding at all these British League tracks, and it was the British promoters who were benefiting [from any profit made], not one single solitary American would benefit from the series, not the AMA, no-one' Bruce points out now.

Writing in his regular new column in the *Daily Mirror*, he put the debate in simple terms with the declaration that 'patriotism doesn't buy tyres', and also suggested that the fee in question would be covered by as little as 150 extra people in attendance at each of the five matches. The remark was scoffed at by those wishing to denounce him, but few people recalled the complaints by the Halifax promotion less than a week earlier, who claimed they had lost as many as 1,000 people through the turnstiles for the League Cup match due to Penhall's non-attendance.

'If you were to ask some of the promoters at the time,' he maintains, 'when I said literally 150 extra people, they would come back and say well we don't know if we can get an extra 150 people, and yet Halifax turns around, which is the other end of the country for us, and say we could have got 1,000 extra people. You're never in a win–win situation. It always comes back to you. The World Champion is greedy, he's a prat or whatever, and you have to hold your ground. Those around me knew that I was worth a certain amount of money, knew that I could pull people in through the gate, therefore they wanted to capitalise on it. Not only for themselves, but for me as well. You gotta remember that this is a very short life and we did whatever we could to be successful [in a dangerous sport] and to put food on the table. You have to capitalise when you can, because who's to know that two weeks from then, there's a chance that you may never be able to race again. Once you become World Champion you have this big target on your back. Everybody's looking to knock you down or get a piece of you, so you *have* to hold your ground.'

Eventually, the BSPA backed down and agreed to pay Bruce the appearance fee he was entitled to. The whole affair was seen to lose him a number of admirers on the terraces – many unjustly, it could be argued, but such was not the case with his fellow riders. 'I explained it to the riders and they were in full agreement. I was riding for America and they knew that they [the BSPA] would come good and pay me the money. It wasn't a matter of patriotism, it was a matter of getting paid what I was entitled to. I don't think it put any extra pressure on me whatsoever. I put the pressure on myself, wherever I went, no matter how much money I would make. If I was to sit on a speedway bike, I would give one hundred and ten per cent.

'I think some of the England team may have rubbed their hands together a little bit, and kinda liked the situation, but I was friends with a lot of the English boys that we rode against. I travelled with them and they were almost as close to me as the American boys. In fact if you look at it, I spent ten times more time with Peter Collins as I did with, say, Kelly Moran. And to be quite frank, Peter Collins was a much better friend to me, as was Michael Lee. They were World Champions too and they understood. They all knew exactly what was going on – it was in the rulebook!'

So, what about the press, who were so quick to stir up the reports and play him as the villain? Bruce is typically gracious in his reflection: 'It was their job! These people also put me where I was – where I am today. They could have forgotten about me, they could have said "who cares?", and I totally understood the way publicity worked, the way journalism worked. I could totally understand it. Sometimes, it hurt my feelings – absolutely. I'd be lying to you if I said it didn't bother me, because I always wanted to be the nice guy out there, I always wanted to be the winner. I always wanted to be the guy in the white leathers, not the guy in the black leathers. I didn't want to be the demon! I wanted to be the guy everybody liked. But I also knew there was a price to pay for that as well. My Dad always told me: "One little mistake, and you're gonna hear about it forever." And quite frankly, I deserved that! But I deserved to win the World Championship too. With a lot of the good that comes, there's also a lot of – I wouldn't say bad – but a lot of negative stuff. And that's just par for the course.'

All along the way, Bruce stuck to his principles. He did only what virtually every World Champion has done, before and since; he tried to capitalise on the success that he had worked so damned hard to achieve. Ivan Mauger had made a similar stance a few years earlier regarding the continental bookings that brought in such much-needed cash boosts, but maybe the extent of public analysis surrounding the dispute simply reflected Penhall's lofty position in the eyes of the media, the promoters and indeed the supporters. It all added to the spice of the Test series, which was being televised by ITV, and for reasons right or wrong, speedway was in the headlines. When the series kicked off, it seemed that the affair had fired everyone up – but none more so than the England team. 'We're just getting flat beat!' was Penhall's characteristic 'no excuses' response to the home side's early mauling of the Americans, midway through the First Test at Wimbledon. England opened with a convincing 63-45 victory, but the stakes were increased in the next clash at Swindon where Steve Bastable and Kenny Carter both hit the deck in hard-fought first bends with Penhall in the very first heat. A few races later, Alan Grahame also found himself in the Blundsdon fence, after Bruce had barged underneath him. There were rumoured to be a few complaints from the England riders, but Bruce revealed that Carter approached him after heat one to admit the accident was not the American's fault. Whether any blame was to be apportioned or not, the Yanks' commitment to their cause was unquestionable, led by their skipper and the series was tied at 1-1. A spanner was thrown in the works three days later when the following Test at Poole was postponed due to a waterlogged track, but the USA edged in front overall in the next at Ipswich, before England levelled the series once more at 2-2, in front of 8,000 people at Belle Vue.

It fell to the rearranged Poole match to decide the competition, but the credibility of the series was thrown into doubt once again when the clash was scheduled for the same day as the practice session for one of the World Longtrack Championship quarter-finals. Both Bruce and Peter Collins were due to be in Herxheim, Germany for the compulsory preparation. For Penhall, this was compounded by a planned trip to the States only the day before, which was reported in the press as an 'urgent business meeting'. It was, in fact, a very first screen test for a starring role in the motorcycle cop show *CHiPs*, as well as a meeting with the president of the MGM film company, which had been set up by his personal management team to pursue Bruce's desire to move into the realm of acting. Once again, his loyalties were divided, but Bruce was determined not to let anyone down, especially considering the appearance payment he had received to compete in the original five Tests, and he embarked on an astonishing travel programme to ensure he met each of the engagements.

Flights in and out of Los Angeles at the beginning of the third week in May took him to the *CHiPs* audition, and from LA it was directly on to Frankfurt in Germany, followed by a short hop to Herxheim on the afternoon of Wednesday 19 May. Taking his place in the obligatory practice session, he cut his preparation for the important championship round to a minimum, preferring to concentrate on the speedway rather than the longtrack part of his racing. He then went to the extraordinary length of arranging a helicopter to collect him from Heathrow airport on his arrival in London, from Frankfurt, which took him straight to the Poole stadium car park, with less than an hour to spare before the tapes went up on the deciding Test match. A burst tyre on the aeroplane upon landing in the UK did nothing to help matters, and after the event it was back in the air to reach Herxheim again for the longtrack meeting itself the very next day.

The punishing dash reaped mixed results. The USA won the final Test in hugely convincing fashion, buoyed by the exceptional efforts of their captain to lead them into action. Bruce returned to Germany on largely untried equipment however, and bowed out of the longtrack championship with a disappointing 8 points, qualifying only as reserve for the semi-final. Preferring to cite his relative lack of prowess in the European–dominated branch of oval racing, rather than the demanding preparation, Bruce was unruffled by the outcome. Suddenly, the lack of patriotism and loyalty seemed a gross exaggeration of the World Champion's attitude. He had been allowed to select the particular longtrack round in which he competed, and chose Herxheim long before the England-USA test match was rearranged, because it was the only quarter-final that didn't clash with Cradley Heath's Saturday night Knock-Out Cup match against Sheffield. The loss of sleep and energy, and the effects of jet lag encountered in tearing around two continents, was bound to take its toll, but no-one would have imagined it when Bruce took his place in the Heathens' line-up in that cup tie at Dudley Wood at the end of the week, to scorch to a 12-point maximum. And no-one seemed to bat an eyelid when England badly missed their own all-action hero, Peter Collins, who elected to stay in Germany for the same longtrack meeting as Bruce, turning down the chance to join his friend in the helicopter dash to the vital Test match. 'Had PC been the World Champion that year, trust me, the press would have been on him. Like they say, the second-place guy at the World Championship is the first loser. They don't watch him, they don't keep him under a microscope. They're watching every single, solitary movement the World Champion makes the following year after he wins, especially the English press. This is not to disrespect them whatsoever, but they are very much aware of what goes on. They are so looking forward to one little mistake, but mind you, they're also looking to reward you. The press in England is far better than anywhere in the world. You can't make a mistake – if you do, you're going to hear about it! But also, if you win, you're going to hear about it. In America, if you do something well, you're going to hear about it, but if you lose they kinda downplay it. There are differences between Los Angeles and New York, and it is also different from New York to England, quite a bit different in fact. But it is their job to do what they have to do, and this is what sells papers.'

In all, Penhall rode in twenty-four meetings in that month of May, on top of the other engagements and personal appearances that were part and parcel of his regular diary. He had earlier calculated that in the space of a few months he had spent 325 hours in the air, flying from country to country, and an average of around 1,000 miles per week travelling by road. Uneasy rests the head who wears the crown, one may suggest, but at least there was the grace of a rare day off when the semi-finals of the longtrack championship came around. Instead of racing, Bruce was at track-side for the round that he had failed to qualify for, merely as friend, coach and mentor to Bobby Schwartz!

A few weeks later, the issue of Bruce's patriotism was brought to the fore once again in an incident on American Independence Day, which has reigned in speedway folklore ever since. Far from the accusation of lacking in commitment to his country, Penhall would be ironically lambasted for showing *too much* national devotion. What started out as an enjoyable and successful afternoon in the 1982 Overseas final at White City deteriorated into one of the worst experiences in his career. He was beginning his World Championship trail at the relatively late stage, after being seeded directly to the round and skipping the preceding US qualifier on account of his status as world number one. He had instead turned commentator for CBS television on that occasion, as he watched fellow countrymen Dennis Sigalos, and the Moran brothers, Shawn and Kelly, fight their way through to join him on the route to the Los Angeles World final.

Memories of previous visits to White City did not bode well, considering the World Championship elimination of 1977 and the Overseas round of 1981 where the ugly public battle with Kenny Carter finally spilled over. Bruce would have been wise to heed the warnings, but still insists that he liked the track and even rated it among his favourites alongside Vojens, Cradley Heath and the bigger oval of Hull. Such an appreciation was wholly evident in his first two rides of the day as he took maximum points, including a defeat of Kenny Carter in his second. By the time every rider had taken four of their five outings, Bruce was still on top of the standings, level on points with England team captain Dave Jessup. He had already comfortably ensured the necessary qualification to the Inter-Continental final in Denmark, which would leave him just one step away from the World final itself. And so came a dreadful dilemma, which would ultimately shape the lasting impression many people held of Bruce Penhall. After Jessup slipped up in his final race, Bruce would be lining up in heat nineteen alongside all three of his competing fellow Americans. He knew he had already made the cut for qualification, but one more victory would cap it all with the

Overseas Championship title and an overall winner's cheque for £1,000. On the other hand, Sigalos and the Morans needed the points to wriggle their way through to the next round, and by not achieving them, one or all would be lost to the World Championship race.

All four riders met in conference with team manager John Scott and World final promoter Harry Oxley at the back of their vans, parked in the stadium car park. They poured over the permutations, each agreeing on one thing – they all wanted to see as many of their compatriots in with a chance of making it to Los Angeles. They knew what was required, and it was Penhall that held the key. While the crowd speculated intensely as to whether the reigning World Champion would be giving his absolute best, given the most unusual circumstances, their golden boy decided to leave them with no uncertainty whatsoever. The tapes went up and before the bikes had hurtled into the first corner, Bruce was left at the back looking left and right like a schoolboy crossing the road. Once assured that his colleagues were safely ahead of him, he waited a couple more laps before utilising all the track space he had engineered for himself in fourth place, to mischievously pop a few wheelies. Sigalos eventually took the hollow victory with Kelly Moran close behind, making sure both riders joined Penhall in the top ten, while Shawn's third place put him into a run-off for qualification. Bruce's last place handed the overseas title to Jessup and allowed Carter to also leapfrog him into the second rostrum position. The White City crowd voiced their uncompromising condemnation with a chorus of boos, and some even went as far as hurling bottles and cans onto the track while the four Yanks made their way back to the pits.

In an immediate interview with Nick Owen of the Central Sports Special TV team, Bruce seemed to suddenly realise the enormity of the public antagonism, and was stunned by the hostility that was vented towards him. Among other things, one of the riders to miss out as a result of the debacle was Cradley teammate Alan Grahame, who was relegated to an unrewarding twelfth position. Taking his place next to Jessup and Carter on the back of the stadium vehicle for a customary victory parade, Bruce was visibly distressed by one of the most venomous and scathing reactions ever seen by a speedway crowd. Enduring a lap of torment, while Carter seemed to revel in the lack of sympathy, he turned around to face away from the ferocious terrace taunts. Never in his five years of British racing had a smile been so far away from Penhall's face.

Media critics who had not forgiven his attitude to the international Test series were outraged once more, and with even less surprise came the predictably derisive Monday morning newspaper headlines. But only a few months earlier, such disapproval for one of the most universally popular riders would have been virtually unheard of. 'There are ups and downs in speedway,' he had told the trackside interviewer, while a meeting commentator labelled his actions 'as a most unselfish and patriotic gesture'. It was the type of impossible situation that Bruce was becoming accustomed to facing. Had he put two or three of his fellow countrymen out of the competition, he would have received equally fierce criticism from fans and press in the States. Furthermore, such similar incidents had occurred on numerous occasions before and have continued to crop up ever since, the result of the formula and an arbitrary draw to decide the racing order, which should surely have been open to equal criticism. Although the debate divided fans nationwide, perhaps what swung the balance of many opinions was the way in which Bruce signalled his intentions in that sinful race. Not with a questionable exclusion from sending his bike through the starting tapes, or from an innocuous slide to the ground when the coast was relatively clear, but by displaying the most blatant of tactics and throwing in the wheelies to rub salt into the English wounds. 'If it was similar circumstances, I would absolutely do it differently,' he now agrees. 'How I would do it, I don't know because no matter how you look at it, I wouldn't be a winner. I was thinking about my teammates, my countrymen. I was looking at a way where I could help out them as well as help myself. I did not want to be the only American in the 1982 World Championship – I needed to take some of the pressure away and bring somebody else into the mix. I would have done everything I could to have helped and they didn't appreciate it by any stretch of the imagination.

'We had a meeting with Harry Oxley and all the riders and we came up with a sort of conclusion – how the race was going to end up. And it didn't end up the way we all spoke about it, other than the fact that I was going to be coming last. Not to point fingers at anyone, because that's not what I want to do, but we had decided on a situation of who was going to win, who was going to come second, third and fourth. That didn't happen though. Not one person followed the plan other than me. I was sat at the back pulling wheelies thinking, they're going to leave it to the last lap. Then we went over the line and I was furious. We all shook on it and made a pact, but I got thrashed for it. I lost a ton of respect and I didn't get one of those guys come to bat for me, expect Harry [Oxley] and he had to. He and I always got along great, he was promoting the World final and I was his boy for that.

'So I guess the way I would do it differently is not to be doing wheelies – that was very, very wrong. [I thought] do I want to break the tapes? No, I'm not going to be a winner that way. Do I lay it down? No, that's not the way either. You can have an engine failure; there's a million ways to do it, but certainly not to pull wheelies at the back. That's the bottom line. But if there's a way that I could help out the others then I would, and I would probably do it again.

'I don't even know what I was thinking, but I was probably showing to everybody that I'm the guy here, and I could have won this, but I'm not – a little big-headedness. In a way, I wanted to show the other riders that I did do it on purpose and they needed to know that I had confidence and I could have won that thing.'

SEVENTEEN

INTERNATIONAL TREBLE

The bitter taste which lingered after the events of the Overseas final was sweetened by a summer in the spotlight for Bruce, for many more positive reasons. A racing schedule as busy as ever was augmented by a series of appearances that more accurately befitted the image-conscious sporting ambassador that he strived to be.

He led a Speedway Riders XI against a photographers and journalists' SWAPA team in a charity football match. Raising funds for the riders' benevolent fund, the game was staged at Port Vale's Stoke-on-Trent stadium only a few days after the hectic helicopter dash between Herxheim and Poole, but it was typical of the World Champion to make time in his diary. Likewise for a speedway 'quiz night' in the bar at Dudley Wood, where his five-man team took top spot. Who was responsible for the majority of correct answers however, from the team of Bruce, Bobby Schwartz, Cradley colleagues Phil Collins and Andy Reid, and a Heathens supporter, depends on which team member you care to believe! And speedway barely had any prominence among the topics of conversation when he appeared on daytime television show *Afternoon Plus*, where the questions focused instead on the subjects of money, relationships and sex!

Bruce concedes that being World Champion can result in the loss of many friends, as everyone wants the champion to get beaten, and regularly likens it to having a big target on your back for everyone to aim at. You can be equally sure though, that there come many perks with the privilege and responsibility of being number one. Not many riders would be invited – or trusted – to drive a £100,000 Rothmans Formula One car around the famous Silverstone racing track in Northamptonshire. Filmed as part of a publicity piece by local television news crews, Bruce was full of witty one-liners when he received the unique opportunity.

'I imagine this would be worse than getting married,' he joked with a smile as he squeezed into the tight driver's space. 'The weather's not the best, but who cares? Probably won't get out of first gear anyway!' Inevitably, he did manage more than first gear, despite feeling trapped inside and being 'totally confused' by having to turn left *and* right, and use the brakes! Completing his circuits with a creditable average speed of 93mph, he concluded 'my Escort will never be the same!'

Back on two wheels, Bruce was leading Cradley Heath to more success following the previously unimaginable heights of 1981. Partnered initially by his young protégé, Lance King, and later Phil Collins, he led the Heathens to the League Cup final in June, where they duly overcame Ipswich for more silverware. With that trophy and the Premiership already locked in the cabinet, the club and its supporters harboured desires of completing a grand slam, backed up by healthy progress in the Knock-Out Cup and pole position in the British League. With Peter Adams firmly established at the helm, not only were Cradley approaching a status of invincibility, they were following in the footsteps of their captain in terms of sheer demand for appearances.

Eager to take the sport to new audiences, Adams teamed up with Ivan Mauger and stock car promoter Robert Mathers, to promote a rare speedway meeting in Northern Ireland. Transforming the stock car circuit at the Ballymena Showground, the league champions were pitched against a Mauger select featuring the former World Champion himself, along with Kenny Carter and others. Bruce was a key part of the attraction for the crowd of nearly 4,000 as he made his way to County Antrim directly from competing in a German grasstrack event in Osnabruck. On the afternoon of the meeting, he was presented on stage at David 'Kid' Jensen's Radio One Roadshow in the town of Port Rush to a fantastic welcome, and an even bigger send-off from the huge audience. When the match itself was underway, Bruce kept his new following entertained with some trademark wheelies and led Cradley to a 40-38 victory in a last-heat decider. In the same month, he stormed to victory in the Yorkshire Television Trophy at Sheffield, and would have been forgiven for feeling a little déjà vu as he accepted the plaudits. For, in his final race, he was faced with the prospect of just needing to finish second behind Carter, to make sure of the title! After apologising to the Dudley Wood crowd on the centre green for his actions in the Overseas final, and for missing an away trip to Hackney when he flew back to the States to be with his sick aunt, Bruce then teamed up with Lance King to win the Multi-National Best Pairs. Still searching for a follow-up to the White City antics, one tabloid capitalised on increasing terrace talk about his future to wrongly suggest that the trip home was for the *CHiPs* audition, which had actually been several weeks earlier, but was at the time being kept officially under wraps. While gossip and guesswork, based on the remarks arising from the winter speculation and his frequent flights across the ocean, suggested that Penhall would be making his television screen debut in one form or another, few were tipping the BBC to win the race for his signature. In a modest step up from just the chat show appearances, Bruce was asked to participate in an edition of *Superstars*, where sporting celebrities were pitched against each other in a range of physical activities, such as weightlifting, archery, shooting and swimming. Filming took place in Oxford over three days at the end of July, and as ever, there was the usual predicament of fitting in the extracurricular activity with the day-to-day business of riding the speedway bike. On this occasion, the dates regrettably clashed with Cradley's Golden Hammer and a memorial meeting for Brett Alderton, who had been killed in a racing accident earlier in the season. As filming took place during the day and the speedway meetings were during the evening, it was all the invitation Bruce required to try to please everyone. After the first two days of strenuous competition, he took his place in an all-star line-up who turned out in memory of Alderton, and gave a good performance after dusting himself down from an innocuous first-race fall. When it seemed everything had gone to plan, the third and final day of *Superstars* events ran frustratingly over schedule, just enough to delay Bruce's journey back along the motorway to the Midlands. He arrived at Dudley Wood for the meeting that had desperately eluded him in the past, just too late to take his first programmed ride. The Hammer had attracted full TV coverage by Central television and sponsorship by the *Daily Mirror*, and Bruce had once again been one of the favourites to finally lift the crown. With his chances of outright victory gone before he took to the shale in his second planned ride, and feeling over-enthusiastic but sadly unprepared, he found himself uncharacteristically sliding along the deck by the seat of his leathers for the second successive night. 'In *Superstars* I thought I was going to do pretty well. I did OK in a couple of events, but a lot of people there trained the full year for the events because they wanted to do so well and I didn't have that luxury. I did pretty well at the swimming, the shooting and the bicycles. Not so much in the weightlifting because there were some pretty big boys, and the canoeing I flipped the thing over straight away. All in all I struggled, but it was a lot of fun and I wish I could have done better. I was so tired when I came back to the Golden Hammer though, I was exhausted.' Kenny Carter won on the night, as Bruce took 7 out of a possible 9 points from his remaining outings, and the Yorkshireman followed up the feat by returning to the top of the British League averages. Bruce was battling it out for the next three places in the league list with Danes, Gundersen and Nielsen, and all four were hitting form at the right time to be touted as red-hot favourites to contest the world title at the end of August. The final qualifying hurdle was the relatively uneventful Inter-Continental final at Vetlanda in Sweden. After the rain-soaked staging of the same round at Vojens in 1981 and the fiasco of the previous championship round in 1982, nerves were unsurprisingly showing in the expressions of the most experienced competitors during the build up to the meeting. Six-times former title winner Ivan Mauger had been one of the casualties of the American tactics at White City, and following his exit at the penultimate hurdle was another multi-champion, Ole Olsen.

Bruce was in scintillating form in his first two rides, collecting two wins and 6 points. It was almost enough to push him above the qualification cut before the interval stage, and he knew it. Meeting the also-unbeaten Kelly Moran in their respective third rides, the American pair found themselves tussling with each other at the back in a very close race, behind eventual winner Les Collins and Dane Bo Petersen. Two more third places followed as he admitted to losing a little bit of interest after making sure of his place in the line-up for the Coliseum. It was unusual of his style, but he was clearly happier for once to stay out of the spotlight, and no doubt glad that there was nothing of any importance resting on his final ride, when once again he was drawn in the same heat as friend and countryman, Sigalos.

When the sixteen riders were determined for the showpiece meeting of the year, Les Collins had thrown his name into the hat as a possible dark horse with first place in Sweden. Carter had endorsed his claims to Penhall's mantle with second place, but the other half of Cradley's dynamic duo, Erik Gundersen had fallen by the wayside as another of the high-profile eliminations. The efforts of the Overseas round proved not to be in vain for team USA, as both Sigalos and Kelly Moran eased all the way through to LA, which meant three riders would together share the burden of expectation from the home nation; a fact that was crucial in Penhall's eyes to relieving at least a little of the pressure from his own shoulders.

With safe passage ensured to the individual World final, Bruce captained his country to further progress in the other World Championship competitions. With regular partner Boogaloo lying on the treatment table, he teamed up with Sigalos in the only qualifying round for the World Pairs, in Prague. If Penhall and Schwartz knew each other's riding style well, then what could be said of his years of experience racing next to his buddy Dennis? And who could have possibly thought that the two eager kids who used to slide their bicycles around their wet concrete garage floor would be teaming up ten years later as America's two representatives in the World Pairs Championship? They revelled in the occasion, scoring a combined total of 26 points, which left them three short of England's winning total of 29. Three countries qualified, so the USA were through to defend their title in the final, which wasn't staged until December, as it was being held in Liverpool, Australia during the Aussie summer.

Two rounds stood in the way of the World Team Cup final, but the Yanks made light work of both. The UK qualifying round was a two-horse race, fought out between England and USA in May, while Australia and New Zealand seemed further and further off the pace of the emergent Americans. It was a measure of how much further Penhall's troops were progressing as they were able to flex their muscles in the team event with five star-quality riders, as well as the pairs. Scott Autrey took Schwartz's place at reserve behind the same four Americans who had been contesting the latter rounds of the individual championship. Sigalos and Shawn Moran only dropped a handful of points between them, while Penhall contributed 10 and Kelly Moran top scored with 12. After a closely fought contest throughout, the top two countries were inseparable at the end of proceedings, resulting in a run-off to decide who moved on as winners, and who followed as runners-up. Peter Collins, although bottom scorer for an evenly balanced England team, was chosen by the home camp, while the Yanks collectively nominated Kelly on account of his performance on the day. Collins won the match race to steal the slightest of psychological advantages before the Inter-Continental round.

At Vojens, the two duelling nations were joined in battle by Denmark and Sweden. This time, with Schwartz back in for Autrey, the USA raced to victory with the Danes narrowly stealing the second qualifying position from England. Bruce and Kelly Moran shared the top-scorers position with 10 points apiece, although Kelly was racing solely on Bruce's equipment after his own bikes had been impounded by his club, Eastbourne, in a contractual row.

Before the proud US riders took their places in the team final several weeks later though, they were all hit by a shattering blow, which forced them all to reassess their commitment to their chosen profession. Twenty-four-year-old Denny Pyeatt, one of the latest American additions to join the ranks of the British League, was killed in a track crash in mid-July. As one of the British-based Yanks, it goes without saying that he was 'one of the boys', but much more than that, he was a close friend and a respected colleague, which made it a personal tragedy for Bruce and the team. Pyeatt had partnered Reading teammate Bobby Schwartz in the multi-national pairs that Bruce and Lance King had won a couple of weeks earlier, and had been due to ride as a guest for Cradley just twenty-four hours after his fatal accident. The American team immediately declared that their forthcoming World Team Cup final performance would be dedicated in memory of Denny, regardless of the result. In additional, as a poignant tribute to their comrade, each rider took to the track with a reminder of his image: 'It was a koala bear! He always had one of those wrapped around his handlebars, because he looked like one! His hair was in a little afro, and he looked like a koala bear, that's how he got that name. So we all put a koala bear on our handlebars. Bobby was the one that instigated the whole deal, and it was for Denny. You know how they hug those trees? Well we got these things in Australia when we were there, and we had 'em on our handlebars like that, and it was like Denny.

'It was devastating [when we had heard of the accident]. Especially as I knew Denny and he was a good friend. Bobby was really close to Denny, as was John Cook – "Cook 'em up". You come across guys who are good friends, and sometimes you lose them, but when it's an American and we were over there together a long way from home, it hits you real hard, and it hit all of us. I was just numb for a week, but we always said that Denny would want us to do this, this is what he would want. He was a racer, this is what he did with his life. He was a good guy, an absolute sweetheart of a guy. Everybody liked him. He wasn't a 10 or 11-point rider, but his passion was speedway. He made the sacrifices, and it hurt us all. I think probably the only thing that helped us at the time was that we were so busy. We could think about him and know that he was watching us, and that he would have wanted us to continue with the sport.'

So it was that the USA embarked on only their second World Team Cup final with very much more than just their usual brimming national pride at stake. With cuddly koala bears clasped to their bikes, they marched back into the same White City arena where they had hit the headlines for the wrong reasons six weeks earlier. With England out of the way, Denmark were their only real threat, even though none of the sunny Californians would have underestimated the powers of Germany and Czechoslovakia to ruin the best-laid plans on a wet London afternoon.

When Penhall took to the track for his first outing in heat four, his country were 2 points ahead of the Danes, and by the time he was back for his second race, the gap had increased to 8. The Yanks never looked back, while their opponents got gradually muddier from the damp shale. Bruce won two and claimed two important second places, while Kelly Moran joined him once again at the top of the charts with the same 10-point haul. The strength that was evident throughout the team carried them all the way to victory, with Bobby Schwartz stepping up from reserve into the main four as a replacement for the injured Sigalos, and Scott Autrey returning to the fold as the fifth man. A picture of Denny was on display in their corner of the pits to urge them on, and the Stars and Stripes-clad squad became like a steamroller out of control. The chequered flags dropped one by one to the sounds of American cheers and the eventual winning margin was an improbable 13 points. It was for themselves and for Denny, and it meant that the USA simultaneously held all three major World Championships at that time. With Penhall as reigning individual champ from 1981, and with his pairs victory with Schwartz also still standing from the previous season, the team trophy made it an incredible treble for a nation who had risen from the speedway wilderness in little more than three years. Penhall revels in the ascendancy just as much to this day as in the sweet moments of victory in 1982.

'They didn't even know who we were [before that]. We had such an impact. It was so good, we just ate it up, we just loved racing on all those tracks. During that time there were like a hundred tracks, we were racing so much, we loved it. It was this new light for us, it wasn't this little bullring. We raced in the mud and we didn't care; we raced against the best and we were there to prove a point.'

While all the Californian clan basked in their success in the aftermath of White City, Bruce Penhall had a different kind of engagement the following morning. He was appearing at a press conference in a plush London hotel to officially announce his retirement from the sport, in order to make the full-time switch into the much-rumoured role of Hollywood actor.

EIGHTEEN

HOLLYWOOD CALLING

Following Bruce's screen test for the *CHiPs* television show in May, he had received an offer to take up a role in the popular American series about California's Highway Patrol Officers. The programme was entering its sixth season, based around the motorcycle-riding police partners played by Erik Estrada and Larry Wilcox. Discussions had already been held for Bruce to play himself in a guest appearance for one episode, which would be based around a plot line featuring speedway racing. However, when a replacement was sought for Wilcox, who was leaving the show, the job offer was presented to Bruce midway through the 1982 speedway season. Although delighted by the success of his screen test, Bruce looked at the proposal – and promptly turned it down. The starring role as one of the lead actors came with the proviso that he would have to quit racing immediately to fit into the imminent filming schedule, two months *before* the Los Angeles World final. 'The role that I went up for was Erik's partner. I was doing some acting classes, and I flew back to do an audition with NBC. I did the screen test and got straight back on the plane to go to the Longtrack Qualifying Round. I ended up getting the role, but they said I had to quit racing straight away, so I rejected it. I told them I had raced all my life, I'd won one championship and the next one was in LA. And they said OK, thank you very much, we'll still have you as a guest star in an episode, but that's it. I wasn't that bummed because I was pretty well focused on my riding and what I wanted to achieve there. Jeff Imediato was probably a little more bummed, but in saying that, he knew I was a racer. Anyway they called Jeff back a couple of weeks later and said they had written a part especially for me. And that was just unbelievable, absolutely unbelievable. Now, that was pretty much the end of it for a while, because I didn't have to go study any more. I had got a role where I just had to go win the championship! There was a lot of work to be done, right after I finished, but at that time I hadn't talked of retiring. I was going to do them both. I wasn't going to run a whole racing schedule, because I couldn't. I was going to compete in some open races and that was it.'

He had been taking acting classes in London since planning to appear as a guest star, but the producers soon told him to stop attending as they still wanted him to be more natural in the role. His first episode, later titled 'Speedway Fever', was to be based around the actual staging of the World final. Bruce Penhall would become Bruce Nelson, younger brother of the new lead character Bobby, and in the plot he would turn from speedway rider into a graduate from the California Highway Patrol Academy. It almost mirrored Penhall's real-life career switch. This time, the chance of a role written especially for him was just too good to turn down, especially as the deal allowed him to still compete in the World final and achieve the ambition of defending his crown on home shale. The drawback was that he would have to quit speedway before the end of the season. In fact, by accepting the offer that was put to him in the second week of August, he would have to agree, under the terms of the studio insurance, not to ride again before the final, and not to ride again in the British League at all.

The dilemma was still difficult to digest. In many ways it was the perfect transition from speedway racing, where Bruce had achieved all his ambitions, into the acting career he had come to crave. The compromise, as he saw it, was the intention to keep a handful of racing engagements in his diary for the foreseeable future, initially hoping to compete in some of the individual open meetings in Britain and in events such as the US National final. He did have to accept, however, that he would not be able to see out the British season, and that he would have to inform the Cradley Heath supporters whom he adored so much: 'I was sorry to leave after the 1982 final for several reasons, one being that I left Cradley and Pete [Adams] high and dry, and also the fans were left high and dry. I was not only leaving behind speedway and what I did on the track, but all the team commitment thing at Cradley. The most difficult part was having to tell Pete and the Cradley fans.'

Once the decision was made, the press conference was arranged for the morning after the World Team Cup final. Bruce spent the preceding weekend under intense media speculation, beginning when Cradley visited arch-rivals Coventry on the night of Saturday 14 August. The slightest of cracks were showing in his normally sparkling exterior. With an unusually low 6-point tally from his first three rides at Brandon, he ended the night with a disastrous fall in the deciding final heat, handing the Bees a 40-38 victory. Bruce's personal score was one of the lowest in his career for the Heathens, and although the retirement news had officially not been announced, it was clear that something just wasn't right. The following day, all the pressure and anxiety over the turmoil that he was facing behind the scenes, had to be put aside once again as he led the American team to the convincing World Championship triumph. And then on Monday morning, the bombshell was dropped – just hours before Cradley were taking on Halifax in a British League tie at Dudley Wood. He informed Peter Adams by telephone on the Sunday evening, and then formally enlightened the rest of the speedway world that he would be departing to realise another dream. The news spread immediately and later in the day, television, radio and newspaper branches of the local and national media were all the carrying the report. Bruce was interviewed by Gary Newbon in the Central TV studios later in the afternoon to elaborate on his position: 'I've got a great opportunity that wouldn't even be here if it wasn't for speedway. Speedway has been great to me and after winning the World Championship, it's brought the great opportunities from the movie industry. And Hollywood won't wait. I've got a great part that I can start my new career in, in the filming industry and I want to get involved with it.'

A huge crowd turned out at Dudley Wood that night, many in a state of stunned surprise that their captain and star attraction was making his final farewell. Public opinion was split for one last time; on one hand Bruce was seen to be accepting an offer that any right-minded fellow would be crazy to refuse, and on the other he was turning his back on the most devoted of followers at the most crucial time in the season. With Imediato still at his side, Bruce was accosted by hundreds of fans wishing to make perfectly clear whichever side of the fence they sat on. He took to the stadium microphone on the centre green of the track and explained his decision, and then blasted away all of his rivals on track to storm to a 12-point maximum, topped with an unbeaten performance in the second-half Star of the Night event. He was overcome with emotion and has never forgotten the send-off given to him by the majority of Heathens fans.

'The hardcore couldn't understand it, but for the most part everybody else understood. I don't think they wanted to accept it, but they understood. I was pretty much inspired to go out and do the best I could that night, but that's what I always gave the Cradley fans.'

Still hoping to return, if there was any possible way, Bruce left three bikes in Britain and the next day packed his belongings to head off to the States. With the World final still almost two weeks away, part of the plan was to reacclimatise himself to the conditions on the other side of the ocean and prepare both physically and mentally in the best way possible before what would turn out to be his last ever competitive speedway meeting. Another part of the plan was simply to take time out from the energy-sapping emotional rollercoaster that he had been on for the preceding weeks. 'We went away up into the mountains. Me, my manager and a couple of girls. I was like a cooked sausage. I just needed to try and recoup and relax a little bit, because the pressure was unbelievable. I felt so worn out by all the travelling and publicity. I just wanted to concentrate on trying to regain my world title. I had done a couple of extra practises at the Coliseum and then I knew that I wanted to retire, if I won. If I didn't win I was going to do a few more races. I asked my manager if I could retire on the podium and he wasn't keen at first, because he knew that if I won the title again I would be worth a lot more to him, as well as myself, commercially, with sponsors and everything else that goes with it. I relied heavily on Jeff to make deals, put deals together, but it was my decision to retire and he agreed with it. If he said that I couldn't, I still would have.

Although the timing of the decision coincided somewhat with the recent tragedy involving his buddy Denny Pyeatt, he makes it clear that, even though it highlighted the enormous dangers of the sport in which all the riders were competing, it did not influence his decision to quit.

'It did cross our minds and with something like that you have to think, 'is it really worth it?' – and absolutely no, it's not. It's not worth losing your life over. But it had no bearing on my decision. My decision was based on the fact that it was going to be a short career, my goal and my ambition was to win the championship and then to do it again in my home country, and then my life was going to change. I was ready to take on a new career that would take me through a longer part of my life, and take me closer to my family. I'm a family guy. I wanted to settle down, and being on the road with kids, I didn't feel would be good. It works for a lot of guys, but it wasn't my idea of raising a family.'

The day that the Los Angeles Coliseum opened its doors to the World Speedway final on 28 August was unique in so many ways. The first final to be held in the USA was always destined to feature the glitz and glamour that the Yanks expected of their sporting entertainment package, but the extent of the Hollywood presence for Penhall was much more than anyone could have realised. The staging of the entire event had been a massive financial gamble, taking speedway's most prestigious meeting to a country with really only a passing interest in the sport. Bruce's 1981 victory had been an enormous shot in the arm though, and his name had rapidly spread around the motorcycling fraternity, not least in the pre-meeting publicity in which he featured so strongly. Ivan Mauger and Barry Briggs, the same pair of multi-World Champions who had virtually kick-started Penhall's career in the 1976 and 1977 touring troupes, teamed up Harry Oxley and former American World Champion Jack Milne to promote the final. The stadium itself was an awesome venue, proving every inch a rival to Wembley, with a whole load of American razzamatazz sprinkled like magic dust over the top.

A modest 40,000 crowd was enough to electrify the stadium on final night and contained a smattering of travelling Cradley Heath fans, whose trip had been made all the more special by a generous invitation to join Bruce at his Newport Beach home a few days before the final. It's hard to imagine any other reigning World Champion, in any other sport, inviting a group of fans around to his own home for beers and snacks on the eve of a title defence. That was the nature of Bruce Penhall.

'They spent the money to come over and support me, so we said let's give 'em a little bit extra. You know, it's a day or whatever out of my life. They gave me time and time again everything they had, and we actually had a good time that day.'

No doubt those Heathens supporters would have been every bit in awe of visiting the Coliseum as they were the Penhall beach residence. The arena was resplendent in bright, clean red, white and blue, positively glittering with excitement and expectation. It was described by one journalist as being 'dressed to kill'. A pre-meeting Wild West parade was provided by the Knotts Berry Farm theme park, and after the anticipation was allowed to build to its absolute peak, Bruce was sent out onto the track in a horse-drawn stagecoach. There were air balloons, fireworks and an electronic scoreboard with streaming video footage and instant action replays. In the Penhall camp of the pits, there were also more than just the usual entourage of managers and mechanics. 'There were actors from *CHiPs* in the pits, in full costume and make-up, shooting segments of the show,' he reveals. 'I had not been pre-warned how much filming would be going on and at first I thought they were going to be there just to cheer me on. There were producers, make-up ladies, script ladies. At one point during the meeting, the producer asked me if I could go stand by some of the actors for a camera shot. If that wasn't enough, then the make-up artist told me they would need to put a little extra dirt on my face for the shot! I had to tell them that I was out in the next-but-one heat and needed to get on with my racing, not stand with dirt being rubbed into my face for the sake of a TV shot!'

Eventually, Bruce was able to get on with the racing, and not before time as the American crowd had been stunned by a brilliant first appearance, when he had lost out in a fantastic tussle with Les Collins. There could hardly have been any more pressure heaped onto his broad shoulders. Not only was he attempting to defend his world title, thus being the one man everybody wanted to beat, but he was doing so in front of a hugely expectant home crowd, and to cap it all, the television script already had him inked in as the champion! He plugged away at the inside line for virtually the entire first race, and despite nosing in front several times, Collins kept on coming back to eventually hang on to his victory with a few metres to spare before the finish line. Any rider

198

wishing to become world champion can scarcely avoid more than one defeat, and Penhall had used up his solitary setback at a very early stage. Any more dropped points would almost certainly cost him the chance of overall victory. He demonstrated his total determination in his next outing with an uncompromising first bend from gate one, and led comfortably for the remaining four laps to get the pursuit back on track. It was enough to relax the nerves a little after he had spent too much time dwelling on his first race – with the opposite build-up to the exhausting 1981 pre-meeting preparation.

Few major championship victories came without a slice of good fortune in any one-off event, and Bruce used up his first minor portion in heat twelve. Attempting to take further advantage from a second successive inside starting lane, but with all the edginess of a man under intense strain, he jumped a second too early and saw his front wheel go right between the two thin starting tapes ahead of him. Breaking them would have meant an instant exclusion and farewell to any hopes of success, but he luckily managed to ease his wheel back into position and, when the delicate white ribbons shot up at last, Penhall's head was down and his machine was stretching out into the first corner. Again, he moved his opponents hard out wide and propelled himself into an unassailable race lead, giving himself 8 out of a possible 9 points and setting up the ultimate showdown between the greatest of all rivals.

The fourteenth heat of the 1982 World final was to prove an even bigger talking point than virtually any other race which preceded it in Penhall's career, and arguably as debatable and controversial as any other speedway race in history. It was Penhall versus Kenny Carter in an epic duel, which could not have been better scripted by the best of the Hollywood movie industry that Bruce was about to join. It was 'The Biggie', said American announcer Bruce Flanders. 'You can put your head out of the commentary box here at the coliseum and grab the atmosphere in great fistfuls,' added Dave Lanning in typical fashion, 'The noise is absolutely deafening. It really is electric out there.'

The riders were justifiably restless before the start and when they finally got into line, and the referee released them from the start, it was Peter Collins from the inside and Phil Crump from the outside who emerged into a shock lead. Sandwiched in between them had been the two protagonists, who were the focus of every spectator in the ground, but who only focused themselves on wrestling with each other. Penhall was stuck in third with the previously unbeaten Carter in fourth, but by the end of lap two they had both swept underneath the Australian to move up a place. That was truly the end of their progression though as they became equally drawn into a private scuffle aboard their machines, which was quite simply the closest thing to a boxing match on motorbikes. On the long straight from the second lap into the third, Carter barged into the inside of Penhall, who held his ground and leaned heavily over to the left, into the Yorkshireman. They separated and then slammed into each other again, pushing and shoving with legs, elbows and helmets flailing into each other. Again they untangled from each other's grip and Carter gave Bruce one more push as they entered the next bend. The American stuck out a leg to retain his balance and then threw the bike sideways to turn hard underneath his rival and steal the inside advantage. Carter hadn't anticipated it and moved slightly off line, leaving a gap for Penhall to seize upon. The momentum of both riders sent them sliding out wide, but as they straightened up to drive out of the bend, it was Bruce who had his nose in front. Carter struggled in vain to keep going around the outside, but refusing to shut off the throttle, he instead ran totally out of room and plunged headlong into the fence.

The incident still has opinions utterly divided to this day, but Norwegian referee Tore Kittilsen blasted Carter's title hopes out of the water by excluding him from the rerun. Whether he fell or was pushed by Penhall is a judgment that every speedway supporter who has watched the event will have their own view about. Carter certainly made his own opinion known in a ten-minute protest, both on the pits phone to the referee, and then on the track where he had to be escorted away to allow the restaging of the heat to take place. With Penhall basing his decision whether or not to retire completely on the outcome of the meeting, and Carter feeling the world was against him winning the crown, so much history was decided in that dramatic and pivotal confrontation. The memory of the entire night is as fresh as ever in Bruce's mind: 'I made a mistake by concentrating more on Kenny in that race than I did on PC and Crumpie. Kenny was fast at that time and I was going to do all I could to block him – not fence him. After we left the start, Kenny had his elbow under my chin and we were fighting on the track. It was ugly and not the first time I'd encountered this with him. Into turn three, he was on the outside and I went up the inside and completely slammed the door on him.

'CBS covered the meeting for American TV but MGM, who were filming as part of my introduction to the *CHiPs* show, had twenty-five cameras around the stadium. The one they had positioned high up at the back of the stand, overlooking turn three, showed that there was a lot of daylight between my back wheel and Kenny's front wheel. Well, three or four inches anyway!

'What was I supposed to do? Put my blinker on and move over to let him past? I'm absolutely sure that I didn't hit Kenny when he went down. We know when we have hit another rider – you feel it happen. I admit that I didn't leave him any room but he just ran out of track and ended up by the hot dog stand!'

It was the final and definitive instalment in the acrimonious rivalry that had raged ever since the first time Penhall and Carter had met on track in 1978. And it was concluded with the decisive race in the World final, at the very end of Bruce's career. The argument between the pair rattled on after the meeting with the Halifax rider issuing the American with a warning not to set foot in England again. Four years later, personal and professional difficulties took their toll on a troubled Kenny Carter and he took the lives of himself and his wife in a tragic incident at their West Yorkshire home. So how does Bruce reflect on his years of conflict with the England international?

'What happened with him is a sad story that I try to keep away from. This is a kid that had a tremendous amount of talent. However, what I think really hurt Kenny as much as anything was his immaturity, as far as decisions about who could do what. And I think he wanted to control everything, and wasn't really willing to listen to others. In my estimation, he felt that everything he was doing, or about to do, was absolutely the right way. Even though he had Ivan Mauger advising him, to be honest with you, I don't really think he listened to Ivan that much. I really truly don't – as far as setting his motorcycles up and as far as his state of mind.

'There comes a time if you're nineteen or twenty years old, you need to start learning from others who have been through it for years and years. I think that was to Kenny's demise in a maturity sense. He was so full of confidence, he didn't think that anyone could ever beat him and you can get to a point when you're over-confident, which will really hurt you. There has to be a ton of confidence, don't get me wrong, but if you're over-confident, that's gonna give you a problem.

'The pressure on him was astronomical as well. There was Michael Lee and PC at the time, and PC handled it well. He was a great ambassador for the sport, he was charismatic. Michael Lee, on the other hand, did not handle it well, not in the slightest. Whenever I was up against [Michael Lee], I had thoughts of him winning. I always knew that if I was leading him, and there were still three feet between me and the fence, Mike could come by me any time. When he was at his best, his most consistent, he was simply awesome. If I made the start on Kenny I usually felt I'd win the race safely. He was fast, always a threat, but I would back myself against him.

'With the amount of publicity that we had in those days, all of the press had hopes on Kenny Carter. They had a bad situation with Michael Lee. Believe me, riding through Great Britain, even though they had their club favourites, they were certainly patriotic as well and they wanted a British boy to win. I think that Kenny's immaturity was his downfall because he just couldn't handle any of that pressure. On the track, sure he could from time to time, he had some brilliant, brilliant rides, but he had several situations where he was hopeless. He had a lot of engine failures, he crashed a lot because he was a hard rider, but I just don't think he could handle the pressure that was thrown in his lap.

'Did I like him off the track? As long as we were well away from the track! We would travel together and we would be on a bus going somewhere with other riders, and we all got along good. But the minute the track was in view, everybody started getting themselves into a different frame of mind. I would never hang out with him, we weren't friends. But there were situations where we would tolerate each other because the situation required it. We both wanted the same thing and we both had our different ways of trying to accomplish it.'

On World final night 1982, the pressure got to Carter. With his chances blown by the exclusion and with the rest of Penhall's biggest rivals dropping points elsewhere, the destiny of the crown fell back into the hands of the reigning champ. Bruce lined up in heat nineteen knowing that he needed to win what was effectively his easiest ride of the night, to be sure of outright victory. He looked across the start line to see scoreless Russian Mikhail Starostin, Czech Vaclav Verner, who was only a single point better off, and almost like a lucky charm, there was Jiri Stancl, who had been alongside Bruce at the start of his final ride of the 1981 final. Within a few yards, Penhall had a bike length over his competitors and despite a brief third-lap challenge from Stancl, he rode a cool and controlled four laps to victory.

Mobbed by his pits team on the track and lifted into the air in triumph, he had repeated his feat of 1981 to become World Champion again. Back to back success was this time capped by achieving the ultimate accolade on American soil. Although interviewed before he could even leave the track amid a crowd of well-wishers, he saved his victory speech for the rostrum when he announced the secret he had kept for almost a week. He had won the title, therefore he would be retiring completely. Another added bonus for the rostrum scene was that Dennis Sigalos had battled his way into third position. The childhood buddies who had started their careers together were able to stand side by side as the American national anthem played out to the final curtain of Penhall's days on the shale.

NINETEEN

MOVIE STAR

'I first walked on the set of MGM one-and-a-half weeks after I retired from speedway and I was amazed to find that it was a complete duplication of the pits scene at the LA Coliseum on World final night, at a cost of $250,000. They even had my programme marked with my races, pinned to the wall! I was a nightmare for the film crew on my first day. They had an hour-and-a-half of my out-takes alone and I put the film company so far behind schedule. And when you think that it costs these guys a $100,000 a minute to film, I was losing them a fortune. I'd hear the producer say "Get the motorcycle guy outta here". I tell you, I sucked so much!'

Under the wing of Erik Estrada, Bruce soon adapted to his new life, albeit without quite demonstrating the natural ease with which he controlled a speedway bike at 70 miles per hour. He starred in nineteen out of the twenty-two episodes in the sixth season of the show, missing only the first three. *CHiPs* was broadcast in the UK as well as the US each week, as the CHP officers rode their motorcycles through Southern California patrolling the streets of LA. When filming, Bruce would have to work up to seventeen hours a day, and found many difficulties with virtually no acting experience behind him. He was given a dialogue coach to help with strategies for remembering lines, but the producers still insisted that they didn't want him to take any more acting classes, as they wanted him to play the character just as himself. He moved house from Newport to Manhattan Beach and won a whole new set of admirers, most of whom knew virtually nothing of his speedway career.

Meanwhile, the promoters at Cradley Heath were still left fuming and the BSPA even threatened legal action against Bruce for breaking his contract. Despite a 'paper trail' for a couple of weeks, the case went no further, and despite the Heathens being awarded a temporary replacement facility in the team, they were overhauled in the British League standings by second-placed Belle Vue, eventually losing the chance of their own back-to-back title success. Peter Adams, who had stood steadfastly at Penhall's side twelve months earlier at Wembley, was so angry that he would not speak to his former rider for several weeks.

Bruce was hardly short of people wanting to get in touch. He had always enjoyed a phenomenally successful speedway fan club in both England and the USA, but by the time *CHiPs* began to air in the States, he was receiving thousands of letters every week, delivered to him in large army duffel bags. He also got to rub shoulders with the rich and famous whom he hoped to emulate.

'I came across quite a few famous people – I fell in love with Victoria Principal out of *Dallas* when I first saw her in the flesh. The sets for *Fame* and *Little House on the Prairie* were just along the way from us, so I'd always be bumping into someone quite famous.'

He wasn't just bumping into them either, especially according to the tabloid newspapers, who even in England featured alleged 'kiss and tell' stories in Bruce's first year as an actor. Most of it he dismisses as 'paper talk', but reveals that he did date Melissa Gilbert, from *Little House on the Prairie*, Morgan Fairchild and even more sensationally Demi Moore, who went on to become one of Hollywood's biggest names, starring in a string of box office hits. 'I actually dated Demi Moore for about five or six months. We hung out together as we shared the same acting coach. She was fun and I had a great time with her.

'Erik Estrada was very good to me and I enjoyed it most when I got to be his partner for the last four episodes. Erik and I would have a lot of fun on set. While he was off camera and I was in shot, he'd often pull silly faces to try and make me mess up my lines, which I found a little hard to cope with at times!'

When filming for the series came to an end, Bruce was ready for a break from the long hours and intense nature of the work, but he hadn't bargained on just how long a break he would be handed. Around a month after the cast and crew had gone their separate ways, the announcement came that *CHiPs* was to be cancelled; there would be no seventh series, despite the show being commendably placed in the top forty of the US television ratings. 'It was a bummer, but I didn't really think much about it because I thought I had a good start in the industry and thought I'd be on another show real soon. In fact what happened was that Universal Studios put me under contract for a year on a lot of money, on a development basis, where if there was any new pilots for Universal, I would be put forward for them. But what it did was take me out of the pilots for Warner Brothers and all of the other big studios – I couldn't go up for any other auditions. The only thing I could do was go for Universal auditions and there wasn't really anything that suited me that year.

'I got paid an astronomical amount of money and I went to quite a few auditions, but nothing was really right for me. I was thrown in at the deep end. I wasn't some stellar actor. I struggled, I really struggled. I didn't know the industry. All of a sudden, I was auditioning and when you go for an audition it is the most nerve-wracking thing. It's like lining up for a World final every single time, especially when you've got several heavy duty producers looking at every single little move you make, knowing that if you miss a line here, you're not going to get the show. It is a huge kind of pressure and I wasn't a good cold reader at all.'

After *CHiPs*, Bruce spent some time, still under the guidance of manager Jeff Imediato, making appearances on celebrity game shows and playing guest roles in TV episodes of programmes such as *Loveboat* and *Facts of Life*. He was a regular pin-up in countless American entertainment magazines, often with his face on the cover alongside the likes of movie star actors Matt Dillon, Rob Lowe and John Travolta. One of those television credits after *CHiPs* was an early version of reality TV and one that ranks as a major personal accomplishment for him. A successful annual event, *Circus of the Stars* would take actors and actresses from different soap operas and other TV shows, and attempt to train them as circus performers. Bruce was invited to learn how to walk the high wire, and took up the three-month challenge. 'I jumped at the chance. I actually had to train every single day for three months on the wire, starting off at two feet and building up to twenty feet. I was able to do somersaults, I could ride a bicycle across the high wire, I would even have a girl on my shoulders while I was walking across. It was quite a feat for me, it was so hard and there was so much pressure again. We would then go to Las Vegas and perform, that's where we would film the show, but nobody would really see the training that was involved – it was a huge amount. There was the trapeze that I really wanted to do, but it involved a little more training and my schedule wouldn't allow for me to be off a month earlier than what I already was.'

He could never quite keep away from any offers of racing either, whether it was on two wheels or four, and competed in the 1983 Pro-Celebrity Toyota race as well as 'The Great American Race', a vintage car race staged over several days through several cities. At the same time, he stayed very loosely connected to speedway, never quite tearing himself away from the sport completely. He appeared as Master of Ceremonies at New York's Oswego track and as ITV commentator for the 1983 British and World finals. He could easily have missed the World final in Germany, however, when, flying via England, he mislaid his passport en route in Europe. He confessed to having crossed three border checkpoints in the boot of Peter Adams' car, in order to arrive safely at trackside in Norden.

His busy schedule did prevent him from spending as much time associated with the sport as he would have liked, but he did manage to set up a racing team to assist two young up-and-coming junior riders, David Busby and a teenage protégé who would go on to become 1997 World Champion, Greg Hancock. Bruce became involved through a friendship with Greg's father, known more commonly through the speedway scene as 'Uncle Bill Hancock'! 'Uncle Bill was always a good friend, and Greg loved to watch me ride and I really liked Greg. His nickname was Grin because he was always smiling. Greg and David were really good buddies back then, along with Uncle Bill. He did a lot with the junior speedway programme, and I was able to help him out. I think we helped Greg out with some bikes, and got him set up with the same sponsors as mine and I was able to help them ride and instruct them a little bit, but not very much. Once I had left the scene, I wasn't around it to help the boys much at all.

'I always had one of my fingers on the pulse around speedway, knowing who the new boys were, who had potential, who really wanted it and who could actually do it over there. There was Greg and Lance [King] and Ricky [Miller], they were all riders who I felt very strongly about doing well over in Britain. I would get several calls during the year from promoters, wondering about certain riders.'

One of those calls was from Colin Pratt, the man who took over the reins at Cradley Heath, after the departure of Peter Adams in 1984. Bruce was happy to help further the American legacy at Dudley Wood by recommending both Hancock and Billy Hamill as potential stars for the Heathens in the late 1980s. 'Billy wasn't around much and I didn't really know him, but I can vividly remember his enthusiasm. He came up to me once at a race and asked me to sponsor him, telling me that he was going to win and he was going to do this and that. He was a lot more outgoing than Greg even thought of being. I loved that side of him. I always told everybody else that Billy Hamill would be a World Champion – before Greg was, but that Greg would probably outlast Billy, because of the difference in their style. Billy was always a lot more aggressive and I knew he had the talent to become World Champion, but I thought that it was going to be somewhat short-lived. He's so good, don't get me wrong, but I thought Greg would be long-lasting in speedway. He wasn't as aggressive and he thought things out more, kind of along the lines of Mike Bast in that respect. Mike Bast had longevity because he thought about his racing a lot more than what his throttle hand did.' Both Hamill and Hancock enjoyed several years as Cradley riders and, true enough, Hamill became World Champion in 1996, one year before Hancock.

Back in the acting industry, Bruce ran into problems with his long-term manager, arguing over a conflict of priorities, both personal and professional. He felt that his career was heading in the direction of more celebrity game shows than anything else, so took the decision to ended his contract prematurely with Jeff Imediato. His manager also disapproved of the fact that Bruce had met and fallen in love with new girlfriend Laurie, the woman he would soon marry. 'Jeff didn't want me seeing Laurie, he wanted me to be linked with the starlets. He actually knew her way before I did and my road manager, who was one of Jeff's employees, knew her too, and they never really wanted to introduce us because they felt that I would fall in love with her. Eventually they did, and one day we went out on a date and we hit it off, just like they said. We had a great night at the comedy store watching some Robin Williams. I didn't think too much about it for a couple of days and then a week went by and I thought that I really wanted to see her again. After that I used to make the trip down to San Diego all the time and spent a lot of time with her. Jeff Imediato hated the fact that I wasn't single and I had a girlfriend, so that contributed to me ending the agreement with him. I broke the contract early and it cost me $40,000 – just prior to getting married. He sued me and I had to give him a cheque for $40,000 but it was good because he was out of my hair, and I was able to move on, and that I did.'

Bruce made the step from television into movies, beginning with a thriller called *Body Count*, which was shot in Italy. He married his fiancée Laurie, and immediately after their honeymoon, flew to Europe for his film debut. Despite fights between the director and producer, the movie was completed and released the following year. It was the first of ten movies in which he would star, as Bruce next linked up with popular American director Andy Sidaris. He was a former ABC Sports director who had moved into the movie business, with a self-styled brand of 'babes, bombs and bullets'. Penhall was a regular star of every further addition to the Sidaris collection, filmed in exotic locations, crammed with bikini-clad playboy models and featuring a range of cars, bikes, boats, helicopters and planes, all of which usually came to an explosive end. After the increasing profitability of three early movies came a title that summed up the principle in one go. *Girls, Games and Guns* (also released as *Do or Die*) not only reunited Bruce with Erik Estrada as a co-star but also featured actor Pat Morita as the villain, better known as the character of Mr Miyagi in the hit *Karate Kid* films. By the early 1990s and after two more similar films as the character Bruce Christian, Penhall was invited by the next generation of the Sidaris family to star in a new role. The formula was the same combination of good-looking girls with a lot of exposed flesh, usually touting some kind of guns or other firepower. This time playing Agent Chris Cannon, Bruce completed two more movies, before taking a semi-permanent break from the industry. In his final production, *The Dallas Connection* – with the tag line of 'Spies, Thighs, Bikinis and Bullets', he took one of the lead roles, appearing first on the credit list but looking visibly older, more than ten years after the crowning glory of his speedway career. He took the conscious decision to break away from the niche, while still doing plenty of other work in the industry, such as sports commentary and commercial work. Once again, Bruce was mindful of missing out on family life and wanted to spend more time at home, rather than being away for weeks or months at a time on the production set of a movie. By this time he had four young children for whom he was happy to refocus his priorities. 'I was able to keep doing the movies, but the producer was getting tired of doing them. They were becoming low budget and they were taking me away from my new family. I had babies to look after! I would have to leave for a month and half and there were times when I would only work two or three times a week, and then I would have to work all week. I didn't think that it was doing anything for my career. It was hurting more because of the amount of girls who were topless in these movies. I didn't want it to affect my kids when they were going to school. It was so hard for us, because we had three kids under the age of five. When I would leave for a month, it was difficult leaving Laurie at home with kids.

'The movies were a lot fun to do, there were a lot of pretty ladies. When we started, they were shot in places like Hawaii, and then they started cutting the budget and winded up in Louisiana and that wasn't as good! It was hard calling my wife every night while I was going to sleep in a hotel room and she was home putting the kids in the bath.'

It seemed like the end of the line as far as Bruce was concerned with motion pictures, but there were plenty of fresh challenges ahead. Bruce Penhall the speedway rider had made the transition to Bruce Penhall the actor, when many people tipped him to fail at the first tough hurdle. He is the first to admit that speedway's loss wasn't exactly Hollywood's gain, but he made a comfortable living and enjoyed many perks of a lifestyle of which many people can only dream. It wasn't long before the transition was being made into Bruce Penhall the family man, Bruce Penhall the businessman and even full circle to Bruce Penhall, World Champion yet again.

TWENTY

WORLD CHAMPION, DAD!

Admitting an ongoing thirst for racing, even during his acting days, Bruce turned to the high-speed world of powerboating. As a child he was taken along to dozens of races to watch his father race, and always loved to watch the action. Feeling a little 'stir crazy' in the movie industry without fulfilling the racing bug, he began making contacts in the world of offshore powerboat racing and received a call from an English man residing in the States. Originally from Staffordshire in the UK, software engineer Nigel Hook was an experienced competitor in the sport and invited Penhall to join his team in the early 1990s.

Unlike any other form of boat racing, in offshore powerboats, two people are required to drive and throttle the boat. When Penhall and Hook teamed up, they enjoyed immediate success and even competed in a World Championship, despite just a handful of prior races together. Bruce was hooked and very quickly became keen to take his involvement one step further, with the idea of setting up his own team, rather than racing for someone else. The sport was expensive, and required two people in the boat with immense trust in each other's talent and judgement. There was one person who Bruce knew he wanted by his side: 'I remember calling Dennis [Sigalos] from Florida during the World Championship, telling him how great it was and that it was something he and I had to do together! He was all for it. When I got home I had a meeting with Dennis and his dad Tony, who used to race boats with my dad in the early 1950s when they were also best friends. Tony agreed to bankroll the team providing I could get sponsorship as well. That wasn't hard because of our past careers, and the *CHiPs* exposure really helped. I also managed the team during the entire time that we raced. We had tremendous luck, and of course there was some skill involved as well.

'The reason you need two people to race is because out in the ocean the swells can reach five to six feet high. The driver will navigate by way of GPS system, while the throttleman has two throttles to work, as well as trim the attitude of the boat, those are called trim tabs. He has his right hand on the throttles and left hand on the tabs, at all times adjusting trim as well as throttling back and forth the entire race. The rougher it is the more he has to work. I thought Dennis would make a good throttleman so I elected him. It was so important, as when the boat comes out of the water, he has to get out of the throttles and back on them as soon as the boat re-enters. If he is off a little bit, he could spin up the engines and simply destroy them, which could cost a mere $200,000!'

It was just the challenge that Bruce in particular was desperate for, and despite being given little chance by some experienced commentators in the sport, the new Ocean Spray 'Crave the Wave' Offshore Racing team built up a sponsorship package of $1.5 million. In their first race, California's Dana Point Challenge in June 1994, the former world speedway champions were successful in their 'Class D' maiden voyage, beating the reigning World Champions' team in the process. Racing in a 37-foot Scarab boat, the pair went on to win the Modified Class World Championship in Key West Florida. A great rookie year followed in 1995 as they won five out of eight national championship races to take the national crown. In the years that followed, Penhall and Sigalos won five World Championships, as well as the national championship, and set a world speed record in the class of Super V-bottoms. Above everything the families of the two buddies were able to share in their success together. And as an extraordinary bonus, Penhall stepped into the very select category of people who have won World Championships in two different sports, possibly even becoming the only person to complete the accomplishments in back-to-back years.

During this time, Bruce was able to venture into a variety of business propositions. He invested in a business refurbishing golf teeing areas, a niche market, but one that became successful and profitable thanks to a link-up with brother-in-law Mark's powder-coating company. With someone else running the business for him, Bruce then took up a sports marketing position with Oakley. Using his acting as an ideal platform for the product placement of Oakley's sports sunglasses, he was able to make further success of his new role. He took particular advantage of his own last movie roles. Instead of paying $25,000 for a thirty-second TV commercial, Bruce could wear the sunglasses in his films and get five minutes of free exposure with added product identification. With a lot of hard work placing the shades in other movies and commercials, he built up an amazing client list that included the likes of Madonna, Tom Cruise, Sylvester Stallone and Robin Williams.

As he got to know the industry better, Bruce decided to branch out from Oakley and set up his own brand of eyewear. With business partner and long-time friend Steve Brereton, he created Penhall Optical Windshades, specialising in high-fashion sunglasses, based in an upmarket resort south of Los Angeles. Within six months of the company starting out, they had outgrown their office with Bruce's original designs for lenses, sunglasses and goggles, and initial signs were all promising. It will come as no surprise to any speedway fan to find that when Bruce visited some manufacturers in Italy to discuss the product, he was met with former supporters who used to watch him race all the time in Europe. He immediately had the Italian manufacturers on board because they knew they'd be working with the former world speedway champion whom they had idolised fifteen years earlier!

Contacts and exposure gained from the worlds of speedway, acting, powerboating and the sunglasses industry itself were all pulled together to make the company a preliminary success. From 1997, a new office manager was employed. Greg Hancock's sister, Carrie, joined the Penhall Optical team, but it proved to be a difficult trade in which to maintain turnover and profits. Three years later, the company had to be wound up. Despite great clients and products, it required huge investors to make the move into a money-making concern, and they could only manage to break even at best.

'The money train just had to keep on coming,' says Bruce. 'In the end, we just needed to stop the bleeding. I eventually lost a million and a half dollars. It was a step that I thought was going to be successful, but it put not only my family in jeopardy, but myself and a partner.'

Since then, Bruce has sold his share in the golf business, in order to whittle down his business commitments and spend more time with his family. With an ironic twist, he has moved back into the demolition business that has been around his family for decades. Not wanting to work for a big company, however, he has instead settled into a role with a relatively new business, working for a friend with about forty employees. They operate in competition with the still hugely successful Penhall Company, the family business that was once run by his father and inherited by Bruce and his siblings.

Acting and performing has continued to play a part in Bruce's life, even after the end of the movies. He was invited back for a reunion with the *CHiPs* cast, when a feature-length movie was made in 1999, including many familiar names from the original series. Set fifteen years after the end of the television series, Bruce's character is promoted to the rank of sergeant. However, after being scripted to crash his bike in the third scene, Sergeant Bruce Nelson spent the rest of the show in a coma! A couple of years earlier, he had made a brief television appearance in the popular series of *Renegade*, which starred Lorenzo Lamas in the lead role. 'Lorenzo was a friend of mine and they asked me to come on the show to play a bad guy. I was doing some drug smuggling – on the show – and I was able to get Larry Huffman to come in to play himself as an announcer.

'We were shooting a scene when I think they dropped Lorenzo out of a helicopter onto the boat that I was on. He had to start a fight with me and ended up throwing me off the boat. It was quite a stunt and my family were down there with us in San Diego. My daughter was watching and we were pretty close to the shore and she was in tears. She was shouting at Lorenzo, "Don't beat up my Daddy." Of course I didn't know this until afterwards. When I got to shore, she came and hugged me and I could tell she was upset and it was Laurie who told me what had been going on. It was pretty funny.

'Also, after that I remember coming home when my kids were literally babies, and they would be watching reruns of *CHiPs*. They would turn around and look at me and couldn't understand it. They looked at me and then looked at the television and couldn't understand why I didn't have a *CHiPs* uniform on. For years, they really thought I was a California Highway Patrolman!'

Bruce has been married since 1985 and now has four children; three boys – Devin, Ryan and Connor – and a daughter, Mckenzie. Two of the boys have already made significant strides in motocross racing, and his youngest son, Connor, has even tried his hand at junior speedway. Such the doting Dad, Bruce has always been keen to play an integral role in the upbringing of his family and loathed the times when business or sporting commitments took him away from home. Even when faced with huge amounts of work through the catalogue of his professional interests, Bruce found time through his children to return to his discarded childhood love of baseball. 'I always loved baseball. To this day I watch quite a bit of baseball, and I've had a lot of fun coaching it. I did it for almost twelve years, from coaching all the way to managing the team. I managed the last four years of my kids' baseball time and my youngest boy had one year left of his major league in the little leagues. He had to make a big decision and he decided he didn't want to play baseball anymore because it affected his motocross. I was kind of relieved, because while managing baseball, we had four practices and two games per week. And it was a huge commitment. I would leave my office at 2.30 p.m. every day to set up the field.

'Now I feel that I am heavily involved with racing through my kids. I'm not the actual guy on the motorcycle, but I'm still heavily involved. And it's something that's in my blood. My father was a huge racer and my kids' kids are going to be racers! That's all my boys want to do, they're fanatical racers. I have to give them the absolute best tools that I can to be successful, but it is really up to them what they want to do and I let them make the decisions.'

It's not surprising then that Bruce has never seriously considered a full-time return to speedway racing, but that's not been through a lack of offers. Cradley Heath audaciously offered him the chance to return to top-flight racing at Dudley Wood in the mid-nineties, twelve years after his retirement from the sport, and further offers have come in since from other British League clubs Coventry and King's Lynn. If he was ever remotely tempted, it was when the chance came to compete in the World Speedway Championship again, when it reverted to a Grand Prix format. He even spoke to Eddie Bull about the possibility and considered the idea of setting up his own training track to get into shape. Not prepared to just turn up and collect the pay cheque and not wanting to dedicate the amount of time and energy required to give the series his full commitment, he eventually abandoned the idea.

There have been occasional glimpses of Bruce Penhall on a speedway track since his retirement, albeit in strictly one-off appearances. He competed against Ivan Mauger at the reopening of the Sydney Showground in Australia, a meeting staged as a memorial to the late Billy Sanders, and teamed up with a host of familiar old faces to take part in one of Barry Briggs' Golden Greats events in Germany before the 1989 World final. He has flown to Britain to appear at testimonials for Erik Gundersen, Rick Miller and Greg Hancock, including riding in a series of match races against old adversary Ole Olsen, for Miller's celebration at Coventry. Most recently, Bruce took up an offer from British promoters Graham Drury and Ian Thomas, to take part in the annual indoor ice racing meetings at Telford in Shropshire. The deal was a tremendous coup for the organisers who staged 'An Evening with Bruce Penhall' on the night prior to the racing where a nostalgic turn out of fans welcomed back their former hero. Preparation hadn't gone too well for the racing itself when he rode in a series of match races in the USA a couple of months beforehand. Falling heavily in one outing, he managed to complete his scheduled appearances, but found later that he had suffered broken ribs in the accident.

Joining him in action at Telford, for what Bruce promised would definitely be his last racing appearance in the UK, was his countryman, friend and former teammate Bobby Schwartz. Penhall was the star attraction of the entire weekend, and he gave a very good account of himself in half a dozen races against Schwartz and Les Collins, despite never racing on ice before his official practice. At the same time, he was considering an option to pursue one more racing dream – the goal of being World Champion in a third different sport, this time drag racing. With the prospect of raising huge amounts of sponsorship all over again and being all too aware of the total devotion required to reach the very pinnacle of any sport, the idea didn't quite have the same appeal as it used to. And nowadays, it just doesn't match up to the sort of life which Bruce enjoys most – being a husband and a father.

There are certainly many facets to the life of Bruce Penhall. He has been around the world as a sportsman and actor, and has turned both businessman and family man. Speedway World Champion. Offshore powerboat World Champion. One thing is for sure, when this man reflects on his accomplishments, he can justifiably do so with a tremendous amount of achievement and personal satisfaction. And with increasing time to contemplate both his past and his future, he is clear about the realisation of one more dream: 'I'm really, really content being at home with my family now. It is everything I ever wanted. It is my life. I'm a family man. It means far more to me than anything else I've ever accomplished. In the past, as a racer I had a lot of time for myself and wanted everything for myself. Over the last six years, I have really come to enjoy my time with my family and let them enjoy their time with what they want to do. It's not all about me, like I've always thought of it. Its time to grow up and mature a little bit.

'I love being around my wife. In the past, at times we just crossed paths, and she was so supportive of what I did, racing the boats and doing the movies, because she knew I wanted to do that, but all of a sudden it's just clicked with me – I really want to be at home. I've been so lucky and so fortunate. Luck comes into it so many times, but I've also worked so hard to try to accomplish my goals.

'I can always look back and say I have certainly lived a great, great life.'

BRITISH LEAGUE CAREER STATISTICS (CRADLEY HEATH)

Year	Matches	Points	Bonus	Rides	Average	Max	Paid Max
1978	48	412	38	201	8.955	3	4
1979	57	582	38	249	9.960	8	4
1980	51	592	11	227	10.626	13	3
1981	43	523	16	197	10.944	15	2
1982	36	384	22	152	10.684	9	5
Career	**235**	**2,493**	**125**	**1,026**	**10.207**	**48**	**18**

Debut: 3 April 1978 (*v.* Sheffield; Challenge)
Final match: 16 August 1982 (*v.* Halifax; British League)

APPENDIX 2

MAJOR SPEEDWAY HONOURS & ACHIEVEMENTS

WORLD INDIVIDUAL CHAMPION (1981 & 1982)
World Pairs Champion (1981 with Bobby Schwartz)
World Team Champion (1982)

US National Champion (1980 & 1981)
American Champion (1980 & 1981)
Inter-Continental Champion (1981)

Master of Speedway (1979)

British League Champions (Cradley Heath, 1981)
Knock-Out Cup Winners (Cradley Heath, 1979 & 1980)
League Cup Winners (Cradley Heath, 1982)
Inter-League Cup Winners (Cradley Heath, 1979)
Premiership Winners (Cradley Heath, 1982)

Skol Masters Winner; Birmingham (1978)
Laurels Championship Winner; Wimbledon (1979)
Yorkshire Television Trophy Winner; Hull (1981)
Blue Riband Winner; Poole (1981)
Brandonapolis Winner; Coventry (1981)

Golden Helmet Holder (1979-80)

APPENDIX 3

OFFSHORE POWERBOAT RACING: MAJOR HONOURS

1993
APBA Class 'A' Western Division Champion

1994
APBA Modified Class World Champion, Key West, Florida
Co-winner, David Albert and Chris Smith Memorial Rookie of
the Year Award

1995
APBA Class 'D' National Champion
APBA Class 'D' World Champion, Key West, Florida

1996
APBA Class 'D' Champion, San Francisco, California
AFIBA Class 'D' Champion, Dana Point, California

1997
APBA Super Vee Class Champion, San Francisco, California
APBA Super Vee Class Champion, Dana Point, California
APBA Super Vee World Champion, Biloxi, Mississippi

APPENDIX 4

FILMOGRAPHY & NOTABLE TELEVISION APPEARANCES

Films

Body Count (1986): Dave Calloway
Picasso Trigger (1988): Hondo
Savage Beach (1989): Bruce Christian
Guns (1990): Bruce Christian
Do or Die (1991): Bruce Christian
Hard Hunted (1992): Bruce Christian
Fit to Kill (1993): Bruce Christian
Enemy Gold (1993): Chris Cannon
The Dallas Connection (1994): Chris Cannon
CHiPs '99 (1998) (TV): Sergeant Bruce Nelson

Notable TV Appearances

CHiPs (1977) TV Series: Cadet/Officer Bruce Nelson (1982–
    1983)
Circus of the Stars #8 (1983) (TV): Performer
Facts of Life, The (1979): Steve Garland in episode: 'All or Nothing'
    (episode 5.16) 18 January 1984
Renegade (1992): Donny in episode: 'Offshore Thunder' (episode
    4.8) 6 November 1995

Other Speedway titles published by Tempus

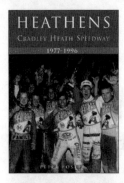

Heathens   Cradley Heath Speedway 1977-1996
PETER FOSTER

After going through the doldrums during the early 1970s, the arrival of promoters Dan McComick and Derek Pugh in 1977 began a golden period at
Dudley Wood that was to set the Heathens on a rollercoaster ride of success.
The mid-1990s saw the end of a fairy tale that had seen a rags-to-riches
speedway team take the name of Cradley Heath all around the world. An
enjoyable and enthralling read for every Heathens fan.
Paperback   £14.99   0 7524 2738 5

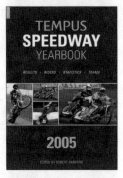

Speedway Yearbook 2005
Comprehensive coverage of the 2004 season
ROBERT BAMFORD

As part of their ongoing association with the sport of speedway, Tempus are
proud to produce the second edition of their national speedway annual. This
volume will appeal to all followers of the shale sport – both old and new.
Containing all the results, teams and riders from the 2004 season, with colour
action shots and personality profiles from an unforgettable campaign.
Paperback   £19.99   0 7524 3396 2

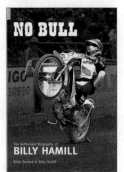

No Bull The Authorised Biography of Billy Hamill
BRIAN BURFORD & BILLY HAMILL
When Billy Hamill embarked on a career as a wild junior, a future as an
international star competing in Europe was a pipe. But in 1996, in a dramatic
final race of the series, the man they call 'the bullet' became the forth
American to win the sport's top individual prize. No Bull is his compelling
biography in which Billy takes a frank, honest and sometime heart-breaking
look back at a distinguished career that saw him compete at the highest level
for over a decade.
Hardback   £19.99   0 7524 3219 2

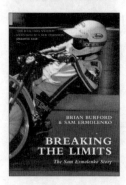

Breaking the Limits   The Sam Ermolenko Story
BRIAN BURFORD & SAM ERMOLENKO
After a horrific road accident in his native sunny California left him virtually
unable to walk, it took Sam Ermolenko an awful lot of bravery and determi-
nation to make a recovery – let alone become a speedway World Champion!
Despite a late start in the sport and a further series of severe injuries, Sam has
overcome all the odds and reached the very top. This is his remarkable story.
Paperback   £14.99   0 7524 3225 7

If you are interested in purchasing other books published by Tempus, or in case you have difficulty finding any Tempus
books in your local bookshop, you can also place orders directly through our website
www.tempus-publishing.com